HEALING BEYOND MEDICINE

HEALING BEYOND MEDICINE

by

William Daniel Snively, Jr., M.D.

and

Jan Thuerbach

Parker Publishing Company, Inc.   **West Nyack, N.Y.**

Library of Congress Cataloging in Publication Data

Snively, William Daniel, date
  Healing beyond medicine.

  Bibliography: p.
  1. Medicine, Psychosomatic. 2. Mind and body.
I. Thuerbach, Jan, date   joint author.
II. Title. [DNLM: 1. Psychosomatic medicine--
Popular works. WM 90 S672h 1972]
RC49.S55   616.08   72-6497
ISBN 0-13-384479-X

Printed in the United States of America

What this book
can do for you . . .

In these pages, you will shortly discover the amazing secret of "healing yourself from within"—a health technique that has helped thousands to find a longer, happier, and more vigorous life.

There are many names for this technique. Some call it "tapping your miracle healing power" . . . some call it re-charging your "health battery" . . . others refer to it as the "X factor." Yet all refer to the same technique, and can be used interchangeably. What's more, this technique is effective in alleviating a wide range of ailments.

Surprising indeed is the list of ailments that may, either partly or entirely, come under this heading: stomach or duodenal ulcers, arthritis, disorders of the heart, arteries, lungs, skin, intestines, muscles—hardly any area of our bodies is excluded.

The ailments that this book covers are those that some physicians call "psychosomatic." This must not be misconstrued, however, to imply that all such ailments are "just in your mind" or that they can't hurt you.

It is a fact that more than 50 per cent, perhaps as many as 80 per cent of all visits to physicians fall into this category. What this means to you is this: the odds are at least fifty-fifty that whatever ailments you have or may develop can be cured or alleviated *by the power of your mind alone.*

This enormous group of ailments differs sharply from mental illness in which a serious derangement of the mind has occurred. They must also be distinguished from somatopsychic disease in which a bodily disorder induces psychic disturbances. To be sure, a clear-cut distinction is not always possible.

Why, then, write a book about psychosomatic illnesses? First, because they play such a large role in today's medicine. Second, because they are so poorly understood by virtually all persons who are neither psychologists nor physicians. Third, but perhaps most important, *your understanding of these ailments may help to prevent them before they develop.* If they have already gained a foothold, we will guide you in learning to cope with them, even effecting a cure. For this type of affliction, there is no magic pill. Nor is it likely that one will be developed. Indeed, medications designed to reduce the tensions causing psychosomatic illness often do just the opposite. Only better insight into the cause of the ailment can hope to produce positive results. Often the measures are relatively simple but amazingly effective.

Are we not all candidates for psychosomatic illness? Indeed, you may even now be an unknowing victim. We hope that from this book you will derive a clearer understanding of the development of these disorders and learn what measures are recommended to combat or cure them.

We have presented in this book cases of psychosomatic disease, thus setting the stage for an introduction to the host of aches, pains, and true physical malfunctions that may at one time or another be identified as psychosomatic. The mechanisms of these manifold ailments are set forth in terms you can readily comprehend. We have written in such a way that you might experience, perhaps for the first time, the feeling that someone truly understands and sympathizes with your dilemma. Graphic examples and case histories are drawn from the medical practice of the senior author of this book. We have especially emphasized the potential hazards of over-zealous drug therapy, an area of gravest concern. Ever leaning upon the great medical minds of this and earlier times, we have made their invaluable counsel available to the lay reader.

Certainly, this book is no panacea for psychosomatic illness. But it does present a wealth of that truth that is alleged to set one free, and will help to release our readers from the miserable shackles of psychosomatic illness.

William Daniel Snively, Jr., M.D.
Jan Thuerbach

Contents

five

What is the respiratory system? . An important balance: oxygen and carbon dioxide . Breathing is both voluntary and involuntary . Emotions reflected in respiration

Shadow symptoms . A classroom incident . Chronic overbreathing adds to fears . Underlying factors in overbreathing . Fear of attending church . Steps for treating overbreathing

Emotional and physical aspects . Personality patterns . Curious psychic influences in asthma . Crying and laughing related to asthma . Lucia was driven to succeed . Physical hazards of asthma

How to protect your "breath of life"

six

What is the digestive tract? . Emotions can disturb digestive activity

Observing the stomach at work . Ulcers—a disease of "civilization" . A shift in sex of persons afflicted . Typical personality . Shadow symptoms . Peptic ulcer can be physical in origin . Ben's job precipitates an ulcer . George's lack of a job precipitates an ulcer . Peptic ulcers in children

Shadow symptoms . Colitis-prone personalities . Delayed grief reactions contributing to ulcerative colitis . Ulcerative colitis in children

Contents

New relief from "nervous stomach" (*cont.*)

Contents 13

A healthy youthful life is no accident (*cont.*)

> *conflicts causing accidents . Accident-prone adolescents . Even children can be accident prone . Today's protesters against the conventional standards . The need for penance as a causative factor*

fifteen

> *A few of life's terrible traps . Tension at work . Inability to break home ties . Repressed desires . Regretted decision . An unhappy marriage . An unwelcome house "guest" . Inconsolable grief . The biblical Job spoke an ageless truth . A vicious circle of psychosomatic illnesses . How the vicious circle operates . How the vicious circle can be broken*

sixteen

> *Symptions of depression*

> *The tightly organized type . The loosely organized type . Miscellaneous types . Chain of events leading to depression . Anxieties as a psychic response . Anxiety states occur in combat areas . Prolonged anxiety can lead to depression . Why Agnes could not find peace of mind at the seashore . How a futile triangle of love led to depression*

> *Adolescents*

> *Small pleasures . Do not live alone . Do not harbor negative memories . Change your attitude to positive ones*

HEALING BEYOND MEDICINE

one

The amazing secret of
"healing from within"

> Body and soul cannot be separated for purposes of treatment, for they are one and indivisible. Sick minds must be healed as sick bodies.
>
> —C. Jeff Miller

An agonizing headache, abdominal pain, a burning sensation in the pit of your stomach are not uncommon symptoms of emotional stress. The prospect of facing a caustically critical employer, a crucial exam, or even dinner guests that you are most anxious to impress can trigger such painful reactions that are far from being imaginary although they originate in the mind. The suffering is real.

This is but a small sampling of what doctors call—with their seeming love of complex terms—psychosomatic illness. "Mind-body illness" would describe the condition quite as well; *psyche* means mind or soul and *soma* means body. But style dictates the use of medical terminology, hence we write of psychosomatic illness.

Unfortunately, psychosomatic illness is not limited to such relatively minor and temporary symptoms as headaches and abdominal discomforts. The mind's influence over the body can create serious physical disturbances and ailments that may be incapacitating, even fatal. The findings may be equally as alarming on X-rays or electrocardiograms as those of diseases with organic causes and represent a genuine physical response to purely mental distress. All illnesses, therefore, must be considered in relation to

17

the whole person, mind and body, for they are indeed indivisible. Each functions to balance and control the other. Dr. Franz Alexander, Director of Chicago's Institute for Psychoanalysis and a bold crusader for psychosomatic medicine, insists that "every bodily process is directly or indirectly influenced by psychological stimuli because the whole organism constitutes a unit with all of its parts interconnected."

The target areas of psychosomatic illness are many. Indigestion, loss of appetite, ulcers, diarrhea, constipation, and colitis are among the afflictions that may beset the digestive system. Heart disease, high blood pressure, hardening of the arteries, skin diseases, asthma and other respiratory ailments, even diabetes and arthritis may be caused or at least aggravated by mental stress. Obesity and chronic pain in the lower part of the back frequently have psychological overtones. Difficulties occurring during menopause and menstrual abnormalities, as well as frigidity and sexual problems, may also fall into this category. Let us emphasize, however, that these conditions are certainly not always of psychological origin but the list serves to illustrate the close kinship between mind and body.

It is a fact that more than half, perhaps as many as 80 per cent, of all the patients in doctors' offices are there with complaints whose origin is emotional, no matter how physical the symptoms may be. And, contrary to the thinking of many, psychosomatic disorders are not limited to the mentally disturbed or even to those persons considered to be extremely nervous or neurotic. Indeed, it is likely that every one of us is affected by some sort of emotional stress with resulting physical disturbances at some time during our lives. Of course, we do not all develop a serious psychosomatic illness but mild reactions are common. On a familiar level, for example, embarrassment is generally followed by an onrush of blood to the face and neck, or blushing. Fear or anxiety may be accompanied by such physical symptoms as excessive sweating, clammy palms, parched throat and pounding heart. And when a strong emotional state persists, physical changes and disorders in our various organs may result.

A glimpse at the past

Great strides have been made during the last few decades on behalf of psychosomatic medicine and even now, considerable research is being conducted in its myriad aspects. From a historical perspective, however, this psychological interest is little more than a revival of pre-scientific views. A look at the long and eventful history of medicine indicates that mind and body were, quite correctly, regarded as one in those extremely early days before the dawn of civilization, when medicine and magic were synonymous.

Scientists have discovered skulls of primitive men, eight thousand to ten thousand years old, with bore or trephine holes representing, no doubt, an attempt to cure illness by releasing evil spirits from the head. Even as man left his home in the cave and proceeded to become civilized, he continued to regard physical and mental diseases as one. Throughout the magnificent Babylonian-Assyrian era that flourished in Mesopotamia and into the great society of the Greeks, this concept prevailed. And though medicine was dominated by religion and employed suggestion as the major tool of treatment, it was modern in the sense that it recognized the powerful influence of mind over body.

The rather curious cult of Aesculapius sprang up in Greece and rapidly attracted a host of ardent believers. Temples were built and thousands of sufferers brought their diseases and woes to be treated. After offering suitable payment, the afflicted would lie down on the hard floor and experience a dream in which the prescribed remedy was revealed. It was usually necessary for the priest-physician of the temple to interpret the meaning of the dream. These temples were essentially the Mayo Clinics of their day and their approach was basically a form of psychotherapy, treatment of the mind.

Although much more enlightened than the cult of Aesculapius, Socrates also recognized the presence of psychosomatic illness for he said, "As it is not proper to cure the eyes without the head, nor the head without the body, so neither is it proper to cure the body without the soul." Hippocrates, who laid the foundations for our modern knowledge of disease, echoes the sentiments of Socrates: "In order to cure the human body it is necessary to have a knowledge of the whole of things." After the death of Hippocrates, however, knowledge of the mind and body as a single unit for the purposes of treatment seems to have largely disappeared, to lie dormant for several thousand years.

During the Dark Ages, disease was looked upon as a direct result of sin; the ill were only receiving their just deserts.

Although this view was far removed from the truth, it did recognize a relationship between mental and physical health.

Then a paradox occurred. The Renaissance, with its monumental advances in mathematics, chemistry, and physics dispelled the depressing mists that had ushered in the Dark Ages. It provided the scientific foundation for the discovery of microscopy, biochemistry, bacteriology, and pathology. But it did something else. Whereas the Dark Ages had regarded the mind or psyche as a mystic force that could inflict physical suffering upon the unjust and the wicked, the Renaissance, in reaction against this concept, relegated the mind strictly to the province of religion and philosophy. Interest in psychiatry and the role of mental stress in physical disorders diminished.

Advent of modern medicine

Then came the beginnings of the modern laboratory-based medicine of Pasteur and Virchow. The cell came into focus as a prime factor in disease. All physical distress was regarded as a direct result of structural cell change and the mind-body approach fell even further into complete disrepute. Diseases, not patients, were treated. One critic of the day wrote: "Disease meant now no longer what happens to the whole man but what happens to his organs . . ." A few bold but lonely voices pointed to the striking relationship between emotions and certain forms of illness, but they were largely disregarded. Pathologists laughed at those who would suggest a possible correlation between laboratory findings and disturbances of the mind.

This unfortunate concept held until Sigmund Freud appeared on the scene in the early 20th century. His revolutionary discoveries led to a new awareness of the importance of emotions in relation to mental and bodily disturbances. Many have disagreed with Freud. Yet he did more than anyone else toward removing the study of the mind from the realms of magic and superstition and elevating it to the level of science. He began a vital phase of psychiatry when he introduced psychoanalysis, a scientific method by which the emotions and the unconscious mind could be studied. The essence of his message still stands and today psychosomatic medicine refers to the interaction between psychological and bodily factors in maintaining health and curing disease.

Edward A. Strecker, known for his work in the field of psychiatry, commented on this new thrust of science: "The accomplishments of psychosomatic medicine are noteworthy; its objective is magnificent, but the name is unfortunate. Its comparatively recent usage makes it sound like the announcement of a marriage between body and mind, with the subdivisions and specialties of medicine and psychiatry in the bridal party. If the union of body and mind has just been consummated, then psychiatry for some time has sanctioned an illicit relationship. Long before the word psychosomatic was compounded, psychiatry had insistently taught that man was a total and indivisible unit, and, therefore, in health and disease, every somatic process at once reverberated in all of the man, and notably in his emotions; conversely, that every emotional reaction, whether it was violent and pathologic, like rage, or merely a feeling tone, like a mild stage of satisfaction, immediately had repercussions in every tissue and cell of the body." In any event, medicine and psychiatry now work hand in hand toward the same goal, healing the whole man.

Psychosomatic illness differs from insanity and hysteria

At this point let us make some important distinctions concerning mind-body disturbances. First, psychosomatic illness is not the same as mental illness, such as schizophrenia. The overwhelming number of people suffering from psychosomatic ailments are completely sane and can be effectively treated by a combination of conventional medical care and some form of psychotherapy. Secondly, psychosomatic disease is quite different from a condition known as hysteria. To clarify this, consider the following examples:

Mary X. is chained in marriage to a tyrant husband with whom she is extremely miserable. She feels that divorce is out of the question because she has no means of making a living. Her suppressed tension and rage cause her, quite unconsciously, to develop muscular spasms in her knees and elbows. The spasms cause alterations in circulation and in the joint surfaces. Arthritis develops. The intense pain and despair of her affliction merely add to her marital woes. Mary's arthritis is psychosomatic.

In contrast, Serviceman Oswald Z. is stationed in Viet Nam when he develops "paralysis" of his legs and is removed to a hospital. The most searching physical examinations reveal nothing to explain his condition. Oswald is reacting to a conflict in which he fears death or mutilation on the one hand and cowardice on the other. His paralysis solves his problem by taking him out of the action. He feels quite blameless, even contented. His ailment is not psychosomatic disease for he has no genuine physical disorder. Instead he is suffering from hysteria, a manifestation of mental illness.

The primary difference between psychosomatic disease and hysteria is that the hysteric solves his problem and the victim of psychosomatic disease generally adds to his suffering. Moreover, the symptoms of the hysteric, be they paralysis or deafness or loss of voice, while quite real are not accompanied by actual physical changes. Psychosomatic disease, on the other hand, is genuinely physical. Indeed, the ailment might progress to death if action is not taken to interrupt the cycle.

What is this strange cycle? How do scientists explain psychosomatic illness? Is there any hope or cure for it? We know that psychosomatic illness is essentially the outer expression of a deep and potentially dangerous struggle going on within. Anxiety, fear, rage, hate, and guilt are our most frequent offenders. But the mechanisms by which these emotions relate to physical changes are poorly understood. The systems involved are unbelievably complex. And yet, the enormous strides that science has taken toward untangling the web of complexity that surrounds our emotions is in itself a cause for hope.

In many persons, merely recognizing the source of the illness can bring about a cure. Even more important, however, psychosomatic illness can be *prevented* through a better insight into the many factors involved and at least a basic understanding of the curious processes by which the mind can wreak havoc in our bodies.

two

How to tap your miracle
healing power

Anxiety is a whisper of danger from the unconscious; whether the danger is real or imagined, the threat to health is real.

—A. A. Hutschnecker, M.D.

Thunder may be ear-splitting but the wee tick of a time bomb alarms us far more. A mother may sleep through loud noises that have no important meaning to her but awaken to the faint cry of her infant. Indeed, shouts may stir us far less than almost inaudible whispers. It all depends on the nature of the message, not on its volume, and seemingly small stimuli can elicit mighty responses. There are tiny but malignant whispers from within our bodies that can shatter our peace of mind, endanger our health, even destroy us, if we ignore or neglect them.

When Freud probed deep into man's inner world he concluded that all of us live another life beyond our conscious existence, beyond our reason and outward control. He declared that the unconscious impulses, fears, and desires cloistered within that hidden continent actually direct our conscious actions. And indeed they do. But we must not hamper our meager understanding of the human mind by even suggesting that the "unconscious" occupies a specific compartment of the brain. It is only one facet of a closely integrated mental facility. The whole human system, in fact, is so completely interrelated that a disturbance in any one of the many subsystems may call for major adjustments in countless others.

23

When the mind decides something is threatening, for example, it promptly commands the body to run or resist. At once breathing increases, the muscles tense for action, the heart begins to pump faster, and special hormones pour into the bloodstream. Intestinal movements come to a standstill and digestive action stops, enabling blood to be shunted to other parts of the body. The pulse quickens and the blood pressure rises. Blood sugar, too, is increased to provide an available source of energy. Such varied reactions occur in virtually all of the body organs until the danger signal is cancelled.

This can best be illustrated by using the digestive system as an example. Indeed, this is a prime target area for psychosomatic disturbances. In the stomach, for instance, gastric juices are secreted at regular intervals to aid in digesting the foods we eat. Under normal conditions, they do their work efficiently and safely. But when the brain signals danger, the secretion of these juices soars to as much as twenty times the ordinary amount although digestive action is interrupted. If the stress continues unabated, as in difficult family problems, unpleasant working conditions, or perhaps overwhelming grief over the loss of a loved one, the acid becomes so concentrated that it literally eats through the lining of the stomach or small intestine, resulting in a peptic or duodenal ulcer, or even ulcerative colitis. Less severe reactions could be loss of appetite, diarrhea, indigestion, or chronic constipation. Other areas of the body respond to danger in much this same manner. Continued emotional tension means increased activity for the heart, lungs, muscles, and glands, just to mention a few. And the long arm of psychosomatic disease takes its toll.

The autonomic nervous system

All of this activity takes place automatically, usually with little or no conscious awareness. Credit must be given to the autonomic division of our central nervous system through which our unconscious mental processes affect our conscious living.

Mind and body are intricately bound together by a network of fibers, conducting billions of electrical messages in a web of complexity that makes the telephone company's switchboard resemble a child's toy. Over part of this system we exert voluntary control; we knowingly signal our foot to take a step or our hand to grasp an object. These messages come primarily from the cerebral cortex, the fantastic thinking portion of our brain.

We normally ignore, however, the vast and variegated autonomic nervous system that regulates our involuntary bodily functions. Autonomic means automatic, which explains the operation of this all-important division of our nervous system—it has a certain degree of independence and functions automatically. Basically it is concerned with such internal activities as the beating of the heart, the secretion of glands, and the movement of food through the digestive tract. Responsibility for these involuntary activities has been assigned to the portion of our brain called the hypothalamus.

Briefly, then, the cerebral cortex is a sort of master switchboard for all incoming calls after they have undergone preliminary sorting and grouping in an area known as the thalamus. The cortex shunts most of its calls, however, to the hypothalamus which then coordinates the appropriate internal activities. In this way the cerebral cortex is relieved of the burden of dealing with the constant demands for routine adjustments but can exert its influence whenever necessary. Although the duties of the voluntary and involuntary nervous systems are not the same, they are tightly interwoven and are constantly being monitored and regulated by the central nervous system.

Dr. Frank G. Slaughter, in his book *The New Way to Mental and Physical Health,* has presented a beautiful analogy of the human body that illustrates some of the various actions of the autonomic nervous system. He compares the human body to a large metropolitan area, with all of the cells and organs representing people who have a wide variety of civic functions. The cerebral cortex portion of the brain serves as mayor of the city. Although the mayor has authority over the entire city, it is not always necessary for him to make the decisions. A disturbance in one area may require the dispatch of police to this section to protect the other citizens. Only when the security of the city itself is threatened is the problem carried to the highest authority.

An example of this sort might arise when bacteria enters the body and infection threatens. The police department goes into action immediately, white blood cells are rushed to the spot, and reserve cells are summoned from the bone marrow. Blood vessels expand so that more blood can be brought to the danger zone. Potent bacteria fighters called antibodies are put into service to combat the bacterial invasion. All of this takes place long before we become aware that anything untoward has happened. Only when swelling, pain, and local redness and heat from increased blood flow attract our attention do we become conscious that something unusual has been going on. The autonomic nervous system has set all these forces in motion automatically.

This great and all-pervading system is divided into two sections: the sympathetic and the parasympathetic. These systems themselves are a sort of paradox for they primarily work against each other in a cooperative manner that attempts to maintain body health. The two systems are generally opposed but counterbalance one another in controlling the myriad involuntary processes that keep us alive and perking. They exert their influences, depending upon the circumstances, on the lungs, heart, liver, spleen, stomach, pancreas, adrenals, kidneys, colon, intestines, sex glands, and bladder.

The sympathetic system usually concerns itself with rapid adjustments in adversity, initiating or increasing activity, and is greatly influenced by changes in the external environment. Although constantly involved in routine day-to-day maintenance, it is sometimes called the "emergency system" because it prepares us for the intense muscular activity that may be involved in meeting a stress situation. The parasympathetic nervous system works most of the time at achieving normalcy, inhibiting or decreasing activity, and repairing the ravages of time throughout the body. For example, impulses from the sympathetic system speed the heart rate and cause digestion to slow down. Parasympathetic impulses do the opposite. Impulses from the one system dilate the blood vessels; from the latter contraction results.

These traditional concepts on the antagonistic functions of the sympathetic and parasympathetic nerve systems have recently been challenged, however, by Dr. Stewart Wolf of Galveston, Texas. He has presented impressive evidence that the two systems are not always opposed in their actions but on occasion work hand in hand in order to serve the needs of the body as a whole. The relevance of these various nerve patterns and the importance of the autonomic nervous system itself will become more discernible as the full story of psychosomatic medicine unfolds.

But invaluable and essential though the autonomic nervous system is, it performs a baleful mission when the mind is deeply disturbed by unfortunate or dismal events: unhappy telegrams surge from the brain along the wires of the autonomic telegraph system carrying news to the organs of the body that create storms of disease. And the nerves themselves have long borne the burden of blame for our emotional weaknesses. We have all heard such comments as, "My nerves are in terrible shape!" or "If only I could do something about my nerves!" Obviously, there is nothing organically wrong with the nerves as such; they merely carry the messages telling the colon to contract or the lungs to breathe faster. Such vital factors as heredity, personality, past experience, and environment can create increased sensitivity in the autonomic nervous system nd determine the innumerable emotional responses that we will experience every day of our lives.

Diseases of stress

Just as there is more than one road to Rome, however, there are routes other than the autonomic nervous system by which our minds can do our bodies harm. Dr. Hans Selye, a great Canadian physician and investigator, discovered through years of research that certain stresses—psychic, physical, or both—can so alarm our mental reaction centers that they will immediately dispatch urgent messages to our endocrine glands calling for emergency action. Again let us emphasize that the functions of all of our body's systems are so interlaced that it would be impossible to eliminate any one of them. Yet these messages of *stress* do not follow the normal route through the autonomic nervous system. They are delivered to the top executive among the endocrine glands and possibly the body's most important organ, the pituitary gland.

The pituitary gland is located at the base of the brain, nestled and cradled in a complete bowl of bone to insure maximum protection from injury. Upon receiving the danger warning, the pituitary promptly signals the adrenal glands, one perched atop each kidney, which serve as indispensable assistants and cooperate in the production of a wide array of hormones that help the body combat the effects of stress situations. If the proper hormones are poured out by the glands in the right quantities to counteract the stress, then all is well. But frequently the glands produce too much or too little of one or more of the hormones and illness results.

If the original stress that sparked the čall for help to the pituitary and adrenal glands was psychic, then the resulting physical ailments can quite properly be regarded as psycho-somatic. These might include disorders of the heart, blood vessels, kidneys, and joints. Or the body's failure to respond appropriately with the precise hormone secretions may contribute to severe headaches, diabetes, peptic ulcer, and to a host of other medical problems. As research progresses, the list becomes longer and longer.

The subject of Selye's "diseases of stress" is admittedly complex but strangely intriguing and will be explored at greater length in a later chapter. It is not nearly as irrelevant as it may appear for, indeed, in this fast-paced, troubled world in which we live, none of us is immune to the perils of stress. And frequently our only clue to the developing disorders, whether they come to us on the pathways of the autonomic nervous system or the hormonal highways of stress, is the almost inaudible whisper of emotion that exudes from somewhere deep within us.

Understanding our emotions

Unfortunately, the term emotion is grossly misunderstood. It is not an emotion, such as fear, that pulls the trigger and sets the wheels of the body's emergency systems into motion. On the contrary, emotion itself is but one phase of our reaction to a particular event or situation that may strike us as pleasing, frightening, or perhaps ominously threatening. Only when the various body systems involved have generated sufficient nervous energy, a process requiring only a tiny fraction of a second, do we become conscious of emotion. It is, therefore, not a *cause* or a *stimulus* but rather a *part* of the body's reaction. When we experience joy, satisfaction, hope, fear, anger, guilt, or whatever, the sensation is simply a conscious expression of our internal response to a given circumstance. In other words, fear itself does not trigger rapid breathing, tense muscles, and so on but is a vital part of that reaction as it is manifested in our conscious minds.

It is of utmost importance that this point be made as clear as possible for it is one of the primary factors in understanding and preventing the development of psychosomatic disease. It is possible, you see, for widespread emergency measures to be taken by the body's involuntary systems, causing undue strain on our various organs and considerably altering our relation to the world about us, with no conscious feelings whatsoever.

Indeed, the whole concept of psychosomatic medicine is based on the certainty that chronic unconscious tension does exert far-reaching effects on the circulatory system, the blood sugar, and most of the internal organs and that it occurs in a large segment of our population. Only when we learn to recognize and interpret the ominous whispers of emotion that filter out from our inner depths can we hope to control or erase these threats.

three

The seed bed of disease

> "Rare is the tree whose every bud develops
> into perfect fruit, and if there be such a
> family tree, I find no adequate evidence of
> it."
>
> —Victor Vaughn, M.D.

It is little help to a person with a migraine headache, for example, to tell him that the headache is "just psychosomatic" and that all he needs to do in order to gain relief is "learn to control his emotions" or "develop more will power." Indeed, that is no simple assignment and, in certain instances, is virtually impossible without competent medical assistance. It would be far easier if the headache were not directly related to emotions but rather the result of obvious physical factors—as excessive smoking or lack of sleep. The cure would be evident and discomfort need only be temporary. But when the problem is of mental origin, there can be no simple remedy.

We have explained that emotions do not cause a physical reaction to a given circumstance but merely represent a conscious manifestation of our inner response to that event. What, then, determines that response? Why can one person bear up under a torrent of troubles while another succumbs to a seemingly insignificant conflict? Why does Mary react so violently to an episode that scarcely fazes her companion? Why does John develop an ulcer when working for an unbearably critical boss while Charlie merely shrugs it off? The answers to these questions and many more lie buried in the seed bed of our minds.

Every one of us is a fantastic composite of heredity, childhood influences, environment, past experiences, motivations, goals, and a host of other elements. If we were to attempt an evaluation of our specific emotional reactions to certain events without considering the whole panorama of life, our conclusions would be as divergent as the "views" of the three blind men who tried to describe an elephant from the portion that each touched first. "It is like a rope," said the man who thoughtfully stroked the tail. "Oh, no!" said the second man, wrapping his arms around one of the elephant's tremendous legs. "It is much more like a tree." "You are both wrong," said the third man as he moved his hands slowly over the elephant's side, "It is definitely flat like a wall." Obviously, we cannot learn much about an elephant, a machine, or, more particularly, the human body by examining an isolated part—a part can only be understood as it relates to the whole.

Heredity

Our life began at the precise moment when egg and sperm united in our mother's womb. Prevailing genetic factors determined such obvious physical features as the color of our hair and eyes, our complexion, bone structure, as well as a potential strength or weakness in our diverse organs and tissues, and a tendency or susceptibility to certain diseases that might have appeared in preceding generations. We do not, however, inherit personality traits as such.

Both physical and mental characteristics do depend to some degree upon experiences in the prenatal period. The embryo, for example, is sensitive to sound; loud noises cause the unborn heart to beat faster. And if the disturbances persist, energy is consumed that might better be used for building body and nerve tissue.

There is also little doubt that if the mother suffers from serious emotional strain during pregnancy, it can have an adverse effect upon the unborn child. Adrenalin secretion, for instance, increases during stress and could be transmitted to the embryo, causing it to be unusually active. It is possible that such children will always carry with them a greater charge of nervous energy than others and be regarded as "nervous" individuals who startle easily and react sharply to any sudden stimulus.

But, as Henrik Ibsen wrote, "What we have inherited from our fathers and mothers is not all that walks in us." For us to dwell upon the factors of heredity can be an extremely depressing and detrimental influence on our emotional stability for we all have at least a few skeletons in the closet—dreaded diseases, neuroses, mental illnesses, even criminal characteristics occurring among our forebears. And by overemphasizing such ailments and negative personality patterns we can, either consciously or unconsciously, "inherit" them.

A young lady whom we shall call Jeannie fell victim to just this sort of psychosomatic illness. Her mother had died of acute diabetes mellitus shortly after Jeannie's birth and her grief-stricken father had never fully recovered enough to marry again. He wanted Jeannie to feel that she had known her mother so he told her often of her mother's wonderful ways, her beautiful smile, how charming and considerate she had been, and how much they had loved one another. And Jeannie grew up loving her.

She was constantly reminded, however, by concerned friends and relatives that she should be extremely cautious—"diabetes is hereditary, you know." An ever-present, conscious horror of the disease was compounded by an unconscious sense of guilt that in some way she had been to blame for her mother's death. During her first pregnancy, Jeannie showed an abnormal amount of sugar in her urine and further tests verified the presence of diabetes. She was panic stricken!

Fortunately, her doctor was familiar with the family history and recognized the possibility that psychological factors had precipitated the illness. He explained to Jeannie the strange mechanisms of the autonomic nervous system; that she had involuntarily inflicted such a relentless strain on her body that it had responded by producing the disease she so feared. And since she had grown to be a strong-willed, capable young lady, she was able to bring her subconscious thoughts out into the open and cast them aside. Medication quickly brought her diabetes under control, she gave birth to a lovely, healthy daughter, and her ailment soon disappeared completely.

Heredity is in itself a temptation for us to "think" ourselves into an illness. But it is not usually the fault of the tree that every bud does not develop into perfect fruit. On the contrary, a bud generally erupts as a potentially good apple. It is the external influences that do the damage and great care must be observed in every state of development to guard against wind, hail, insects, blight, and the whole army of environmental enemies.

Childhood influences

Many of us will never again experience a shock comparable to that of birth. Psychologists believe that unless the trauma of this shock and the associated fear for safety are overcome by tender loving care during the early months of life, they may instill within us a sense of uncertainty and fear that will not be easily conquered. Indeed, birth is when a beginning must be made in building a sound mind in a sound body. And feelings of security, harmony and affection are essential in laying the foundation.

The newborn infant has a mind that is far more susceptible to outside impressions than one might suppose. He has a depth and degree of sensitivity like that of an unexposed photographic film. The emotional atmosphere in which he finds himself will leave its imprint on his unconscious mind for years to come. Particularly unfortunate are those infants conceived under the illusion that the patter of little feet can resolve marital maladjustments. Much to the contrary, the children usually become the principal victims.

Dr. Flanders Dunbar, a pioneer in the field of psychosomatic medicine, writes of what she refers to as "emotional contagion." The youngest infant can be infected with fear or anger or disgust even more easily than with the measles, but the discerning parent can see the symptoms long before they develop into major tragedies. By the same token, the child can "catch" love and trust and respect.

She tells an amusing story of a four-month-old girl who suddenly was unable to tolerate liver soup after eating it with obvious enjoyment for a month. It developed that an aunt who kept the child while the mother worked had a distinct dislike for "eating the insides of animals." Although she offered the baby "just one more spoonful of that nice liver," her real sentiments were transmitted, simply by emotional contagion, and the child refused to eat. The solution was simple: Auntie should not attempt to feed the child liver soup.

Such emotional contagion confined to a distaste for liver would not be a great danger except for the possibility of setting up an allergic pattern. But just as an infant is sensitive to his elders' likes and dislikes in food, even when concealed, so he reacts to other factors. No amount of dramatic acting can prevent the unwanted child from knowing his real place in the family affections. The feeling of rejection may emerge years later in the form of loneliness or a crushed spirit or rebellion, or it may be repressed and covered over with other experiences, but it will remain a menace to health and happiness. The pattern of a good many bodily ailments contains the thread of the unwanted child.

Problems incurred during toilet training of the child can also have far-reaching effects. If the process is not handled properly or if the child is punished severely and shamed for his delay in changing his habits, he may store away his resentment and inhibitions in the dark recesses of his unconscious mind with resulting psychosomatic disturbances of bowel function much later in life. Indeed, there appears to be no limit to the role that childhood influences can play in our adult years.

Environment

Environment, especially within the family, has more to do with molding our personalities and our ability to handle difficult situations than any other element. As stated previously, we do not inherit personality traits as such; they are the result of our environment, particularly in the formative years. Comprehensive studies of infants adopted shortly after birth reveal that these children grow up reflecting the personality patterns of their adopted families and surroundings rather than those of their natural parents.

If, for example, a child is reared in an atmosphere of constant gloom, pessimism, and complaining, he is likely to become a confirmed hypochondriac. Excessive criticism or lack of affection in the home can retard or destroy one's pride and self-esteem to such an extent that he develops a crushing inferiority complex. This lack of confidence, either in school or, later, in an occupation, will lead to a life of worry and anxiety . . . and psychosomatic illness.

Dr. John Schindler, in his book *How to Live 365 Days a Year*, elaborates on the various family atmospheres that can produce immaturity and emotional stress. In the "kill-joy atmosphere," for example, he describes a patient named Betty who came from a family of constant gloom and sour grapes. Like the rest of her family, Betty had no sparkle or lustre because any hint of humor or joy was nipped in the bud. She developed none of the qualities that would make her popular at school. Her negative attitude prompted both students and teachers to avoid her. By the time she was 13, Betty's gloomy emotions had produced numerous real and imagined physical ailments; these became her major concern. Her first thought each morning was, "How am I sick today?" And from that time on, she was never without medical attention any year of her life. By the age of 40, she had undergone five major operations, including a hysterectomy.

Betty's dilemma, which is not at all uncommon, might have been avoided had the family merely taken the time to enjoy life. Such little things as setting aside one night each week to just sit in front of the television *together* and eat popcorn, or play a game of checkers, or attend a family movie. When a busy father can take time to "wrestle" on the floor with his boys, or play baseball with them, or build a model, he will endow them with treasures that money can't buy. And a mother who invites her daughters into the kitchen for sheer enjoyment rather than begrudged assistance, or listens intently to their "impossible" problems, or has time for a pleasant game of Scrabble will find that the generation gap is not nearly as wide as it would appear. The whole idea is to willingly utilize the little, ever-present opportunities for pleasantry and simply be nice to each other. Indeed, this is a good rule to employ in all walks of life.

Certain psychiatrists have suggested that specific "family types" might well be associated with particular psychosomatic diseases. In a study conducted at Stanford University in California, for instance, it was learned that ulcerative colitis—inflammation and ulceration of the colon—was frequently linked to "restricted" families. In these familier, humor, novelty, and creative response seemed to be discouraged. They spoke quietly and with little expression in their voices. Arguments and emotional comments, anger and affective responses, were generally avoided. There appeared to be a conscious awareness of disharmony in the family and yet an agreement that this will not be mentioned in front of other family members. Characteristically these families held themselves in rigid, wooden attitudes and their restrictiveness even extended to physical posture.

It was concluded in the study that such family restrictiveness does not in itself cause ulcerative colitis. Rather the stress produced in these families by the repressed emotions and desires may enhance what is already a genetic predisposition, an inherited tendency, to the disorder.

Even temporary household difficulties can have a pervasive influence on one's health. This has been termed "the family factor" and was the subject of an entire symposium at the annual meeting of the American Academy of Pediatrics in Chicago several years ago.

One rather typical case that they cited concerned a seven-year-old girl named Judy who suffered from a persistent skin rash. A salve prescribed by the family pediatrician had no effect. When subsequent treatments also failed, an allergist was consulted. He determined that the child was sensitive to eggs but, even after eggs had been omitted from the diet for over a week, the rash continued to spread. Judy was then hospitalized for further testing. But before the results of the tests could be interpreted, the skin began to clear.

Obviously, her affliction had been related to something to which she was exposed at home. When the pediatrician made further inquiries, Judy's mother happened to remark that her husband had been fired from his job at about the time the rash had first appeared but she couldn't see where that could be important. Quite to the contrary, the strained temperament of the parents had greatly disturbed the child and induced the physical reaction. A few days in the hospital, away from the tensions at home, had relieved her anxiety. Hopefully, when the parents realized the effect of their emotions, they would provide a healthier atmosphere for Judy's return.

Crises in the family can also alter a child's resistance to the ever-threatening bacteria that precipitate colds, ear infections, even strep throat. Such occurrences as the death of a grandparent, moving to another home, loss of a job, or the onset of a serious illness in a loved one have been noted frequently just before a child exhibited signs of infection. And children are certainly not alone in this sensitivity to strenuous conditions, either in the home or elsewhere in the environment. Numerous infectious diseases have been traced to undue emotional strain or depression.

What can be done to curb the family factor and relieve strenuous situations in our environment? One leading authority has stated, "We must educate families to meet crises and reduce household disorganizations." And that is, indeed, the answer to the problem—the desired end—but grossly oversimplified. Unfortunately, the means by which we can achieve that end have thus far eluded us. We might also say that to achieve world peace we have only to educate the nations of the world to settle their differences peacefully and be friends. But wars continue. We can begin, however, by securing peace in our own backyards and, similarly, easing tensions as best we can in our own environments. Great strength can be found in the words of this little verse:

> I am but one, but I am one.
> I cannot do everything, but I can do something.
> What I can do, I ought to do.
> What I ought to do, with the help of God, I shall do.

Improving our emotional environments is no simple assignment, to be sure, but with bullish determination and cooperation, it can be done. And although our ability to change our own emotional atmosphere depends immensely on the environment in which we ourselves were reared, that need not be an insurmountable obstacle.

Past experiences

Lucretius once said, "I am a part of all that I have seen." We prefer, however, Stewart Wolf's recent inversion of that statement,

"All that I have seen is a part of me." Traumatic experiences, whether physical or emotional, will have a definite effect on a person's reaction to a given circumstance.

If, for example, Mary had been driving a car some years ago and inadvertently struck and killed a child who darted out from between two parked cars, merely seeing a child standing on the curb near two cars might trigger an hysterical outburst. Or if Mary, either consciously or unconsciously, harbored a sense of guilt because of the child's death, it might reveal itself years later as a seemingly unrelated physical ailment.

Even our reaction to such everyday events as a knock on the door or a ringing phone is largely determined by our past experiences, in combination with our present environment. One who has heard the ominous words come through the wires of the telephone, "This is the Hospital Emergency Room . . . there's been an accident!" may cringe in terror every time the phone rings. To the lonely shut-in, starved for companionship, the ringing of the telephone is a moment of anxious expectation. The busy executive, crowded by a rapidly approaching deadline, responds with increased tension and anger as he hears the interrupting ring.

Countless times each day we experience emotional responses determined by our peculiar backgrounds. But just as often, we suppress emotions with little or no conscious awareness that we have done so. Unless these emotions are a healthy blend of the pleasant and the unpleasant, we soon become prey for somatic assault.

Although it seems rather far-fetched, it is even possible for psychosomatic illness to be linked to the date of a tragic event in a person's life. This strange manifestation has been referred to as an "anniversary reaction." A person may, for example, experience severe shortness of breath exactly one year after a serious heart attack. Or he may develop such a related symptom on the anniversary of a parent's death.

One patient, an elderly widow, suffered from three such reactions—hay fever, diarrhea, and a bothersome skin rash on both forearms and hands—which occurred every year at a specific time, then disappeared. No physical signs, such as allergy or intestinal trouble, were found to account for her disorders. But a careful interview turned up three dramatic events in her past that had occurred on the dates she experienced her ailments.

Such "anniversary reactions" as these are not too unusual and further attest to the devious mechanisms of the body's autonomic nervous system.

On call from the unconscious

In order to better explain the mystifying processes of the mind and its uncanny ability to store factors of heredity, environment and experience in a sort of seed bed, let us again borrow an analogy from Dr. Frank Slaughter. He proposes that we consider the mind as a house. Much of our daily living involves the kitchen, so we will label it the conscious portion of our minds. All of the articles that are essential for everyday activities are assembled there within reach.

Just outside the kitchen is the pantry or utility room that houses those items we use from time to time but which need not clutter the kitchen. They are easily accessible; we have only to open the pantry door and take them out. The pantry thus represents the preconscious, or subconscious, portion of our minds—a sort of halfway point between the conscious and the unconscious levels. Here we assemble the mental perceptions that are called upon occasionally but not regularly.

Many of the things in our house, however, are not needed at all in normal living. We therefore carry them into the attic, which represents the unconscious mind. All that we have ever experienced, painful or pleasant, even racial instincts, are stored in the attic of the unconscious.

We usually manage to achieve a certain amount of emotional stability by shoving the memories we particularly fear or dislike into the attic, but we do not always arrange them in such a manner that they will not be shaken loose in a storm. And just when we think we have our lives running smoothly, lightning strikes and something tucked away in the attic comes tumbling down into the kitchen, producing an acute emotional reaction. Ordinarily, we take such unpleasant offenders and replace them in the attic at once, being certain to put them away more carefully.

Or we may take a good look at them and find they are not nearly so painful and unpleasant as we thought they were; they no longer pose a threat. This, indeed, is the principle of psychotherapy.

If we have haphazardly stored too many items away in our unconscious minds, they will continually filter down into our lives and we will be referred to as "neurotic." Or we may experience severe storms or emotional earthquakes during which, in spite of our best efforts, all sorts of unpleasant memories and impulses surge down the stairs and threaten to inundate our very sanity. These earthquakes may be caused, at least in part, by puberty, marriage or the lack of marriage, death of loved ones, the menopause, occupational difficulties, serious illnesses, or other occasions of extreme tension or crises.

There is yet another room to our house, however, a most important room, which represents the autonomic nervous system. It is the bedroom. As a barrier against unwelcome visitors from the unconscious, we often place a board in front of the kitchen door so that anything tumbling down from the attic will be deflected into the bedroom. This board might be called "repression." It keeps us from seeing the skeletons falling out of the attic, but it does not prevent them from disrupting the all-important autonomic activities of the body. And we know that continued disruption can only wreak havoc in various target organs. The heart, in particular, frequently comes under attack.

four

Miracle healing power
for heart troubles
and high blood pressure

> When man is serene and healthy the pulse of
> the heart flows and connects, just as pearls
> are joined together or like a string of red
> jade—then one can speak of a healthy heart.
>
> Huang Ti
> (The Yellow Emperor
> 2697-2597 B.C.)

Until five o'clock on the evening of his admission to the hospital, Elmer had apparently been in good health. But while preparing to leave his office he suddenly developed a sharp pain in his chest and collapsed; within minutes he was in a hospital bed in an oxygen tent and described by his doctor as being in a state of shock. His illness was diagnosed as coronary thrombosis—heart attack!

Elmer was only one of countless thousands of persons who suffered heart attacks last year and his story was not unlike a great many of theirs. Characteristically, they were competitive, driving individuals, hell-bent on success, proud of the long hours they labored and maybe even a little resentful of the lack of appreciation they received for it—our success-conscious society molds them. Yet they were not merely victims of overwork. They were victims of the psychological factors that spurred their apparent ambition.

Elmer, for example, was a building contractor, financially sound but under a tremendous amount of pressure from the competition. His job was seven days a week, day and night, for he felt that he could not afford to be rude to prospective customers who called at nine o'clock at night or on Sunday afternoon. The business had come down to him from his father who had worked slavishly to build it. And although a heart condition had forced his retirement several years back, he still kept one foot in the door, constantly reminding Elmer of the importance of turning out good work. "That's what built this business, you know."

But it was becoming increasingly difficult to hire efficient, conscientious workers. "You just can't depend on people anymore," Elmer had often complained. "They don't want to accept responsibility. My foremen come to me with every little problem. I go to work in the morning feeling refreshed but by noon I'm exhausted, ready to give it all up. Why, if I had fifty dollars a week and was happy, that's all I'd really need." But he didn't give it up; he kept right on plodding away—until five o'clock one evening.

Elmer's heart attack, from which he did recover, was most certainly a physical ailment—it left scar tissue on his heart about the size of a small marble. But it was also psychosomatic. Even the untrained eye can readily detect some of the offending circumstances: inherited predisposition to heart disease, repressed hostility toward inconsiderate customers, pressure to conform to his father's rigid standards, competition from other businesses, constant emotional tensions related to his employees, and a host of other factors. This is a picture that is being repeated all too frequently in our culture today, a man caught up in a highly competitive business struggling to manage his labor and please his customers, and finally getting caught in the middle—in Elmer's case by a heart attack.

Diseases of the heart differ almost as much as the emotional factors involved. And our knowledge concerning those diseases, as well as the emotional involvements, is rapidly expanding. Almost instinctively, however, the heart has been held in awe since earliest times. Folklore held it to be the seat of the emotions, both love and hate. Valentines, symbols of love, are supposedly heartshaped. We say that the heart leaps for joy, stops for fear, breaks for grief, palpitates for love, throbs for sympathy, beats for courage, flutters in modesty, and even that it moves about the body, appearing in the mouth for fright and descending to the shoes in sadness. Perhaps more has been written of the heart than of any other organ.

How the heart works

Yet one who knew the heart only through the outpourings of centuries of romantic writers would never recognize this important muscle if he saw it on the dissecting table. It weighs about 12 ounces, is reddish brown in color, and has an unimpressive shape—more like a pear or a clinched fist than a Valentine. It is about six inches long, three inches thick, and, at the broadest point, about four inches across. A powerful, hardworking four-chambered pump, it circulates our blood by alternately contracting and relaxing. Its rhythmic beat is, indeed, the rhythm of life.

Every day the heart pumps over 3,000 gallons of blood through nearly 60,000 miles of blood vessels at the rate of four quarts a minute. Its only rest is the half second between contractions and the slightly relaxed heart rate permitted during sleep when a large percentage of our capillaries are inactive—the beat slows from a normal around 70 down to about 55.

The heart, like other muscles, works because it receives impulses from nerves. The impulses that make it beat come from delicate nerve cells and fibers which are complete in the heart, with no outside connection. Thus the heart is truly automatic and can operate quite independently; when all nerves are cut, as in a heart transplant, the newly implanted heart goes merrily and efficiently about its business of circulating blood in its new home.

But the impulses that regulate the *rate* of the heartbeat come through two pairs of nerves outside the heart—one from the spinal cord and one from the medulla, the lowest portion of the brain that adjoins the spinal cord. These nerves receive messages from other parts of the body and pass them along to the heart. No other body organ responds more quickly and delicately to changes in the autonomic system.

Since society frowns on spontaneous outbursts of rage or even unrestrained shouts of enthusiasm, we have learned to repress our emotions, keeping them pent up inside us. And unlike most other body organs, the heart and blood vessels have no means of working off emotional conflicts by external discharges. They can respond only by increased or decreased heart rate, an irregular beat, or high or low blood pressure. It is not surprising, then, when we consider the hair-trigger mechanisms under which the heart operates, its vital role in body functions, and its inevitable reactions to emotional conflicts, that the heart is extremely susceptible to psychosomatic disturbances. Indeed, coronary artery damage, clotting, circulatory disturbances, high blood pressure, even a sudden halt of all heart action can result from prolonged tensions.

Shadow symptoms of heart disease

Under the bombardment of disturbing messages from the brain, the heart may begin to act in an abnormal manner. A typical symptom might be extra beats. Actually, every heart misfires on occasion, piling one beat on top of another. This does not mean that there is anything wrong with the heart. But if it occurs repeatedly, it can be regarded as a shadow—the shadow of potential heart trouble—for the basic stress that causes such symptoms can ultimately lead to either structural or organic heart disease. Or it can worsen organic heart disease that is already present.

Strictly speaking, shadow symptoms of themselves are harmless and cannot be called psychosomatic disease since organic changes have not yet occurred. But the grave danger lies in our failure to establish the basic cause or causes of the symptoms and to take whatever steps are necessary to alleviate the problem. When shadow symptoms are allowed to continue for a long period of time, organic changes usually do occur; then we have psychosomatic disease.

A familiar shadow symptom is palpitations, or fluttering, of the heart. This rapid beating, even throbbing, of the heart is basically an abnormal consciousness of the heartbeat. And like most of the psychosomatic heart abnormalities, it is closely related to anxiety, rage and repressed hostility. Unfortunately, hostility can create anxiety and anxiety of itself can cause more hostility. We find ourselves being drawn into a whirlpool of self-destruction.

Margie, for example, was a chronic worrier. Almost every night she would lie awake listening to the thump, thump, thump of her heart, pounding as if it were trying to jump out of her chest, and, even more alarming, it would often seem to add an extra beat. Her doctor assured her on several occasions that the condition was merely a by-product of her unhappy emotions; fretting about it would only tend to worsen it. But Margie could not free herself from the vicious cycle of anxiety—shadow symptoms—increased anxiety—more pronounced symptoms—greater anxiety, and so on and on. And in her continuing trek from clinic to clinic, she will no doubt be assured someday that she shows evidence of true heart disease—self-inflicted.

Some persons are bothered by an irregular heartbeat—sort of a hop, skip, and a jump. Or, the heart may race, for short periods or for days or weeks on end, depending on the psychic stimulus. In some instances, the heart rate may actually decrease.

Breathlessness, too, can be a shadow symptom of potential heart disease. Emotional upsets are often accompanied by gasping, sighing, even choking, frequently with dramatic overtones. And although they are not of a physical nature, such symptoms do represent a basic need for adjustments in our emotional behavior.

Pain over the heart may afflict some of us when we are exposed to unpleasant or strenuous situations, or when unrecognized stress has set the wheels of the autonomic nervous system into motion. This is especially true if we have, at some time during our lives, witnessed a dramatic heart seizure or been deeply hurt by the death of a close friend or relative from a heart attack, even if these experiences have been consciously forgotten but stored away in the attics of our minds. Usually this type of pain has nothing to do with the heart but it does constitute a shadow symptom; chronic heart and chest pains can lead to physical disorders if the underlying cause is not sought out and corrected.

There is a distinct difference between real heart pain and the shadow symptom. Pain *over* the heart in the lower left chest usually stems from intense anxiety or similar emotions. Genuine heart pain is deep, often in the upper abdomen as though it were an attack of acute indigestion. Or it may come from behind the breast bone, or sternum, move to the left shoulder and then radiate down the left arm. The victim of a severe heart attack suffers from a feeling of profound constriction, gasping and choking for breath, and a horrible sense of impending disaster. The scene is generally more terrifying than dramatic; dramatic attacks arouse suspicions that a strong conscious factor might be involved.

Coronary artery disease

Although the heart is quite fragile and delicate, it is one of the hardest working muscles in the body. J.D. Ratcliff has said that the heart works twice as hard as the leg muscles of a dash runner, or the arm muscles of a heavyweight boxing champ. Such exertion demands considerable nourishment and, indeed, the heart consumes about ten times the nourishment required by the body's other organs and tissues. This means it must have an efficient, rich blood supply. And so it does.

But the heart does not extract nourishment from the blood that flows through its chambers almost constantly. Instead, it is fed by its own two arteries, called the left and right coronary arteries, which are charged with the crucial task of supplying blood to all segments of the heart muscle. These arteries are not much larger than soda straws at their trunks, encircling the heart, then branching out to thoroughly infiltrate its many cells.

Our coronary arteries are a particularly weak spot in the circulatory system and can be subject to several types of ailments. In fact, such disorders constitute one of the chief causes of death and disability in western civilization.

Any interference with the normal flow of blood through the coronary vessels may result in a malfunction of the heart. Muscle spasms might occur in the walls of the arteries and cause such a narrowing of the vessels that blood flow is temporarily shut off. Or, the walls of the coronary arteries might harden, as in arteriosclerosis. Or they might be narrowed by layers of a fatty substance, as in atherosclerosis. And when the heart demands an extra measure of oxygen and nutrients, as in acute emotional states or during undue physical strain, the constricted arteries simply cannot furnish ample blood. A cardinal symptom of insufficient oxygen is angina pectoris, or pain over the chest and in the left arm—a shadow symptom indicating a potentially dangerous condition. For if the narrowing continues, or a sudden, crippling muscle spasm occurs, or a blood clot forms or becomes lodged in a coronary artery, the blood supply to the heart becomes blocked, resulting in coronary thrombosis or coronary infraction, both terms referring to the cutting off of the blood supply to the heart.

When an artery shuts down, the section of the heart muscle it feeds promptly dies. The dead tissue is gradually absorbed into the bloodstream and replaced with scar tissue. And although the scar may not be much larger than a garden pea, it can be half the size of a tennis ball. The degree of danger depends on the size and location of the plugged artery.

Organic factors play an important role in causing coronary artery disease. High intake of animal fat, excessive smoking, and lack of reasonable daily exercise are important. But psychic turmoil can also contribute or perhaps even be the chief culprit and it is then that a heart disorder becomes a psychosomatic illness.

Psychic trauma can have a harmful influence on our body chemistry and the level of fats in our blood, not to mention tightened arteries, blood clotting, higher blood pressure, and generally a faster pace for the heart. For the patient who already has heart trouble, it may impose an additional load that a diseased heart simply cannot bear. When the heart muscle is operating at its peak, the added burden of unhappy autonomic or glandular discharges caused by emotional disturbances may overwhelm it.

Few of us have not come into contact with coronary artery disease in one way or another. We particularly recall a man, we'll call him Jim, who paid dearly for his failure to heed his doctor's warnings.

Jim was born and reared on a small farm in Arkansas. Money was scarce and the work-load was heavy, so he was only able to complete the ninth grade of school. But he learned well the lessons of the land and became an excellent practical farmer. He was extremely conscientious in his work and not only did well on the family farm but hired out on occasion to the large farmers in the region. Later he went north to Iowa where he found employment on a prosperous vegetable farm. His hard work did not go unnoticed and over the course of the years he was promoted first to assistant foreman and then to general manager of the entire farming operation. His performance was consistently excellent. Jim had no time for marriage or relaxation, however, no hobbies or diversions of any kind—he was married to his job.

When he was forty he began noticing palpitation of the heart, occasionally his pulse would race, he would have extra heart beats. Worried, he consulted a physician. After a thorough examination revealed no evidence of organic heart disease, the doctor warned Jim to slow down, to "take it easy and enjoy life a little more." But Jim didn't think he was the type to slow down, convinced that doing his job properly required full effort and was the only enjoyment he needed. He continued to work hard, harder than anyone else on the farm. And although he felt reassured by the results of his examination, his symptoms persisted.

At the age of fifty he began having chest pains. Again he went to a physician and again no organic damage was found. The doctor urged Jim emphatically to follow a slower pace, but to no avail. The pains gradually increased, both in intensity and in frequency. When he finally did slow up some, he worried enough to more than compensate for the decrease in his work effort. At the age of fifty-six he was seized one day with a deep, excruciating pain in his chest. He collapsed and was taken to a hospital where coronary thrombosis was diagnosed.

Jim was in the hospital for two months. After his release he found it difficult to work because of recurring pains. His worry increased and he found it almost impossible to sleep nights. Some eight months later he suffered another attack—his last.

Although other factors in his background no doubt contributed to his illness, Jim's chief problem was his obsessive, driving ambition and his extreme conscientiousness. Pride in one's work and the determination to succeed are certainly admirable qualities and should not be discouraged. But they must be tempered with sufficient pleasure and relaxation if we are to enjoy good health, both physically and emotionally. All work and no play not only makes Jack a dull boy, it could even make him a dead one—as it did in Jim's case.

Disturbed blood circulation

Frequent fainting might be considered a forewarning, a shadow symptom, of a disturbance in our blood circulation. But occasional "blacking out" is not at all uncommon, even in completely healthy, well-adjusted persons, particularly in circumstances when they are expected not to show fear. This is why strong, healthy men frequently faint when facing an injection, drawing of blood, or minor surgical or dental procedures. It is considered disgraceful for a man to exhibit fear so he represses it, but the autonomic nervous system is not easily deceived. It knows that the person would much rather run than resist so it prepares the body for escape.

The muscles begin to fill with blood, borrowed from the general body circulation. But the person cannot take flight, cannot even relieve himself by screaming. What would people think? He *must* take the needle or be sewn up without flinching. He remains· motionless instead of fleeing as he would like to. The muscles continue to fill with blood. The blood pressure drops, circulation to the brain is curtailed, vision becomes blurred, and the darkness of unconsciousness descends. Some people are able to fight off the actual fainting, others are not. Parents in particular, who attempt to watch or assist while their child gets a broken bone set or a laceration sutured or a tooth pulled, are prime candidates for this type of fainting.

One does not faint when he is reclining. Therefore, placing the person in the horizontal position or lowering the head toward the floor to aid in returning blood to the brain promptly cures the ailment. We cannot say with conviction that fainting, even repeated fainting, leads to true psychosomatic disease. But it does reflect an undue response to psychic influences. Certainly no good can come from even brief periods of impaired circulation to the brain.

Fainting that results from a disturbance in blood circulation can readily be distinguished from hysterical fainting in which there is a symbolic conscious expression of psychic conflict. Hysterical fainting is much more dramatic and there are no actual changes in the circulatory system.

More serious than fainting are a cluster of symptoms of disturbed circulation induced by psychic repression that includes numbness, tingling, coldness, and an unpleasant crawling sensation of the fingers, sometimes the toes. These symptoms can be viewed as shadows of circulatory disease which may become manifest if the cause is not determined and relieved.

We have seen a thirty-year-old school teacher, intelligent and graduated with a master's degree, who exhibited this very symptom. After a number of years of teaching English in a small private college, Jenny began to experience an occasional tingling in her fingers and thumbs. Sometimes they appeared blanched and felt cold and numb. When her symptoms did not disappear, she consulted her physician. He examined her thoroughly and found no physical disorder but suggested that the problem might well be psychosomatic. He referred Jenny to a psychotherapist.

She was reluctant to follow her doctor's advice, she was not "crazy," her fingers really did feel numb. But finally she gave in and after only a few sessions, the psychotherapist determined Jenny's trouble. He also succeeded in convincing her that you don't have to be mentally disturbed to need the services of a psychotherapist. Quite unconsciously, Jenny envied her fellow teachers who were married and had families while she had none. She was greatly surprised when it was explained to her that the circulatory problem stemmed from this repressed hostility, coupled with the fear that she might never marry. She had no idea that unrecognized emotional turmoil could reflect itself in physical symptoms of this nature and could, in time, lead to serious impairment of circulation and permanent organic changes.

Jenny decided to take forthright steps to meet more young men and to make herself more attractive. Before the end of another year had passed, the "right" man came along. Jenny's symptoms disappeared, however, not when the young man proposed but long before that: indeed, when she understood the basis for the symptoms and started doing something about the problem. Truly, a disease known is half cured!

High blood pressure

Our blood pressure represents one of the best indexes we have to the health of our circulatory system. It is of a dual nature, with the *systolic* pressure representing the pressure within the blood vessels when the heart is pumping blood out through the arteries and the *diastolic* pressure giving the reading when the heart is relaxed after pumping. The figures are expressed in terms of the height of a column of mercury on a standard scale. Normally, the systolic pressure should read about 120 millimeters of mercury or less and the diastolic pressure 80 millimeters of mercury or less, referred to orally as "120 over 80," or written in this manner: 120/80.

Many persons live long lives with pressures somewhat higher than these. In fact few people over forty maintain pressures this low. Nevertheless, these are the normals.

Why should we be interested in high blood pressure, or hypertension as it is usually called? Mainly because it is the major cause of death or disability. Perhaps as many as half of the deaths in people over the age of fifty are the result of some form of hypertensive disease. If prolonged, it can lead to kidney disease, coronary disease, stroke, brain alterations, and a host of other unpleasant ailments. And it seems to be intimately associated with the speed and strain of our modern, high-pressure civilization.

Indeed, hypertension is almost unknown in primitive countries. This was borne out in a study of a group of black men living in native Africa and an equal number of the black race living in the United States. Hypertension was extremely rare in the African group but relatively common in the American black men. It would appear that the difficulties inherent in the social adjustments that the black man must make in most areas of our country induce the need for an extraordinary degree of self-control. And repression is the crucial factor in causing high blood pressure.

There are many physical causes of hypertension. The dismal list includes malfunction of the kidneys, overactivity of the thyroid gland, tumors or overgrowth of the adrenal glands, drugs, and disease of the blood vessels, including arteriosclerosis—related to aging—and atherosclerosis—believed to be closely related to our intake of animal fats such as fat in meat, cheese, and butter. But another cause, and probably the most significant, is mental and emotional trauma.

Hostility and the closely-associated emotions of anxiety and rage, even envy and hate, are prominent figures in the development of high blood pressure. Many persons who succumb to hypertension, including all too many young people in the late teens and early twenties, appear on the surface to be well-adjusted and mature, pleasant and agreeable. But they seem to have a hang-up when it comes to unburdening themselves of their aggressive emotions. In our society we cannot express hostility freely, and rightfully so. Some people have a sort of inborn ability to protest gracefully—others do not. They live in a continually restrained, chaotic state which inevitably results in psychic trauma and, in those who are susceptible, in high blood pressure or hypertension.

Repressed rage and anxiety works exactly like a pressure cooker with a lid screwed down tightly. As pressure builds, the petcock must be opened to release pressure; if it is not properly released the consequences could be tragic. The pattern is often as follows:

A hostile feeling, leads to
Fear of retaliation of others, plus
Dependent longings, and
Feelings of inferiority, with subsequent
Reactivation of hostility, followed by
Anxiety and further restraint of hostile feelings, then
Hypertension

Or the source of the trouble may be hidden in the vast attic storehouse of unpleasant emotions, childhood experiences, and inherited tendencies—the reservoir from which might trickle the feelings of uncertainty, resentment, fear, and hate that can overwhelm us. Even those people who exhibit a great deal of restrictiveness and self-control might be carrying around a live and bubbling volcano beneath the surface of the unconscious. And when the emotional tension is continually disrupting the autonomic system, causing faster heartbeats and rising blood pressure, the chain of heart, blood vessel, and other physical changes can eventually cause the volcano to erupt; a real explosion might occur in one of the blood vessels of the brain—a cerebral hemorrhage.

Unfortunately, hypertension appears to have few heart shadow symptoms, although the patient may well have shadow symptoms in other segments of the circulatory system or in other areas of the body. It can therefore reach a serious level before it is discovered, usually in a routine or annual physical examination. A delay in discovery will permit the condition to become unpleasantly advanced. Regular check-ups are *so* important! Only through prompt detection of the problem, elimination of all possible organic factors, and, if necessary, psychotherapy can psychosomatically-induced hypertension be controlled.

But frequently we can reorder our own lives without resorting to a specialist in this field. After consulting your physician and having a thorough physical examination with electrocardiogram and all other advisable tests, you may be restricted to a low salt diet and given some form of drug therapy. Strictly speaking, however, these are not cures. They are essential, to be sure, in order to control the high blood pressure and prevent further organic damage.

They do not ease the basic emotional disorder, however, that is causing your high blood pressure. Only *you* can do that. Realization of the part emotion plays in hypertension and a concerted effort to avoid upsetting situations will greatly help. Often the sort of measures suggested in the last chapter of this book on self helps will be effective. The reader is referred to that chapter.

It is almost inconceivable that Huang Ti, who was quoted at the beginning of this chapter, could have perceived the great truth over 4,500 years ago that "when man is serene and healthy the pulse of the heart flows and connects . . . then one can speak of a healthy heart." Truly, in all of our impressive laboratories and with all of our advanced equipment, we have yet to devise a better treatment for psychosomatic heart disease.

five

How to prevent, retard,
and cure breathing ailments

The average unmarried female, basically
insecure
Due to some long frustration, may react
With psychosomatic symptoms, difficult to
endure,
Affecting the upper respiratory tract.
In other words, just from waiting around
For that plain little band of gold
A person . . . can develop a cold.

Frank Loesser

Ten, twelve, perhaps fifteen times per minute your lungs expand and contract. Under normal conditions you probably give little or no heed to your breathing, although your lungs provide you, quite literally, with the breath of life. It may even surprise you to learn that the most common psychosomatic ailments for which help is requested involve disturbed breathing. And because these various breathing irregularities can mimic almost any clinical disorder, their diagnosis is difficult and frequently overlooked, thus allowing them to become chronic, severely disabling, or even fatal. Hopefully, by gaining some insight into the nature of the respiratory system and its weaknesses, and by clarifying some rather simple treatment techniques, we can prevent, retard, or even cure a broad measure of psychosomatic respiratory ailments.

What is the respiratory system?

Essential though the lungs are they represent only part—although certainly a vital part—of the greater body function that we call *respiration*. It can be defined as the exchange of gases between a living organism and its environment. For in a creature as complex as man, some sort of provision must be made for the trillions of cells to receive and dispose of certain elements. To solve the problem, a masterful plan was devised that involves close cooperation between the lungs and the heart and blood vessels. The heart and blood vessels, which we have already examined, concern themselves with what might be termed internal respiration—transporting substances to and from the cells. The lungs and their assistants are involved with external respiration—carrying oxygen from the air to the blood and disposing of wastes, primarily carbon dioxide. In order for these exchanges to occur, we require a large, moist surface where air and blood can come closely together so that the process of exchange can take place. The lungs were designed precisely for such a purpose. Then there must be a pathway through which fresh air can be moved into the lungs and stale air removed. Finally we need a bellows—the chest cage fills this order—with nerves to control it and muscles to power it, so that air can be breathed in and out of the lungs.

Specifically, the respiratory system consists of the lungs and the numerous passages leading to the lungs from the outside of the body. Inhaled air first passes through the *nose* or *nasal cavity*, then through the passages back of the nose or *nasal pharynx*. It then passes downward into the *throat* or *pharynx*. The pharynx divides into two sections: the esophagus, which leads into the stomach, and the *trachea*, a large, cartilage-ringed tube carrying air downward toward the lungs. The trachea splits into two slightly smaller tubes designated *bronchi* that pass directly into the lungs. In the lungs the bronchi divide into finer tubes named *bronchioles*. At the upper part of the trachea is the *voice box* or *larynx*, which makes speech possible. It can properly be regarded as part of the respiratory system.

An important balance: oxygen and carbon dioxide

As we inhale, the lungs fill with oxygen-rich air. In the interior of the lungs, the red blood cells pick up oxygen and release carbon dioxide. Oxygen is essential for the vital functioning of our diverse body cells; carbon dioxide is a waste material thrown off by the cells. We must retain, however, a certain minimal amount of carbon dioxide in our blood stream if we are to remain healthy. Impaired or improper breathing can seriously alter this precarious balance and produce illness.

Breathing is both voluntary and involuntary

The function of breathing involves a strange combination of voluntary and involuntary control. We can inhale and exhale at will but when we try to hold our breath for more than a limited period an irrepressible urge forces us to start breathing again. Also, many chemical and nervous factors influence breathing. And as is true with so many body actions, they are not all completely understood.

Emotions reflected in respiration

Since breathing bears such an intimate relationship to life itself, it is not surprising that emotion-charged experiences would be reflected in changes in respiration. Sadness or discouragement may bring on sighing respirations. A stunning sunset might evoke a deep lingering breath. Or sudden fright may cause us to "catch" our breath. Worrisome problems are referred to as "weights on the chest." Or we may get something "off the chest" by confiding in a friend or by sounding off to an antagonist. If we keep a painful subject to ourselves for a long period we may be said to harbor a "smothered" feeling. Unhappiness may cause us to feel a "lump in the throat."

Even many of baby's first experiences are closely related to breathing: he cries, smells, coughs, and sneezes. When he drinks, he must coordinate sucking, swallowing, and breathing. His lungs make it possible for him to express unhappiness or hunger by crying; they allow him to show happiness or contentment through cooing. Breathing and its associated actions thus play a key role in helping baby to begin communicating with the members of his family. So from the very first, breathing is interlaced with a host of emotional activities.

It is not difficult to see, then, why various psychosomatic ailments involving the respiratory system might result from intense or prolonged psychic stimuli. Indeed, the respiratory apparatus is richly supplied with nerve connections of the autonomic nervous system. This was borne out by a laboratory experiment in which several persons were given painful stimuli, causing their breathing to quicken. Later, when they were merely reminded of the painful experience their respiration increased just as it had during the original suffering. But unpleasant mental or emotional experiences can do far more than merely change the breathing pattern: they can and do cause psychosomatic illness in which the mind induces a harmful change in the body.

HYPERVENTILATION

Hyperventilation, also referred to as overbreathing, usually stems from serious anxiety. It is not, of course, the only physiologic reaction to anxiety; blushing, paleness, quickening of the heart rate occur frequently. But scientific articles support the assertion that as many as one in ten patients who consult physicians suffer from overbreathing.

Shadow symptoms

The shadow symptoms of overbreathing are many. They include chest pain; dizziness; numbness or tingling of various parts of the body; headache; feeling of impending doom; fear of insanity, heart disease, or fatal illness; and the chief complaint—difficulty in catching one's breath. Frequently, however, a person may become so preoccupied by one or another of his other symptoms that he may be totally unaware of the overbreathing itself.

In its early stages, overbreathing is in itself a shadow symptom since there are no organic or physical changes. The victim reacts to anxiety with heavy sighing, or perhaps deep, rapid breathing that proceeds for hours, days, or even longer. In time the body becomes involved: prolonged overbreathing means that the person blows off excessive quantities of carbon dioxide, gradually depleting his blood supply of this gas. Recall that although carbon dioxide is largely a waste material, a precise level must be maintained in the blood for normal respiratory activity to occur. As the level of carbon dioxide decreases, symptoms appear. At first the fingers or toes begin to tingle. Then the patient becomes giddy or light-headed. He may feel faint or his vision may blur. His arms and legs twitch or even undergo mild spasms or jerking. Should the overbreathing be severe or prolonged the person may lose consciousness. If he has been taking tranquilizers or sedatives—and many anxious persons do—he may even stop breathing for half a minute or more, throwing those about him into a panic. It may well be that in some such cases breathing will not be resumed at all unless artificial respiration (mouth to mouth breathing being the preferred method) is given.

The line between the shadow symptom of overbreathing and organic changes is thin, but when chronic anxiety causes the persons to repeatedly overbreathe, the reaction becomes a fixed habit, organic changes in the form of depleted blood carbon dioxide occur, and psychosomatic disease is present. Here, as always, the name of the game is to prevent the shadow from developing into the substance.

A classroom incident

An incident occurring in a classroom training young men for highly specialized work in industry introduced us to a classical case of hyperventilation, or overbreathing. Thirty students were taking a final examination, the climax of many weeks of intensive study, when one of them, a husky young man in the first row, suddenly collapsed and fell from his seat to the floor. The instructor was aghast and immediately sent for a physician who happened to be working in the building at the time. Making his way through the excited crowd that had promptly gathered, the doctor made a hasty examination but could find nothing to explain the loss of consciousness. He summoned an ambulance and the youth was rushed to a hospital. Hardly had the stretcher been wheeled into the emergency room when the patient suddenly woke up, looked about in confusion, and asked, "Where am I? What happened?"

A thorough examination failed to reveal any organic cause for the seizure. But careful questioning made it apparent that the student, who had been for some days deeply concerned with his studies, was a victim of hyperventilation. He freely admitted that he had been extremely concerned over passing the test and that his breathing had been both deep and rapid for at least three days. Ultimately he had exhaled sufficient carbon dioxide to cause him to faint. The physician explained the syndrome to the student and administered a mild sedative. The instructor talked with the young man, reassuring him, and a make-up examination was set for a few days later.

In this instance recognition of the nature of the problem, coupled with competent reassurance of the physician and sympathetic understanding from the instructor were all the medicine the patient needed. He did not, to our knowledge, suffer any recurrence of hyperventilation.

Chronic overbreathing adds to fears

The importance of arresting overbreathing before it becomes a true psychosomatic ailment is highlighted by the possible consequences. The person who has had several attacks, losing consciousness, will begin to restrict his activities for fear he will have an attack in a public place, causing embarrassment, or even that his life would be in danger if he should faint under certain circumstances, as in traffic or while driving a car. He will become fearful of leaving his house or traveling any distance at all. And there is the very real danger that if he should have an attack while under sedation, the possibility exists that it could be fatal. An example has been described in a well-known medical journal of a student who died from experimental overbreathing. It is not hard to understand, then, why persons who have suffered from repeated episodes of overbreathing "run scared." They lead fear-ridden lives, which only compounds their original problem.

All sorts of events can trigger attacks of overbreathing: witnessing a violent act, hearing a police or ambulance siren, watching a violent television program, receiving a telephone call late at night, even reading an alarming report in the newspaper. In recent years the sudden deaths of such nationally known figures as President Kennedy and Martin Luther King, receiving as they did such wide coverage by the mass media, reportedly triggered a great many episodes of hyperventilation.

Underlying factors in overbreathing

Many persons have no idea what constitutes the source of their fear. Still others show a strong tendency to hide—either consciously or unconsciously—the underlying factors or events. Most often it is anxiety associated with death, or the fear of death. The loss, either real or threatened, of loved ones through death, separation, or divorce is most typical. The fear of having or developing a fatal illness, as cancer, heart disease, or brain tumor, is frequently a cause of overbreathing.

The symptoms of hyperventilation itself, including dizziness, numbness, and giddiness, further contribute to the victim's insecurity and often instill the fear of insanity. He may begin to disassociate himself from the world, feeling as if things are not quite real, or that he is an outsider looking in. Such persons have described a sort of "floating sensation" that is experienced as a barrier between himself and the real world. He thus becomes increasingly concerned about his sanity.

Fear of attending church

It is not uncommon for persons who harbor guilt complexes because of real or imagined sins to experience attacks of hyperventilation while at their place of worship. The fear of punishment, or of eternal death, or of estrangement from God, can cause such intense emotional conflicts that overbreathing occurs, resulting in loss of consciousness.

A lady, whom we shall call Agnes, suffers repeatedly from fainting during church but refuses to believe that it might be of psychic origin. The evidence, however, is conclusive. She has a long history of conflict about religious belief. During childhood, she was taken to church frequently, if not regularly, by her mother who clung doggedly to her faith against the strong opposition of her father, a zealous atheist. Family quarrels were frequent, bitter, and painful.

When Agnes married, her religious problems were only magnified because she married a man of a faith quite different from her own. Reluctant to relive the unbearable conflict she had known at home, she decided to join his church although her heart was not in it. Her husband's untimely death from heart failure a few years ago left her grief-stricken. After several months, however, she transferred her membership back to the church she had attended before her marriage.

Shortly thereafter Agnes began to experience dizziness. The spells gradually worsened, her hands and feet became numb and cold with a strange tingling sensation. When chest pains beset her she feared, quite understandably, that she was suffering from heart disease. Her doctor examined her thoroughly and assured her that her heart was amazingly strong and healthy. But her dizziness has continued. On at least three occasions during the past year she has fainted during church. Each time she has been rushed to the hospital but ECG findings indicated no heart damage or irregularities, although her pulse was quite rapid.

Her doctor explained the possible existence of hyperventilation and suggested psychotherapy but she vehemently refused, criticizing him for his "lack of understanding" and his reluctance to prescribe tranquilizers that might relax her. Unfortunately, she appears destined to follow a collision course and her fear of death may indeed become a reality.

Steps for treating overbreathing

Until the person who suffers from overbreathing is convinced that his symptoms are of psychic origin, and faces squarely the events or circumstances that are responsible, there is scant chance that the condition will be relieved. This is where the person will usually require help from psychotherapy.

The steps in treatment include these:

1) Serious physical disease must be searched for and ruled out. Such physical problems as high fever, hot weather, brain infection, aspirin poisoning, high altitudes can all bring on hyperventilation.
2) The patient must be reassured that his condition, however distressing, is completely curable.
3) The therapist must demonstrate to the patient how the symptoms are related to overbreathing—by having him overbreathe.
4) The patient must be made to see clearly and beyond doubt how the precipitating factors have led to the hyperventilation response. Seeing the link between psychic tension and the hyperventilation is probably the most important object of all. If the overbreathing was initiated by an unhappy event then that event must be explored, however painful to the patient, until doubt concerning the connection between the event and the overbreathing has been resolved.

Early diagnosis and treatment is emphasized in order to prevent chronic disability. Even more important, however, is prevention which rests on our understanding of the syndrome and imminent dangers of exaggerated fears and anxieties.

ASTHMA

Asthma represents a breathing problem that often stems from a combination of physical and psychic problems. It involves a constriction or tightening of the bronchioles of the lungs to the extent that the air passages are obstructed, especially when exhaling. Excessive amounts of secretions pour into the bronchioles making a bad situation worse.

Emotional and physical aspects

Certainly, many physical factors are involved in the production of asthma. It may be in part—perhaps largely—caused by an allergy or sensitivity to a great variety of substances ranging from dust and pollen to food. Infection can play a role. Heart disease can help bring it on. Heredity may provide the background. Nevertheless the role of psychic pressures is unquestionable.

An emotional disturbance can increase the severity of asthma that is primarily due to exposure to pollen or mold to which the person is sensitive. For without the psychic problem the allergic factor might not have been sufficient to bring on the asthma. One authority assures us: "Bronchial asthma is a psychosomatic problem. . . . Probably two-thirds of these asthmatic conditions are emotionally caused. . . ."

Powerful psychic stresses help bring about asthma by affecting the brain control of the bronchioles, causing them to shrink or contract. The "order" for this constriction rides to the lungs over the wires of the ubiquitous autonomic nervous system. As long ago as 1887 a scientist found that an electric shock to the brain of a guinea pig caused the animal's bronchioles to constrict. This is quite similar to what happens to human bronchioles when an unpleasant stimulus surges from the brain to the lungs.

Personality patterns

Although there is no one personality that is particularly prone to develop asthma, some physicians believe that attacks are more likely to occur in persons with an exaggerated need for love and a great fear of losing loved ones. Others have been known to develop attacks after sexual temptation, severe competition, anger, or intense anxiety. Suppressed or frustrated longings may produce symptoms that would never have been caused by an allergic irritant alone.

Curious psychic influences in asthma

Yes, psychic influences rate a high priority in causing asthma. We remember a fine and enormously talented young man who was allergically sensitive to egg. If he unknowingly ate egg in a pudding or cake he would become violently ill and would also develop an attack of asthma. But on one occasion he developed asthma—just as severe—when he knowingly ate chicken. He had no allergy to chicken and he knew that he didn't. But chickens, he explained, lay eggs and that was reason enough to develop asthma. He likewise suffered from asthma after eating eggplant—again knowingly—just because *egg* is part of the name of the vegetable. He was not allergic to eggplant.

Quite similarly, artificial roses have been known to cause asthma in persons allergic to real roses. A person suffered a miserable case of asthma after driving down a road lined by ragweed, a frequent allergic irritant. But later he developed an equally violent attack on the same road long after all the ragweed had disappeared, buried under the snows of winter. Indeed, an idea, a fear, or a feeling can set off an attack of asthma at least as readily as a whiff of pollen or a luscious bowl of strawberries. And the desensitization to such sensitivity must be psychic!

Crying and laughing related to asthma

A curious relationship has appeared between asthma and crying—or, strangely, laughter. Scientific studies have revealed that an asthmatic attack might well represent a substitute for a crying spell induced by anxiety or rage. Some asthmatic children appear unable or unwilling to cry. Some asthmatic patients assert that they have not cried for years. Still others have suddenly developed crying spells after their asthmatic attacks ceased.

Lucia was driven to succeed

Let us consider the case history of a charming young girl, Lucia, who came perilously close to dying from asthma. Lucia, who was sweet sixteen in 1940, was an extraordinarily bright teenager whose prime goal was to obtain superlative grades in school. In this she was not only encouraged but driven on by her parents. Neither of them, though both highly intelligent and ambitious, had been financially able to secure a college education. So Lucia, an unusually attractive young lady, became imbued with the goal of superlative—not just good—grades.

Bright though Lucia was, she was sometimes hard-pressed to top her class. And, like so many other intelligent, strongly motivated persons, she had more than her share of allergies. Hers included some sensitivity to uncooked corn, raw onions, chocolate, peanuts, molds, and ragweed. No reaction reared its head upon exposure to these irritants, however, unless she happened to fall under psychic pressure—as she did at exam time.

Then, given an allergic irritant, Lucia would explode—no other term could explain her situation—into an acute asthmatic attack. She would sit on the very edge of her bed—the only position in which she could find relief—hands supporting her extended trunk. She would hungrily draw in each breath of the life-giving oxygen. And you could not escape the impression that she believed that each gasp would be her last. Injections of epinephrine—this was before the advent of cortisone—would provide temporary relief. But it was only temporary and Lucia's ordeal (the doctor's, too) would go on for days. Then the easing of psychic tensions and the effect of medication would relieve the attack. Lucia's doctor was all too aware of the terrible possibility of "status asthmaticus," a condition in which the asthma may not be relieved by *anything* and the patient descends the path beyond the point of no return.

Happily Lucia recovered. An easing of parental pressures for extraordinary grades and a more realistic viewpoint on Lucia's part as to what is really important resulted in a complete halt of asthmatic attacks.

Physical hazards of asthma

But what might have happened had Lucia's attacks not been interrupted? She could have gone on to attack after attack. Her schooling would have inevitably been piecemeal. Worse, she would have accumulated the dreadful physical alterations of asthma: thinning and eventual scarring of the lung passages, emphysema, and finally—and most dreadfully—a barrel chest in which every breath is a painful exertion and a prayer for relief from a miserable existence.

If it is not possible to improve the environmental conditions, family conflicts, or emotional problems within the confines of the home, manipulation in the form of removal from the family home and temporary placement in an institution often helps relieve asthma. Most desirable, of course, is control within the familiar settings which depends heavily upon the sufferer's determination to adjust his life accordingly.

HAY FEVER

Some persons, like the disconsolate unhappy maiden descirbed in the quote at the beginning of this chapter, develop what appears to be hay fever or a head cold because of mental or emotional frustration. Technically termed *rhinitis* and often accompanied by red and weeping eyes, this unattractive and distressing condition closely resembles a virus infection or allergic hay fever.

Indeed, it may represent the combined result of allergic sensitivity to inhalant or food and psychic stress, just as does bronchial asthma. The shadow symptoms of temporary irritation of the mucous membranes of nose and eyes progress to permanent changes in the tissues with time; at this point psychosomatic disease is present and real cure can be protracted and difficult. Here again, an ounce of prevention is worth a pound of cure.

BREATHHOLDING

Young children can create quite a panic and invent a scene at the highest dramatic level when they choose to hold their breath. Typically, the child shows his resentment against not having his way by holding his breath until he loses consciousness.

In one case of record, a physician was called to see a twenty-one-month-old child who had been holding his breath until he passed out. The household was nothing short of chaotic when the doctor arrived. Parents, brothers and sisters, even grandmother and aunt were madly rushing about, screaming frantically for the baby to wake up. Several questions revealed that this was not the first time baby had terrorized the family in this way. And he seemed to delight in doing so.

The doctor examined the child in a most casual manner and urged the family to calm down and act as if nothing unusual was happening. When the baby regained consciousness, all was placid and in order. Baby did attempt several attacks in the future, but finding a completely unreceptive audience, gave it up as a bad job.

TICS

Tics can be cited as another form of psychosomatic respiratory disease, minor but potentially bothersome and even, in certain circumstances, disastrous. These consist of grunting, snorting, coughing, or speech peculiarities such as excessive *oh*ing or *ah*ing. They begin as symbolic or defensive movements, shadow symptoms in reality. But should they persist they can become fixed in the nervous system and defy uprooting. At this point they have become organic and can only be viewed as true psychosomatic disease, even though they will never threaten life. But they may prejudice employers or associates and have, in our experience, contributed to loss of jobs.

Tics often appear in childhood, disappear for years, then reappear in adolescence or adulthood. They can always be eliminated when the patient is sympathetically given to understand their basis and makes a determined effort to eliminate them.

LOSS OF VOICE

Sometimes anxiety and tension can cause loss of voice or laryngitis, especially in public speakers. We knew a young woman, "supercharged" with nervous tension, who habitually spoke loudly and rapidly. Not until she began to lose her voice was she ready to listen to counsel. Then, with the help of a mild sedative and a large dose of restraint on her part, she was successful in toning down her speaking so that her normal voice returned. Even now it retains a raspy quality that will probably remain.

How to protect your "breath of life"

As in the case of all psychosomatic disease, whether in the shadow symptom stage or full-blown, the first step is a careful diagnostic check-up to determine if psychosomatic illness is indeed present or if the ailment is partially or completely organic. Then follow the doctor's recommendations. If your problem does have a psychosomatic factor he may recommend psychotherapy or he may feel as the physician did in Shakespeare's *MacBeth:*

Macbeth:	How does your patient, doctor?
Doctor:	Not so sick, my lord,
	As she is troubled with thick-coming fancies,
	That keep her from her rest.
Macbeth:	Cure her of that.
	Canst thou not minister to a mind diseased,
	Pluck from the memory a rooted sorrow,
	. . . .
	Cleanse the stuff'd bosom of that perilous stuff
	Which weighs upon the heart?
Doctor:	Therein the patient Must minister to himself.

The last chapter, titled "A Treasury of Wonder-Working Remedies" will aid the reader in "ministering to himself."

six

New relief from
"nervous stomach": how to gain
back youthful digestion

> You can't ignore the importance of a good
> digestion. The joy of life ... depends on a
> sound stomach, whereas a bad digestion
> inclines one to skepticism, incredulity,
> breeds black fancies and thoughts of death.
> Joseph Conrad

If we were to compile a list of factors that contribute to good mental health, hence to good physical health, it would seem to be without end. Yet, the entire list might then be condensed into five words which would encompass all the rest: *Enjoy Life at Its Fullest.* For a person who truly enjoys living has no time for psychosomatic ailments. Unfortunately, however, too few of us ever achieve that lofty goal.

Being human, we are plagued by all sorts of unpleasant emotions and mental hazards that threaten to tear us down each time we climb to a new level of happiness. Anger, hostility, rejection, dissatisfaction, compounded by tension and the occasional feelings of inadequacy that beset us all, constantly prey on our peace of mind. In defense, we try to swallow the distasteful emotions that well up in us, but we don't digest them. They linger in the digestive tract producing such reactions as nausea, vomiting, heartburn, diarrhea, constipation, even ulcers and colitis. For, next to the heart, the digestive system is most responsive to the emotions. Indeed, in biblical times the "bowels" were even thought to be the seat of the emotions.

What is the digestive tract?

The digestive tract is essentially a long, hollow muscular tube, extending from mouth to anus, and lined throughout with mucous membrance, as the inside of your mouth. The various *salivary glands* pour their secretions into the *mouth* where a tiny amount of food digestion occurs. The *pharynx* leads from the mouth downward toward the stomach, changing to the *esophagus* as it descends. The esophagus leads into the top of the *stomach.* And while the stomach is foremost in our minds when we speak of digestion, it actually absorbs few nutrients of the food passing through it. Through its mechanical, churning actions and the secretions of gastric acids, food is prepared for digestion. This important function is carried out almost exclusively by the next section of the digestive tract, the long and snake-like *small intestine,* which consists of three parts: the *duodenum,* the *jejunum* and the *ileum.* Without the small intestine we could not digest and absorb enough food to stay alive. After digestion has taken place, the liquid food wastes are passed on to the *large intestine* where water is extracted and food wastes are concentrated. The large intestine continues downward until it becomes the *rectum,* then the *anus.* And every part of this long tract responds to emotion, being richly supplied with fibers from the autonomic nervous system.

Emotions can disturb digestive activity

C. T. Copeland once said, "To eat is human; to digest divine," paraphrasing a more familiar quotation. And indeed, the mere swallowing of food by no means indicates that it will be used by the body for it must first be digested and absorbed. Even such auxiliary organs as the liver, the pancreas, and the gall bladder play a part in digestion. And unhappy emotional responses can disrupt this process at any point along the entire route.

Fear, alarm, or depression can cause the salivary glands of the mouth to stop functioning, resulting in great difficulty in swallowing and a dry, "cotton mouth" condition. The glands of the stomach temporarily cease their production of gastric juices. The muscle walls of the esophagus, stomach, intestines, even the rectum, tighten up like a fist. The many "entrances" and "exits" along the digestive tube become immobile. Digestive activity screeches to a painful halt. And you have *nervous indigestion!*

Emotional conflict and anxiety can also produce the opposite effect—overactivity—including an overproduction of digestive acids and an increase in the normal contraction and relaxation motions of the muscular walls by which food is moved along. If this stepped up pace is prolonged, the mucous membranes become fragile and oversensitive; tiny breaks occur. The excessive amount of acids in the various portions of the tract can further irritate the breaks, finally resulting in ulceration.

When nervous indigestion, ulceration, or any other physical changes occur in the digestive tract in association with emotional turmoil or upsetting life situations or undue mental strain, the condition is rightfully classified as psychosomatic, although the patient requires definite medical attention. Indeed, one authority has estimated that 85 per cent of all digestive disturbances are the result of emotional problems. And perhaps the most frequent and important of these ailments is peptic ulcer.

PEPTIC ULCERS

Peptic ulcers represent little erosions in the lining either of the stomach or of the duodenum, the first part of the small intestine just below the stomach. The exact cause of peptic ulcers remains elusive although poor or irregular eating habits are known to contribute. Gastric acids are secreted into the stomach at regular intervals and if there is no food present, the acids will become concentrated and can eventually burn through the mucous membrane, causing ulcers.

But psychic conflict and tension and the damaging impulses that flow down the nerves of the autonomic nervous system as a result are certainly liable for much of the blame. X-ray and laboratory studies verify their guilt. For that matter, however, even poor eating habits, skipping meals, or eating late might well be associated with emotion-charged circumstances. Thus the line between psychic and physical causes is again uncertain.

Observing the stomach at work

Drs. Stewart Wolf and H. G. Wolff were permitted to observe the lining of the stomach itself under varying conditions, witnessing first hand the formation of stomach ulcers as a result of emotional conflict. A man who worked in their laboratory had scalded his throat so severely that he was unable to swallow. This had happened forty-seven years earlier when, at the age of nine, he had swallowed boiling hot clam chowder. Through a remarkable surgical operation, a permanent opening was made through his abdomen so that food could be put directly into his stomach through a funnel. He chewed the food first to start the digestive processes, and perhaps to retain some of the pleasure of eating. This sounds grotesque but the man actually managed quite well. Or so it appeared. But there must have been some emotional difficulties because the two doctors, who observed the mechanical and chemical behavior of the stomach by looking directly through the hole in the abdomen, recorded the development of stomach ulcers as a result of emotional maladjustments. They concluded, "It appears likely, then, that the chain of events which begins with anxiety and conflict and their associated overactivity of the stomach and ends with hemorrhage or perforation is that which is involved in the natural history of peptic ulcers in human beings."

Stimulation of the autonomic nervous system, then, causes increased secretion of stomach juices, including hydrochloric acid and certain protein-digesting enzymes, which, in proper amounts, serve a useful purpose in breaking down food; when they are produced in excessive quantities the stomach begins to eat itself. Ulcers form.

Ulcers—a disease of "civilization"

Peptic ulcers rarely occur in such countries as northern India or South Africa. Rather, they represent a disease of "civilization."

And they occur more frequently in cities than in suburban or rural areas. Among men in administrative and professional fields they are especially prevalent. Peptic ulcer has frequently been thought to be limited to persons in the higher socio-economic groups. This is not true! Dr. William J. Mayo points out, "Unfortunately only a small number of patients with peptic ulcer are financially able to make a pet of the ulcer." No, the ulcer cannot be regarded as a badge of financial success.

A shift in sex of persons afflicted

One of the interesting aspects of peptic ulcer is the fact that there has been a remarkable shift in the sex of persons afflicted in western civilization. Before 1900 peptic ulcers occurred far more frequently in women than they do today. About 1910, the sex incidence became nearly equal and since that time more and more men and fewer and fewer women have been developing peptic ulcers. This has happened in spite of the fact that the total number of ulcers has been constant, total population taken into consideration.

Why should this be? Before 1900 women experienced deprived lives; they were severely restricted in their personal freedom, had little opportunity for self-expression, often spent their lives in virtual slavery. As one explores old cemeteries he is impressed by the numbers of men buried alongside two, three, even four wives—and in a day when divorce was almost unheard of. The wives had been worn out, one after another, by the harsh work of a farm woman in that day before "modern conveniences." Men, on the other hand, enjoyed a highly favored social and economic status.

Now, however, women have been largely "liberated" and it is the men who, for the most part, are caught in the well-named rat race of modern competitive life. So it is the men who now possess more peptic ulcers, four times as many as women. And this shifting incidence of the disease provides excellent evidence that peptic ulcer is, to a large extent, a psychosomatic disease, stemming from psychic pressures. Perhaps, as women advance into more and more executive positions in the business world, their "liberation" might backfire and the incidence of peptic ulcers will again be equally divided between the sexes.

Typical personality

The typical person with an ulcer has been described as a tough, hard-driving individual, who refuses to acknowledge, even to himself, his dependency on others. He is hypersensitive and hyperirritable. His compulsion to succeed might stem from a deep inner sense of failure to adjust to the world in the process of development into an adult. It may relate to an inability to find the love and affection so badly needed in his home life. Attaining success in the world is his mask of strength and independence, although underneath his frustrations are only heightened because he is rewarded with increasing responsibilities. As a rule, this person plays as hard as he works, obsessed with winning. If he plays golf or tennis, for example, and competition becomes keen, the ulcer patient will not profit from his recreation because of his burning desire to win.

It has been estimated that approximately 10 per cent of the population will suffer at some time in their lives from peptic ulcer. And 50 per cent of those persons will have recurrence of ulcer symptoms within a year, and 75 per cent within two years. These crises in physical symptoms usually coincide with crises in emotional tension, when minor psychic earthquakes shake out the old fears, guilt, and resentment from the unconscious and allow them to prey upon the sensitive lining of the stomach. When an ulcer becomes acute, it may erode through a blood vessel–bleeding ulcer–and the consequences could be tragic.

Shadow symptoms

How can you recognize the symptoms of peptic ulcer? Suppose that a person becomes disturbed because he finds himself in a position considerably beyond his capabilities. Or perhaps he has landed in a vocational field for which he is not equipped by either training or experience. Or perhaps the work-load becomes unbearable. Refusing to admit to weakness, the person struggles to prove himself. At first the work stresses only make him uncomfortable. But even this mild discomfort can be the first shadow symptom.

Then he has difficulty sleeping. His disposition, formerly pleasant, suffers. He snaps at his wife and children for little or no reason. Then a vague, pit-of-the-stomach fullness occurs after meals. He attributes this to "acid indigestion" and takes one of the remedies so enthusiastically recommended on television. But the discomfort persists. He begins to notice "hunger pains" before meals. Or they might wake him in the middle of the night. And he finds that food or antacids will relieve the discomfort, at least temporarily. Days, weeks, months, perhaps several years later, the distress becomes unbearable because he has a real ulcer in his stomach or duodenum. His initial discomfort was but an ominous shadow of what lay ahead. With an organic lesion in the form of an ulcer, he now has a psychosomatic disease.

Peptic ulcer can be physical in origin

We must emphasize that peptic ulcer can result from non-psychic factors. One type occurs when the brain is injured. Blood vessel disease can bring about an ulcer. Surgery on the brain or a severe burn can stimulate ulcer formation. So can disease of the pancreas or of other endocrine glands. Certain drugs can induce ulcer. So naturally, a thorough examination by a physician is the first step if you suspect an ulcer. Only when organic causes are ruled out can you assume that your ulcer stems from psychic tensions. But when it is concluded that the initial cause of the ulcer is emotional stress, immediate steps should be taken to eliminate the unpleasant influences, if at all possible.

Ben's job precipitates an ulcer

Ben was in his middle years and had worked at a railroad headquarters office in a midwestern city since graduating from high school. He was a conscientious, hard-working employee. His family life was happy. But Ben was basically insecure. Both of his parents had been cursed with nervous temperaments, easily upset, and Ben showed his heritage. He found it difficult to accept even mild criticism but managed to swallow his anger and embarrassment. He found it particularly difficult to contain himself, however, when the division inspector for the railroad visited the office where he worked.

Over the course of the years, Ben had suffered from a "nervous stomach." He always carried antacid tablets for his "acid indigestion." But his condition became worse rather than better. He began experiencing pain before meals. Eating seemed to help only temporarily. When it became evident that his condition was worsening, he consulted his doctor.

X-rays were taken that revealed a large duodenal ulcer. In addition to giving medication and prescribing a bland diet for a limited period, including frequent feedings of certain highly alkaline foods, the doctor talked with Ben about his work. When he learned how tense Ben became each time the inspector made his visits and how "critical" everyone was of Ben's work, he urged him to enjoy himself more and not to take his work so seriously. Frequent weekend trips with his family, fishing outings, and simply "relaxing" would be, according to the doctor, just as effective as medication—perhaps more so. Because unless Ben could see his life and work in the proper perspective, medication would only relieve the symptoms temporarily; he would probably resume his suffering within a year.

With this new insight into his ailment, Ben determined to follow the doctor's advice and start "enjoying life for the first time in my life." He now looks forward to retiring and having more time to "go fishing and just putter around the house." He no longer requires medication; he doesn't even carry his antacid tablets anymore.

George's lack of a job precipitates an ulcer

But unfortunately, not all persons who suffer from ulcers can alleviate their problem so efficiently. Unpleasant influences, inescapable environment, even physical handicaps, can pose seemingly insurmountable problems. Whereas Ben's difficulty stemmed from his maladjustment to his job, George developed an ulcer, along with a host of other ailments, primarily because he was physically unable to hold a job. Or, more precisely, he could not hold a job that he deemed "worthwhile" or whieh offered him the prestige that his insecurity demanded.

George had been the oldest of eight children, growing up during the 1920's with scarcely enough to eat. His father shuttled from one job to another, moving the family each time to a new location. Being the oldest, George was expected to carry a large share of the chores. He had to quit school after the fifth grade in order to help out at home; all seven of the other children were allowed to finish high school. And when George took a job on a nearby farm once, his mother promptly took the money he brought home to "buy little Johnny some new pants and a pair of shoes." George felt that he deserved some new pants and a pair of shoes just as badly as little Johnny. Similar incidents laid a firm foundation for a life plagued by insecurity, hostility, and resentment, and the determination to be "somebody."

Then came World War II and George was called upon to serve. Three years later he returned with shrapnel wounds in his left shoulder and his left arm hanging lifeless at his side. Although several jobs were offered to him, he turned them down remarking, "They just feel sorry for me and I don't need their sympathy!" or that the job wasn't worth having. He finally took a job as a salesman but it lasted only a few months. Other jobs came and went but George failed to find the security and prestige he so bitterly craved.

Five years after he had come home from the war, he learned from his doctor that the terrible pains he had been suffering were from peptic ulcer. He took medication but was unable to adjust his life accordingly; other complications developed—diabetes, heart trouble, and circulatory problems—and George died at the age of forty-two. Heart attack, the doctor had said, possibly brought on by a ruptured ulcer. He might just as well have said that George had died because he could not adapt to living. His insuperable emotional problems prevented him from finding any joy whatsoever in life.

Peptic ulcers in children

Not only adults but children as well develop peptic ulcers. Strangely enough, peptic ulcers have even been known to occur when the baby was still in the mother's womb. About 56 per cent of the children afflicted have a history of peptic ulcer in their families. And the overwhelming majority are associated with an extremely unhappy home situation.

Beginning with the age of six, children resemble adults in the symptoms they experience, although their symptoms are more vague and eating frequently causes pain rather than relieving it. The child may complain of vague pains in the abdomen for months or even years, often associated with unpleasant events, before the disease is suspected.

The successful management of peptic ulcers in children depends on the same principles as does management in the adult: change the life situation that brought about the ulcer in the first place. Tragic indeed are those children who are victims of parents who do not want them and do not love them. For such persons, the outlook is not bright unless they receive much help and understanding from outside the home. It must be emphasized, however, that emotionally induced peptic ulcers, or any other psychosomatic ailments for that matter, that occur in children must not always be blamed on parental neglect or abuse or even overindulgence. Indeed, countless other influences affect a child's development and should be considered when maladjustment or misbehavior occur. If the child fails to respond to treatment, psychotherapy will no doubt provide valuable assistance.

ULCERATIVE COLITIS

Another ailment that frequently develops in the digestive tract as a result of unpleasant emotional responses is ulcerative colitis, a serious inflammation of all or part of the mucous membrane that lines the large intestine, or colon. It tends to be chronic, recurring again and again. Diarrhea, containing blood, mucus, or pus, is accompanied by abdominal pain and the patient feels extremely miserable. Elevated temperature, weakness, anemia, and loss of weight might occur.

The exact cause of ulcerative colitis is not certain. Bacteria have been indicted; allergy has been charged. Frequently, however, ulcerative colitis appears, or reappears, following some emotional trauma or psychic disturbance in which nervous stimuli induce spasms, damaging the colon and so ·weakening it that bacteria find it easy prey. In such instances, the disease is truly a psychosomatic ailment. It often strikes young adults, either sex, in their twenties, thirties, or forties, although children have been known to develop it.

Shadow symptoms

The onset of ulcerative colitis is usually gradual. It starts with the shadow symptom of an increased urgency to move the bowels. Then cramps appear in the lower abdomen. Diarrhea begins; the stools become loose and filled with mucus. The patient may eventually have as many as ten to twenty bowel movements daily, often associated with pain and severe cramps which continue through the night. Loss of appetite, weakness, and fever might follow.

Many persons with ulcerative colitis have experienced conflicts centering about their marriages, unsatisfactory sexual relations, heartache and tension related to their children's lives, or any of the other innumerable life events that bring on unpleasant emotions. Some patients have gone through a period in which they were frustrated in carrying out an obligation; the obligation might be biologic, moral, or material. Others were frustrated in their search for happiness which persistently eluded them. Financial pressures have played an important role. In almost every case, the person was involved in a situation that demanded difficult adjustments. He responded with tension, anxiety and—ulcerative colitis. And to make therapy more difficult, this conflict is sometimes in the unconscious mind sending its damaging reactive impulses via the autonomic nervous system so that the victim is unaware of the impending danger. The whispers of emotions that filter out, causing a vague nervousness and jittery feeling, might be the only clue—until the first shadow symptoms appear.

Colitis-prone personalities

Personality tendencies for persons suffering from ulcerative colitis present a sharp and interesting contrast to the personalities of peptic ulcer sufferers. Whereas the peptic ulcer patient often compensates for his dependency by a vigorous striving for success, the patient with ulcerative colitis tends to be extremely dependent, shy and passive, emotionally restricted and even restrained in his posture and movements, exhibiting little drive or motivation. Such persons are meticulous and extremely sensitive, frequently brooding over minor incidents which appear to them to be major insults. Inner conflicts result in grave difficulty in meeting everyday problems and in adjusting to life in general.

When serious obstacles or events arise, as death of a loved one, they are frequently overwhelmed but repress their emotions. Charles Darwin wrote in 1872 of this type of person: ". . . He who remains passive when overwhelmed with grief loses his best chance of recovering elasticity of mind." Indeed, the passive exterior is but a facade that veils an internal volcano, which is akindle with fire and spews out nervous impulses that cause muscle spasms and serious malfunctioning throughout the digestive tube. And although colitis and peptic ulcer are both reactions to resentment, the two diseases rarely coexist in the same individual, no doubt because of their varying personality patterns.

There are many people in our midst with colitis-prone personalities who obviously do not have and will not develop ulcerative colitis, so that emotional problems are not the sole factor involved. An inherited organic weakness or predisposition certainly contributes. Various infections might precipitate ulcerative colitis. Yet, emotional conflicts are by far the most frequent and significant offenders.

Delayed grief reactions contributing to ulcerative colitis

In a study of forty-five patients with ulcerative colitis, twenty-six were found to have suffered the loss of loved ones immediately prior to the onset of illness. Indeed, delayed grief reactions appear to be a prime factor. Thomas, a forty-year-old bookkeeper, presents a classic example of ulcerative colitis associated with loss of a loved one and marked inner conflict.

Entering the hospital for the third time in a year with recurring ulcerative colitis, Thomas expressed a desire to talk to the chaplain after Sunday service in the hospital chapel. And he poured out a tearful confession of an illicit romance in which he had become involved after the death of his wife. Six months prior to his first hospitalization his wife had died. He explained that he was completely lost and alone when she died for she had handled all the bills, managed the house, even picked out his clothes.

Following her death, Thomas began to eat his meals at a boarding house near his home. The couple who ran the boarding house had been friends for several years and he turned to them often in times of need. His dependency gradually turned to infatuation with the lady and led to an affair about six months after his wife died. Shortly thereafter, his ulcerative colitis appeared. His inability to cope with grief had produced great tension, complicated by marked feelings of guilt, and the colon bore the brunt of his emotions.

After Thomas had ended his confession, completely exhausted, the chaplain reminded him of the scripture: "If we confess our sins, He is faithful and just to forgive us our sins, and to cleanse us fron all unrighteousness." (I John 1:9) Several subsequent sessions with the chaplain and medical explanations from his doctor provided Thomas with a deeper understanding of his way of life and the importance of giving vent to his cmotions. After release from the hospital he joined a group of friends who met regularly and through their support he was able to successfully control his ulcerative colitis.

Ulcerative colitis in children

Just as peptic ulcer, usually thought of as an adult disease, can afflict children, so can ulcerative colitis. Although it can strike in early infancy, most children who develop it are over eight. The child with ulcerative colitis does not exist in isolation; the behavior of aunts, uncles, parents, grandparents, brothers, and sisters invariably contributes to his disease. It is, therefore, necessary to examine the entire family constellation. A chief goal must be to stimulate a concern among all members of the family so that they will examine their own actions and personalities.

Linda, a thirteen-year-old girl, began having diarrhea and abdominal cramps following her thirteenth birthday. Just a few weeks earlier, her older sister had left home to attend college and her younger sister began to share Linda's room. This minor conflict provided the key by which the attending -physician unlocked Linda's psyche and drew out the factors that precipitated her illness. For Linda had been a superior student in school and had had no serious difficulties until the bloody diarrhea, diagnosed in the hospital as ulcerative colitis, had started.

Linda appeared calm but underneath the placid surface she was teeming with suppressed rage. Not particularly concerned with her bowel complaints, she admitted during her first interview with a psychotherapist that her main problem was difficulty in "getting along with others." She was obviously jealous of her mother's attentions to others, which was doubtlessly related to her objection to sharing a room with her younger sister. And, indeed, further talks revealed that she had resented the younger sister since her mother's pregnancy. She even recalled becoming violently ill when her mother was honored at a "shower" preceding her younger sister's birth.

Linda showed great antagonism against her mother, whom she viewed as cold and inattentive. Her father, on the other hand, came out as a gentle, kind man whom the children loved dearly. So the physician attacked not only Linda's problem but the problem of the family as a whole. Repeated sessions were held with various members of the family until gradually, the family members began to have greater concern for personal and interpersonal fulfillment. The mother came to respect the father's gentleness and the father began to appreciate the mother's virtues. Linda realized that it was not her sister that she disliked but the loss of her mother's attentions. Encouraged to participate in more community projects and activities that she had never experienced before, she soon found much satisfaction. And her ulcerative colitis has not recurred.

CONSTIPATION

Constipation, or difficulty in moving the bowels (not merely infrequent bowel movements) can also represent a psychosomatic ailment. Prolonged constipation can be harmful, particularly if the patient has a weak colon. Impacted or "locked" bowels can result and the consequences can be serious.

Many patients who are chronically constipated tend to worry excessively, and are prone to be mistrustful and pessimistic. This attitude manifests itself in constipation. And although simple dietary adjustments, enemas, laxatives, or other measures usually relieve the problem, the constipation may be a shadow symptom of a deep seated psychic disturbance; their problem may be far more serious than just constipation.

HOW TO AVOID INDIGESTION AND ITS COMPLICATIONS

If you would truly desire to live life at its fullest, then by all means, don't try to live against the flow of your own personality. A rather wealthy man once remarked that he disliked his work so intensely that he dreaded getting up each morning. He had worked for the company for a number of years and had reached an enviable position among the management. Yet he hated it! "For a dime I'd quit this job," he said. His listener offered him a dime and asked him what other incentive he needed. And he decided then and there to make a fresh new start; he is enjoying life much more today than he has in many years.

It is unrealistic to suggest that we can sidestep all our difficulties and ignore all our conflicts and simply enjoy life. But by making certain attitude adjustments, perhaps incentive adjustments, we can certainly learn to avoid many unpleasant emotions that can disrupt our digestive processes and lead to peptic ulcers, ulcerative colitis, or a host of other digestive disorders. The last chapter will lead you in this direction.

seven

Lifelong help for
sufferers from arthritis

> He spent eight years watching his hands
> become claws and waking in screams when
> he turned on his hot swollen knees in his
> dreams...
>
> K. D. Beernink, M.D.
> *Ward Rounds*

The heart-rending patient described by Dr. Beernink was suffering from the mysterious and agonizing disease, rheumatoid arthritis, only one of a cluster of ailments frequently associated with physical or mental stress. You will recall that we referred to "diseases of stress" briefly in Chapter Two, pointing out that they differ sharply from other emotional distrubances. Because of the singular importance of stress as a cause of serious, but preventable, disease, we shall focus on it here in considerably more detail.

Stress, a word that generally suggests strain, tension, pressure, or overwork, takes on a special meaning in regard to psychosomatic illness; it refers specifically to the effect on the body of strenuous or threatening conditions or events. The various threats to the safety of the body, then, are referred to as "stressors." Certainly we have all experienced stress in one form or another. Just as surely we differ, one from the other, in our ability to withstand its ravages.

Since we have defined psychosomatic disease as physical illness caused by psychic turmoil, obviously an ailment caused by emotional stress would represent a psychosomatic illness. Usually there exists no sharp dividing line between physical and psychic stress. For example, if you are heavily overburdened with physical work, or involved in a serious accident, or caught in a severe storm or hurricane, the physical and psychic elements of the stress are indivisible. But if there could be such a stressor as a purely physical one anɑ if that stressor caused disease, then the disease would *not* be psychosomatic. So let us confine our consideration of stress-caused ailments to those resulting, in part at least, from psychic stresses—with or without a physical element.

We have a three-step reaction to stress

Diseases of stress have no doubt plagued Man since he first appeared on this planet a million or more years ago although we had little inkling of their nature until quite recently. Even our early ancestors, however, who had no sophisticated knowledge of disease, must have recognized the exhaustion that assailed them after they had pursued (or been pursued by) a wild animal, had been exposed for long periods to extremes of hot or cold, had fought savagely with another cave man, or perhaps had been desperately frightened. They might even have observed the human's three-step reaction to severe stress, a vital factor in our present day understanding of diseases related to stress. For when our primitive forebear swam across a freezing stream, or fled for miles from a vicious enemy, or engaged in grueling manual labor, he at first experienced a real hardship. After a period of continual exposure to the arduous condition, however, he seemed to get a "second wind," so to speak, and was able to carry on. But if the stress was too demanding or if it continued too long, he finally reached a stage where he could take no more.

SELYE'S DISCOVERY OF STRESS SYNDROME

Dr. Hans Selye, of the McGill University of Montreal, was the first to recognize that a long list of ailments could be related to the human body's inability to adapt to prolonged stress situations.

Through his carefully documented and reported observations, a whole new realm of medicine has been opened to us. And his first clue was the instinctive three-step response to severe stress, which he interprets as a general law that regulates every man's performance under difficulty. Moreover, he shows us how we can spare ourselves from serious, even fatal, disease by understanding the body's efforts to withstand stress.

It was in 1926, as a second year medical student, that Selye became aware that anyone who performed an exacting task reacted in a more or less standard manner: First the individual faced the task and was hard put to carry on; then he gradually adapted to it and found the going much easier; finally, if the task continued to be difficult, he became completely exhausted.

A concern for patients who are "just sick"

Next, Selye noticed that patients suffering from a wide variety of diseases had many symptoms in common, such as loss of appetite, generalized weakness, disappearance of ambition, loss of weight, and a haggard facial expression. Whatever the illness, the patients looked much the same. They were, as Selye put it, "just sick." So he inquired into the scientific basis of just being sick. He wondered if the way in which these symptoms developed could be analyzed by modern scientific techniques; he felt sure that they could.

Search for hormone produces startling results

Selye had no opportunity to test his theories, however, until 1936 at the biochemistry department of McGill University. There, while searching for a new hormone from the ovaries of cattle, he made a startling discovery: Every time he injected extracts from the ovaries of cattle into experimental animals, precisely the same physical changes occurred—enlargment of the adrenal glands, ulcers of the intestinal tract, shrinkage of the thymus gland and lymph nodes, and loss of weight. He assumed that the effects were caused specifically by ovarian hormones. But when he injected various other substances and found that they produced the identical changes, he knew he had opened the door on something pretty exciting. These symptoms must be the result of the burden placed on the body by the various substances and not the chemical properties of the substances themselves. These physical changes would explain the symptoms he had observed in those patients he had labeled as "just sick."

He named the group of symptoms or changes (meaning syndrome) the *stress syndrome*. And he subsequently found that the degree of enlargement of the adrenal glands, the severity of the intestinal ulcers, the amount of shrinkage of the thymus gland and lymph nodes, the extent of weight loss, could be used as a measure of the stress.

Three stages in the body's response to stress

Then the realization struck him that his injections had been producing, in an experimental way, the same three-step reaction that he had recognized ten years earlier in persons facing heavy physical or mental strain. He proceeded to name the three steps: The initial response to stress-producing agents he called the *alarm reaction*. The next stage, when the animal began to get used to the stress ("adapted" to it), he called the *stage of adaptation*. It might also have been called the stage of successful resistance. The third stage occurred if the stress continued in such severity that the animal could not cope with it. He was overwhelmed and the stage was appropriately named the *stage of exhaustion*.

As Selye became more deeply involved in his investigation he found that the first and second stages differed in many respects. During the alarm reaction, for example, the cells of the outer layer or cortex of the adrenal glands discharged tiny portions of hormones into the blood stream until the source was depleted. But during the stage of adaptation, the hormone stores were restored and the glands even accumulated a reserve supply. Also, during the alarm reaction the blood became concentrated and body weight decreased; during the stage of adaptation, blood became more dilute and body weight climbed toward normal. When stress had been sufficiently severe and prolonged, the animal entered the stage of exhaustion, all capacity to resist had been spent, and he died.

Selye coined a term to include all three stages of the body's response to stress, the *general adaptation syndrome* (GAS).

THE NATURE OF OUR DEFENSES AGAINST STRESS

How does the body manage to adapt to stress? What is the nature of its defenses? And what does all this have to do with us and our efforts to control psychosomatic illness? It is most essential that we understand the answers to the first two questions, the mechanisms by which the body attempts to adapt, so that we can fully comprehend the importance of preventing stress-caused ailments. For although we may not be able to change a stressful situation, we can learn to control our response to it and thereby avoid much trouble, even tragedy.

The pituitary gland—a tiny giant

Primarily, when stressors assail the body, messages pass quickly to the brain from the affected part of the body. The brain immediately dispatches a call for help. But rather than following the usual route along the wires of the autonomic nervous system, these messages of stress are sent directly to the pituitary gland, located on the underside of the brain. And although the pituitary gland is negligible in size, little larger than an overgrown pea, it is a giant when it comes to performance and has rightfully been dubbed our "master gland."

The pituitary manufactures or distributes at least nine hormones, which are essentially messengers carried in the blood. These hormones each have specified duties, including the control of blood pressure, muscle contraction, urine production within the kidneys, and other equally vital functions. In addition, certain of the hormones act upon other glands, stimulating the production of still more hormones. In this manner, the pituitary ultimately controls just about everything that goes on in our bodies. And with all its essential functions in health, it adds the defense of the body against stress.

Upon receiving the messages of stress from the brain, the pituitary sends a hormone, called ACTH, to the adrenal glands; ACTH stimulates them to produce increased amounts of an anti-stress hormone called cortisol. It is cortisol, then, that valiantly defends the body and enables it to enter into the stage of adaptation, or resistance. All of the changes we mentioned as characteristic of this stage are produced by the effects of cortisol.

An error in adaptation to stress causes disease

The same set of signals that calls forth cortisol, however, sometimes causes the release of another quite different type of hormone, actually a pro-stress hormone, called aldosterone. Why this occurs is one of the unsolved mysteries of physiology. The mystery is deepened by the fact that sometimes so much aldosterone is released into the blood stream that disease is produced. Indeed, there is a cluster of such ailments and they are not at all uncommon. Since they result from an error in the body's adaptation to stress, they are properly called the *diseases of maladaptation.*

Included among these ailments are some forms of high blood pressure, various diseases of the kidneys, inflammation of the skin and eyes, and the dreaded form of joint disease mentioned at the beginning of this chapter—rheumatoid arthritis.

RHEUMATOID ARTHRITIS

It is generally accepted that rheumatoid arthritis results, at least in some instances, from maladaptation to stress. Usually the onset is gradual although in some instances it may be abrupt. The joints of the fingers, wrists, knees, and feet begin to swell and become red and painful. The adjoining muscles become stiff and "splinted." They often go into spasm, causing almost unbearable torment. The muscles above and below the affected joints tend to wither and give the joint a spindle appearance. As muscles deteriorate, the bones of the toes, fingers and wrists are pulled to the side, resulting in extreme deformity. Patients have difficulty in walking, if indeed they can walk. And because this horrible affliction is basically a psychosomatic ailment, it might possibly be avoided if the sufferer accepts counsel when the first shadow symptoms appear.

Shadow symptoms

Shadow symptoms that may indicate the coming of rheumatoid arthritis include continuous fatigue, loss of appetite, weight loss, sweating, diarrhea, and stiffness in the morning. The actual onset of the disease often follows psychic or physical strain or infection. Prolonged grief or separation from loved ones has appeared to precipitate the disease.

Arthritis-prone personalities

That rheumatoid arthritis is most often a disease of maladaptation to stress is borne out time and again by studies of the personal histories and emotional environments of its many victims. From such studies it has also been determined that the sort of persons who are most likely to develop rheumatoid arthritis are characteristically inhibited, self-conscious, self-sacrificing, conforming, compulsive, but capable of strong control of their emotions. They appear to want both to dominate and to serve.

It is interesting to note, too, that they often have revealed a greater than normal muscular response to emotional stimuli, frequently displaying a distinct interest in participating sports and physical activities. Indeed, this may well be explained by the fact that many such people like to work off repressed rage through physical means. Active physical exercise is, in fact, recommended as an outlet for tensions to reduce the danger of stress-caused ailments. This advice seems to conflict with the findings that many persons who have a high interest in physical activities are prone to develop rheumatoid arthritis; obviously, they are attempting to release their tensions rather than to resolve them. But the body is not easily deceived and stress continues.

The course of rheumatoid arthritis is capricious; it may become better or worse and for no apparent reason. Some patients have had flare-ups of joint symptoms on anniversaries of deaths of loved ones. The courage with which victims fight the ailment appears to have much to do with their progress. Those who are determined to keep up with their usual activities do far better than those who give in to the ailment.

Medical treatment of the disorder

As in other psychosomatic diseases, the physical disorder must be actively treated if one is to cure the patient. Dr. Philip Hench and his co-workers at the Mayo Clinic made a great contribution to treatment of rheumatoid arthritis when they found that use of the hormones ACTH and cortisone provided a remarkable suppression of the symptoms. Apparently these natural agents restore a broken link in the body's effort to maintain or regain balance, at the point where prolonged stress has caused a breakdown. Other medicinal agents have also been effective in some instances.

Exercise and physical therapy are essential in treatment of arthritic joints. Surgical operations are sometimes recommended to help those who are already suffering from deformities.

Yet medical treatment alone cannot effect a cure of rheumatoid arthritis or any other stress-caused ailments. Even the powerful hormones do not constitute a cure. Hench explained that both ACTH and cortisone "affect not the cause of a disease but the reaction of the tissue to the irritant or cause." They will do no more than repair what the inner conflict will again break down. It is sometimes necessary for the individual to seek out psychotherapy in order to get at the source of the stress that is forcing the body to make continuous efforts to adapt.

A revealing case history

The case of a man we shall call Wendel highlights the fact that psychic trauma can play a major role in causing such diseases of stress as rheumatoid arthritis and that the disease is not only an instance of disease caused by maladaptation to stress but is a psychosomatic ailment as well.

Wendel was a vigorous young engineer who had worked his way through college, obtaining such outstanding grades that he had no problem in finding a splendid position. Shortly after starting to work he married his childhood sweetheart. Both looked forward to a joyful life together. Wendel was a highly conscientious young man, deeply aware of his obligations to others. He tended to hide his emotions, relieving his feelings by strenuous athletic activities, which he enjoyed immensely.

For a few years all went well. Two children were born to the marriage and Wendel continued to progress, earning several substantial promotions. World War I began to run its horrid course but he was excused from service because of the essential nature of his work.

Then tragedy struck in the form of the great influenza epidemic of 1917, one of the killer plagues of all time. Wendel's wife contracted the disease and, like so many others, developed the bacterial pneumonia that so often accompanied it. She apparently was recovering and had resumed her housework when, suddenly and without warning, she died in her sleep. Wendel was overwhelmed; he had not anticipated the catastrophe. Nevertheless, after a few days of mourning, he pulled himself together, outwardly at least, and went on about his work. But his heart was no longer in it.

It wasn't long before he began to notice vague aches and pains, some abdominal discomfort, stiffness in the morning. Then he experienced the rapid onset of rheumatoid arthritis with hot swollen joints, fever, pain, and general fatigue. He forced himself to keep on with his work, ever fighting the torturous pain. He kept going, despite the fact that medicines then available provided him with scant relief.

Never forgetting his deep love for his wife, he raised the children and saw that they received splendid educations. Then, tired and wracked with pain but still in the harness of his work, he died. The year was 1940, just a few years before Hench was to appear on the scene with his magical anti-stress hormone treatment of rheumatoid arthritis.

A host of circumstances can cause rheumatoid arthritis

Some of the terrible traps of life that can bring on this dread disorder are exemplified by the following:

A housewife developed rheumatoid arthritis when her husband fathered a child by another woman and the patient's mother deserted her. . . . A man experienced the onset of the disease when he lost his home and property and his children moved away from home. . . . A woman developed rheumatoid arthritis when her children left her alone with her alcoholic husband. . . . One woman became arthritic when her husband became an invalid because of serious heart disease. . . . Symptoms of rheumatoid arthritis struck another woman following an operation and a serious squabble with her daughter-in-law. . . . A woman's illness began following conflict with her husband over the fact that her elderly father was living with the pair. . . . A woman's rheumatoid arthritis started after her family refused to help her locate a job. . . . Still another woman experienced a worsening of rheumatoid arthritis when her son's mental illness became more serious and she became estranged from her husband. . . . A woman's illness started when her invalid mother moved in with her. It became worse when she transferred her mother to a nursing home and became still worse when she had an altercation with her husband and mother-in-law. . . . Severe financial and job problems plus separation from family and home brought another woman her arthritis. . . . A young woman developed the disorder when she quarreled with her fiance before marriage. The disease worsened after marriage but cleared after the inevitable divorce! . . . A bitter conflict with a 19-year-old son, plus severe disappointment in her oldest daughter brought the disease to still another woman. The backdrop for the disease was life-long conflict with her dependent husband.

OTHER DISEASES RELATED TO MALADAPTATION

We mentioned several of the ailments, other than rheumatoid arthritis, that are generally considered to be diseases of maladaptation. These included some forms of high blood pressure, certain kidney diseases, inflammation of the skin and eyes, to mention a few.

But stress is also closely related to allergies, mental derangements, sexual problems, digestive diseases, metabolic diseases, perhaps even to some forms of cancer. Obviously, we are still in somewhat of a shadowland when we discuss this group of ailments. As Selye has pointed out, "It is still largely a matter of debate which of the diseases of adaptation are due to an actual overproduction, or of hypersensitivity to adaptive hormones." We can only hope that, as new evidence is uncovered, long-awaited breakthroughs may come in many of these areas. The use of the hormones ACTH and cortisone has already demonstrated that it is possible to "reverse" a number of diseases that were formerly considered incurable.

We are clearly in deep scientific water when we deal with diseases of the maladaptation syndrome. The field is a new one, the complexities are baffling, the explanations incomplete. Yet awareness of this group of diseases, as exemplified by rheumatoid arthritis, and of the insidious way in which they come about, can be of enormous help in preventing the ailments. The concept of stress and of our resistance to it lies at the heart of the subject of diseases of maladaptation. Whether one develops one of these ailments or not is largely determined by his personality structure and by how he reacts to stress.

Is there a limit to our "adaptive energy"?

We are all born with ability to adapt to stress. Obviously this will vary from person to person. To some extent our adaptive competence can be measured by our ability to marshall anti-stress hormones. There are probably other as yet unknown yardsticks. But whatever the basis for our power to resist and adapt, Selye believes that we are all born with a fixed quota of what he calls *adaptive energy* and that when this "energy" is exhausted there is no way of regenerating more. We can at least hope that this pessimistic view does not prove correct.

Biography of Ishi is encouraging

Anyone who reads the fascinating biography of Ishi, the last wild Indian of North America, who emerged from the mountains of northern California in 1911, can be optimistic regarding the human stores of adaptive energy. As told in *Ishi*, by Theodora Kroeber, University of California Press, Ishi had been a lonely fugitive from the white civilization of northern California for many years. The last of his murdered tribe, he was subjected to almost unbelievably severe hardships; he responded to the stresses and adapted.

But finally, after years of struggle, he appeared to have exhausted his adaptive energy. Completely lonely, completely despairing, completely hopeless, he shuffled down from the hills that had given him shelter. He had every reason to believe that the whites who had murdered his people would also kill him, and his fears were on solid grounds.

When Ishi approached the town of Oroville, California, his adaptive energy was apparently exhausted. He should have died at this point. But he did not. Befriended by kind and understanding scientists, he made a magnificent, heroic comeback. His contributions during his remaining years of life should be a source of inspiration to us all. It should also encourage us to believe that adaptive energy can be regenerated!

ONLY *YOU* CAN EFFECT A CURE!

Certainly the picture of fully developed disease of maladaptation is a grim one, particularly if the ailment is as disabling and painful as rheumatoid arthritis. But the very grimness makes both prevention and treatment all the more important. At the outset let's grant that a real catastrophe—and life offers all too many of them—might impose a disease of maladaptation on anyone. But the body is capable of forceful resistance. Even when its resources are depleted, we can supply medically the help that will restore it. The relief, however, will only be temporary; true recovery is still in our hands.

It is when we permit stress to continue, unrestrained, that we suffer damage. The chances of developing stress-caused ailments would be far less if the individual did not possess the backdrop of the arthritis-prone personality. If your personality fits this pattern, as we've described it, take steps to induce sound mental hygiene:

1) Verbalize your frustrations, speak them out. You can do this without being unpleasant and without making yourself persona non

grata. Hostilities and hang-ups do harm when they are kept inside. Repressed emotions tend to lose their potency when they are exposed to the world of reality.

2) If you will take part in an active physical exercise program it will help get rid of those repressed feelings. Walk, run in place indoors, ride a bicycle or an exercizer, play tennis or golf—you name it. Fatigue produced by physical exertion is healthy, within reasonable limits. But don't try to deceive your body. In conjunction with a program of exercise, you must still work to improve your emotional environment, hence your state of mind.

If it is within your power, correct the situation that is causing your stress. Admittedly, this is not always possible. But if we cannot change the situation, we can at least work at changing our emotional response to it. In many instances, the source of the stress is not readily apparent; it may be tucked away in one of the dark recesses of the unconscious. Then it is advisable to obtain psychotherapy from a reputable professional.

But suppose you have already experienced shadow symptoms of rheumatoid arthritis—coldness of the hands and feet, abdominal discomfort, morning stiffness in the joints. By all means consult your physician at once. Ask for a thorough examination and follow the doctor's recommendations. He will be able to aid you in procuring relief. But remember: *Only you can effect a cure!*

eight

How to lose weight
quickly, easily, and safely

Since eating occupies such an important part of our lives during our sojourn from the cradle to the grave, it should come as no surprise that a wide variety of psychic tensions can distort our eating pattern. The result can be obesity—overweight—on the one hand and diminished appetite—underweight—on the other.

OBESITY

Obesity is a mental state,
A disease brought on by boredom and disappointment.

Cyril Connolly
The Unique Grave

Obesity really represents an excessive accumulation of fat in the body. We can regard it as being present when body weight exceeds the standard weight listed in the usual height-weight tables by 20 per cent.

The obese in history

Throughout history fat people have often been regarded with amused tolerance. Sometimes, however, tolerance has given way to scorn, as when Shakespeare had a character say, "Falstaff sweats to death and lards the lean earth as he walks along; were't not for laughing I should pity him." On the other hand, Shakespeare also gives us reason for believing that fat men are safer to have around when he puts these words in the mouth of Julius Caeser: "Let me have men about me that are fat; sleek-headed men and such as sleep o' nights; yond Cassius has a lean and hungry look; he thinks too much; such men are dangerous."

In the past obesity was often regarded as somewhat of a status symbol; it is so regarded today in some regions. Why should this be? Rarely throughout the long course of history has an entire nation had more than enough to eat for a prolonged period. Frequently it was only the highly privileged who could afford to be fat. Obesity came to be an admired and respected trait in some cultures. Every year, for example, the Aga Khan was weighed and the degree of rejoicing following the weighing paralleled the weight increase over the previous year. Obviously the *size* of the leader represented a point of pride for the entire country. In Germany and in India studies have revealed that obesity and importance were associated.

Today, however, the story is changing in many countries. In the United States the slim executive represents an ideal; the fat—even moderately fat—executive is frowned upon and may be asked to reduce his avoirdupois. Those in this country who enjoy higher income show considerably less obesity than those of low economic status. One study revealed that obesity is six times as common in lower economic groups as in economically privileged classes. Social class influences obesity, not obesity social class.

Why is obesity a psychosomatic ailment?

We have defined psychosomatic disease as organic changes resulting from psychic factors. We see precisely this situation in many obese persons. When psychic tension causes obesity, as it often does, we have a physical change in the individual, specifically in his bulk. This, as we shall see, is followed by diverse harmful bodily effects. The statement, "He dug his grave with his teeth," appears to have great meaning.

Causes of obesity

The immediate cause of overweight is crystal clear: *Caloric intake persistently exceeds caloric output.* Food that exceeds the needs for growth, tissue replacement, and energy is changed to fat and stored as fat. But although obesity results from excessive food intake, the latter often originates either in psychic or physiologic disturbances. Even though simple overeating or lack of exercise or both appear to be responsible for a given case of obesity, the individual deserves a careful study to determine whether mental or physical factors might be at the base of the problem.

Increasing age

Age bears importantly on obesity since the incidence of the condition nearly doubles between the ages of 20 and 50. Since the percentage of body weight that is fat increases with increasing age, overweight persons in the older age groups tend to be *fatter* than younger overweights. Decreased growth requirements and energy output are obvious explanations for the effects of age on body weight.

Heredity

Without question, the chemistry one inherits from his ancestors has some bearing on whether he becomes obese or not. Short, broad body types put on fat far more readily than tall persons, partly because they have less body surface area in proportion to their weight. And one's loss of heat, and hence of energy, depends on body surface area. One's surroundings are also influential; a child brought up in a family that customarily overeats will probably be overweight himself.

Three researchers at New York's Rockefeller University, Doctors Jules Hersch, Jerome Knittle, and Lester Salans, believe infant eating habits may shape the adult figure. On a basis of preliminary laboratory work with animals, these doctors have suggested that the number of fat cells become fixed in childhood and cannot change later on. Thus, the child who overeats in infancy increases the size and number of his fat cells, which "play a significant role in the carbohydrate and insulin abnormalities of obese persons." These researchers further say that once the individuals mature, the number of their fat cells remains fixed, although diet can modify the amount of fat these cells store. It would thus appear best not to overfeed infants. A chubby, overweight child is not necessarily a healthy child; in fact, the opposite may be true.

Physical activity

Another factor important in obesity is physical activity. In the lusty pioneer days when men, women, and children all performed the heavy physical work necessary for day to day existence, there was scant problem of becoming overweight. But today most persons live fairly sedentary lives. The danger of taking in food in excess of need is great, particularly in our relatively affluent society.

Many fat persons tend to become less and less active. This tends to make them fatter which, in turn, makes them still less active. A truly vicious circle is thus set in motion.

Restriction of physical activity causes a surplus of calories in two different ways: First, there is a reduction in the expenditure of energy, derived from calories, and second, appetite does not necessarily decrease with decreased exercise. Indeed, the low level of physical activity of some obese persons can entirely account for their obesity. Such reduced exercise tends to be more important in women than in men, since many obese men are forced to be active in their jobs. The energy expended by such subjects in moving their heavier bodies can produce a caloric expenditure that equals or exceeds that of lean men.

Physiologic malfunctions

Sometimes we hear that persons become obese because their digestion or absorption is more efficient. This is seldom—if ever—the case. Nor does the body of the fat persons have an unusual tendency to retain fat. Disorders of the glands of internal secretion (the endocrine glands) can favor the development of obesity by encouraging increased food intake or decreased output or both. But they are not the primary causes.

Certain brain disorders cause obesity by impairing one's sense of satiety: the patient can't tell when he's had enough to eat! If that important gland, the pancreas, secretes excessive insulin (the carbohydrate burning hormone), the person tends to eat more and may therefore become obese. Diseases of the adrenal glands can also cause overeating and obesity. The same can occur following removal or destructive disease of the sex glands. Overweight often occurs after delivery of a baby. Or during enforced inactivity because of injury or illness. Indeed, limitation of energy output from any cause favors development of obesity.

And yet, overweight usually boils down to one, perhaps embarrassing but inescapable, truth: the person simply eats too much!

Psychic tensions

The primary reasons, however, why many people over-indulge in food may be related to psychic tension of one type or another. To be sure, many people just naturally enjoy eating good food. But for others, being obese can serve as a means of escape from social interaction, maturity, responsibility, reality, and other aspects of modern life. Layers of fat can insulate the person in many ways. Obesity can be used as a defense against participation in undesired activities. It can justify withdrawal from normal pursuits. It can serve as a protection against frustrations caused by lack or loss of physical attractiveness. It can become an excuse for inefficiency.

Some persons overeat because of an unmet need for love, security, and pleasure. Some overeat because of hostility and aggression. Among the psychologic factors responsible for obesity must be listed habit, improper childhood training, frustrations, and dissatisfaction. Any of these can lead to increased food intake or decreased physical activity. The pleasure of eating can become a dominant personality trait: the person does not eat to live, *he lives to eat.* Eating thus serves as a substitute for unsatisfied business, career, personal, or sexual achievement.

Problems in the home affect children

Even small children can develop obesity because of psychic factors. Prolonged mother-child separation proved to be linked to childhood obesity in a study of 72 ghetto patients in a Harlem obesity clinic. The children were all under the age of 12; 23 of the patients had been living in a home apart from their mothers for six months. When a comparable group of 72 non-obese patients were reviewed it was found that only 6 had been separated from their mothers for extensive periods. When a mother was absent from the home for part of a day because of work, however, the incidence of obesity did not appear to increase.

Frequently problem children become obese. They indulge in eating to satisfy unmet needs or frustrations and then use the state of obesity to demand special attention. And, indeed, they usually deserve special attention in an effort to solve their psychic problems.

No specific personality types

From all this we can safely conclude that psychic disturbances, of one type or another, are enormously important in causing overweight. Many obese persons have stated that they eat more when under stress or when mentally upset; obese persons certainly show a higher incidence of emotional upsets and neurotic traits than do those of normal weight. Despite this fact scientists have failed to uncover any one personality type for obese persons. They have also failed to reveal any common psychic conflict related to overeating. However, studies of large numbers of obese persons have uncovered two small groups who do have common patterns of food intake: the night eating syndrome and the binge eating syndrome.

Night eating syndrome

This pattern of eating is found in about 10 per cent of obese persons, more commonly in women. These women have no appetite in the morning but experience ravenous hunger at night. Moreover, they have trouble sleeping. The eating pattern is precipitated by tense life situations. Once the pattern has started it tends to recur every day until relief of the situation has been achieved. And attempts to diet while the pattern is active are usually futile. Nor does the syndrome respond readily to psychotherapy. Only when the stressful situation is alleviated or the person becomes more capable of coping with it will dieting stand a chance.

Binge eating syndrome

A second group of obese persons have what has been called the binge eating syndrome. Less than 5 per cent of the obese belong to it. These persons have a sudden compulsive desire to eat large amounts of food in a short period. Their binge is followed by agitation and self-condemnation. Like the night-eating syndrome, binge eating represents a reaction to tension. It differs, however, in that the bouts of overeating are not usually periodic. But they tend to be closely linked to specific events. Indeed, a binge may occur within minutes of a particularly frustrating experience. Sometimes binge eaters can lose amazingly large amounts of weight by rigid and unrealistic diets, but their efforts are usually thwarted by resumption of the eating binges.

Body changes

In obesity excessive storage of fat occurs throughout the body. Special accumulations are to be found in the abdomen, around the kidneys, and surrounding the heart. Fat may be found in the pancreas and in the muscles of the skeleton and heart. The liver may enlarge because of fat accumulation within the liver cells. Fatigue, shortage of breath, and aching of legs, back, knees, and feet are often complaints of the obese. The skin beneath massive rolls of fat may soften and deteriorate; skin may become infected due to extreme obesity.

Outlook for the obese

There are two distinct disadvantages of being overweight. First, it is generally agreed that the obese person is less attractive than he or she would be at a normal weight; some overweight people have the fixed idea that their body is loathesome and grotesque and that others can view it only with hostility. One fat woman was quoted, "I look in the mirror and I call myself a slob and a pig!" An obese man was reported as saying, "Just looking at myself in a store window makes me feel terrible. It's gotten so that I am very careful not to look. I feel that people have the right to hate me and anyone else who is as fat as I am. When I look at myself I feel an uncontrollable burst of hatred." Such attitudes may well color every personal relationship. The body becomes the excuse for all failures and disappointments. And the mental anguish over appearance merely compounds the problem or problems that first led the person to overeat.

This type of misperception of the body occurs in persons who become fat before adulthood. It is probably imprinted on the personality before adolescence. Indeed, 8 of 10 obese children remain obese as adults.

Health hazards

The second disadvantage is the definite health hazard of being overweight. Even relatively small amounts of overweight, such as 5, 10, or 20 per cent above the ideal can pose a problem. There is a considerably increased incidence of high blood pressure, heart failure, respiratory failure, and diabetes to name just a few. Diseases of the kidneys, liver, and gall bladder strike the obese more than others who are within the normal weight range. So do complications following surgical operations. Even deaths from accidents are more common among the obese. Degenerative arthritis of the back and of the knees, various bone disorders,

varicose veins and leg ulcers afflict the obese in increased incidence. Menstrual disorders are more frequent and there is more
likelihood of complications accompanying pregnancy.

It is interesting to note that if all the blood vessels in one
pound of body fat were straightened out, they would total
five-sixths of a mile. Thus, thirty pounds of excess fat tissue add
twenty-five miles to the blood vessels through which your heart
must pump your blood. This adds tremendously to the load your
heart must carry, as well as causing your kidneys to work
overtime. It is obvious, then, why even a small amount of extra
weight places a hardship on our bodies.

Increased death rates

Insurance companies, whose financial solvency depends upon
their being right, take a dark view of being "just a little"
overweight; extra pounds carry a measurable decrease in life
expectancy. From age 45 to 50, persons who are 10 pounds
overweight have a death rate 8 per cent above the average. Thirty
pounds overweight carries a 28 per cent penalty and 50 pounds
overweight 56 per cent! Overweight persons succumb to disorders
of the heart and kidneys some 60 per cent more frequently than
do those of normal weight. In other words, avoid being overweight
if you would prolong your stay in the land of the living!

Johann's bad habits

Johann, or so we will call him, was a 45-year-old bartender of
average weight who smoked and drank heavily. About fifteen
years before we saw him he had stopped smoking; five years after
that he gave up drinking. Obviously, he possessed admirable
self-control to set aside both of these habits. But he missed them
more than he cared to admit and in compensation took to eating.
The result was such a rapid gain in weight that he soon tipped the
scales beyond 300 pounds.

Being overweight was not his complaint, however, when he
sought out medical help; rather it was shortness of breath on even

slight exertion. After a careful examination, which revealed that the patient's extra weight was placing a serious burden on his heart, the doctor probed, as tactfully as possible, into Johann's private life. It developed that his marriage was unsatisfactory, his job boring, and he had no hobbies or pastime activities. The chief pleasure in his drab life was eating.

The doctor prescribed a diet consisting exclusively of high protein foods such as meat, fowl, eggs, cheese, and fish, plus 8 glasses of water a day. Johann was to starve completely one day a week, except for celery, a little salt, and water. And to this the doctor added the suggestion that he take up hunting and fishing seriously or some other pastime that would require some physical exertion; he was to get a minimum of one-half hour exercise every day.

Johann did follow the recreational and exercise programs and the diet. Over a period of months his weight loss averaged half a pound a day. By the time he had achieved his ideal weight, it appeared he would be able to maintain it because he had developed other enjoyments and a new pattern of living.

Response to treatment

Unfortunately, many persons who are extremely overweight do not meet with the success realized by Johann. And to be sure, prevention of obesity is far better than cure. When you first begin to gain weight, take stock of your life style. Is something lacking that you've begun to seek enjoyment via food? Perhaps your between meal cravings or mid-afternoon hunger pangs are symptoms of more than an empty space in the stomach. Analyze your emotional responses that might seek satisfaction through eating. Then offer them more healthful appeasement. For example, many persons eat simply because they don't have anything else to do at that moment. But why not call a friend, write a letter, work on a hobby, or just sit down and relax. Whatever your need to eat excessively, work to correct it.

Dieting requires perseverance

There are various sensible ways to reduce. In most obese persons a moderately restricted diet plus a program of exercise is the first step. An initial period of fasting for a few days can make caloric restriction more acceptable. It "shrinks" the stomach and even a little food is welcomed. Then, merely eat less of the usual foods. This method has certain advantages over stringent diet regimes. For when the special dieting period is over and the person returns to normal foods, he frequently resumes heavy eating and regains all the pounds he worked so hard to lose, perhaps more. In contrast, if the short fasting period is observed and followed by judicious limiting of the usual foods, reduced weight can be maintained.

But the person who is really determined to permanently achieve a normal weight must become emotionally adjusted to the prospect of living for years, probably the rest of his life, on a moderately restricted diet. And this is no easy assignment for those who truly enjoy eating good food.

Benefits of exercise

Regardless of what reducing program you decide upon, don't neglect to exercise. True, it requires a great deal of activity to burn up even a few calories. Nevertheless, a period of exercise approached gradually but consistently appears to reduce rather than to increase the appetite. It improves muscle tone, perhaps even your outlook on life, so that you find living bearable even though your caloric intake is sharply curtailed. A brisk walk, a bicycle ride, nine holes of golf, or a game of tennis or handball are all good exercises. Jogging around the block or simply running "in place" in your bedroom arc beneficial. Indeed, exercise should be a daily, year-round practice even after you have attained your ideal weight.

Some psychological "tricks" for dieters

There are several useful tricks that have proved helpful to many dieters, employing psychology to get maximum results from one's efforts:
1) Use small dishes. It makes the food look like more.
2) Drink more water. This helps to keep your stomach comfortable as well as aiding in digestion. It also discourages drinking calorie-rich carbonated beverages.

3) Eat slowly and chew leisurely. Take time to fully enjoy every mouthful so that you will not feel so deprived.

4) Buy new clothes a little bit tight. This offers an incentive to cut down on your food intake for a few days.

5) Weigh yourself only once a week. Weight loss occurs in spurts, and running to the scales constantly can become depressing. Be sure to keep a record of your weight so you will have a long-range view of your progress.

Controlling psychic factors

Psychic tension is unquestionably related to overeating. Good mental hygiene, therefore, is of utmost importance in treating obesity, helping overweight persons to lead less stressful, more gratifying lives. Group therapy has proved especially helpful because of the direct association with others who share the burden of being overweight. Not only are the participants encouraged by the progress of others but they receive guidance in improving their outlook on life. And merely belonging to such groups as TOPS—Take Off Pounds Sensibly—provides a diversion from eating.

Since overeating often represents an escape from the harsh realities of living, you might do well to ask yourself, "Is my life truly meaningful?" All of us, regardless of weight, should have as a primary goal the creation of a meaningful life. A group of ex-drug addicts, who call themselves "The Family," at Mendocino State Hospital in California, have described a meaningful life as possessing these traits:

1) It should have some warm, human relationship.

2) It should hold the opportunity for self-expression and honesty without penalty.

3) It should have a sense of structure and hope for the future.

4) It should provide a person with a sense of belonging to something larger than himself that is worthwhile.

5) It should be a life to which the individual feels he has made significant contributions through his own efforts.

Surely anyone who can adopt such a "prescription" for living can certainly do without overeating.

APPETITE LOSS

> He . . . threw off his spirit, his appetite, his
> sleep, and downright languish'd.
>
> William Shakespeare
> *The Winter's Tale*

Just as psychic disturbances can cause overeating, so can they cause loss of appetite and produce an underweight condition. All of us have experienced a decrease or loss of appetite due to disappointments, unpleasant events, or emotional tension from one cause or another. But when the condition becomes chronic and the normal urge to eat does not return, it becomes a serious ailment known medically as *anorexia nervosa,* meaning loss of appetite from nervous influences.

Physical changes from anorexia nervosa

Anorexia nervosa is indeed a psychosomatic disorder since it originates as a nervous reaction to tension and can well result in serious physical changes. For when a person does not receive his required quota of calories, he begins to consume himself, unconsciously but literally. He loses weight and may actually become emaciated. Growth may stop, causing some children to become dwarfs. The pulse slows down and even the slightest exertion brings shortness of breath and fatigue. Underarm hair may be lost. Sexual desire may disappear. Women may experience irregularity or even a stoppage of menstruation. Glands of internal secretion are curtailed in their activities, causing further loss of appetite. Mental depression, apprehension, and jitteriness occur. Indeed, once anorexia takes hold, a vicious cycle is set in motion that is not easily reversed.

About 90 per cent of the victims of anorexia nervosa are women. And while some begin by curbing an intense desire for food, others actually lose their appetites. They may consume less than 1000 calories a day.

Psychic causes

Just as obesity can stem from different types of psychic disturbances, so there is no one psychic cause of anorexia nervosa. The adolescent patient may, because of self-condemnation and ridicule, worry about extra pounds to such an extent that she becomes obsessed with dieting, restricting her food intake so completely that she reaches the opposite extreme—underweight. And she no longer has any desire for food.

Some anorexic persons appear to be punishing themselves; a guilty conscience will not permit the person to grant himself the pleasure of eating. (For centuries, fasting has been a common form of repentance.) Quite unconsciously, he refuses food until his "hunger mechanism" becomes inactive.

Jealousy, resentment, rejection, all of the emotional responses might be involved in precipitating anorexia. Sometimes the cause is quite obvious; on other occasions it defies recognition. In Christy's case, the cure was relatively simple once the problem came to our attention. Although only 8 years old, she had developed a full-blown "jealousy-guilt-penitence syndrome."

Christy's self punishment

Christy's family owned a summer home in a Midwest resort area and spent much time there during June, July and August. And Christy had always enjoyed it thoroughly. But one particular summer she became quite listless, refused to eat, and soon began to lose weight. Her parents were enormously disturbed and sought medical help. A thorough examination revealed nothing to account for her malnutrition and it appeared obvious that some sort of emotional disturbance had caused her to stop eating.

The doctor asked several questions and then suggested that the parents wait in the outer office while he talked to Christy. At first she was quiet and withdrawn but within minutes she had revealed her problem. For although her parents had failed to mention that there was a five-month old baby in the house, Christy referred to her repeatedly.

"Do you like your baby sister?" the doctor asked. Dropping her head just a little, Christy replied, "Well, I should like her, shouldn't I?" Then she went on to tell how much Mother liked the new baby and how long it took to feed her. And that Mother no longer had as much time to play outside or to help her read. And that Mother said, "Shh-h-h!" all the time because baby sister was sleeping. Indeed, it became quite apparent that Christy experienced strong jealousy toward her tiny sister.

At first she had refused to eat so as to capture her mother's attention. Then she began to feel guilty, sensing that what she was doing was wrong and that she really should love her sister. For this she had to do penance, so she continued to refuse food as a form of self-punishment. The results could have been disastrous had they been allowed to continue. But when the parents were led to understand the problem, they took careful steps to include Christy in all the baby's feedings, allowing her to care for her sister, "change" the diaper, and to go about her normal activities even if baby was sleeping. And the problem soon disappeared.

"The pediatrician's disease"

A prevalent form of anorexia occurs in young children whose mothers attempt, with the best intentions, to force them to eat. This type of eating problem can bring about serious malnutrition and an unhappy, pale, underdeveloped child. Since the physical state stems from psychic tension, childhood anorexia is indeed a psychosomatic disease. And it is quite different from Christy's problem.

Why does childhood anorexia develop? Up to about 14 months the infant has an enormous appetite. He has been growing rapidly, gaining as much during the first year of life as he will for the next five years added together. His appetite, therefore, is ravenous. But shortly after the end of the first year, his growth rate drops sharply. Appetite depends upon growth, not upon expenditure of energy, so his appetite also decreases. But Mother, who has been enormously happy with baby's hearty appetite, becomes concerned. She consults her pediatrician. One pediatrician jokingly said, "Pediatricians eat because babies don't." For that reason this decrease in appetite has been dubbed "The Pediatrician's Disease." The doctor reassures Mother that her baby is healthy and completely normal, that she should let the baby eat what he wants and no more, and that all will be well.

Forcing children to eat

But suppose that Mother does not seek the doctor's help. She may well attempt to compensate for baby's lack of appetite by forcing food on him. This, like all forcing, creates psychic tension. And baby rebels.

Mother, of course, does her forcing at mealtime. So mealtime becomes an unpleasant experience for baby and he loses what little appetite he had. Then, between meals, he becomes hungry. He is given tasty carbohydrate tidbits and milk to wash them down. Now milk is a good food in some respects but it is low in protein and high in fat, and the latter of itself tends to decrease appetite. If this program of between-meal eating is allowed to go on, the preschool child is in physical trouble. His intake of proteins, the important structural foods, has been woefully inadequate. And the diet has other inadequacies. Baby becomes protein deficient, iron deficient, and probably deficient in other substances as well. And he fails to develop a normal mealtime appetite!

Such children have a characteristic look about them: their facial expression is woeful, teeth often decayed, posture poor. Their ghostly pallor has caused a famous pediatrician, Dr. Preston McLendon, to call these children the "Children in Pastel Tints."

An easy remedy

The remedy for childhood anorexia caused by forcing of food is simple: permit the child to eat what he wants and not more than he wants at *mealtime*. Forcing is taboo! Place an assortment of proper foods—including generous amounts of protein foods—before him, then leave him alone. Most children will develop an appetite within days. In others it may take longer. Bear in mind, there are no appetite problems in countries plagued by starvation.

Anorexia nervosa can affect social life

Strange as it may seem, anorexia can have detrimental effects on social life and can lead to serious complications in marriage, even to no marriage at all. Mary Ann, for example, was unable to eat in public or with people whom she did not know well. She suffered great embarrassment and anxiety because of her refusal to join friends, particularly young men, for dinner. But when she forced herself to accept a dinner date, she became nauseated and had even fainted on one occasion. Her social life became nil.

Mary Ann's problem was complex and required much probing to discover its origin. It finally emerged that being the oldest of seven children, Mary Ann had bitterly resented her mother's repeated pregnancies by her lazy ne'er-do-well father. Every new child deprived her further of her mother's attention. She had always enjoyed her mother's cooking, however, and considered the gift of food as a most touching expression of love. Gradually, her repressed bitterness against her mother had resulted in a sense of guilt and the guilt attached itself to eating and to sexuality. Hence, she was unable to eat without restraint, particularly in the presence of members of the opposite sex.

When the problem was brought out into the open, Mary Ann began to make some progress. Unfortunately, her social life had already been sorely damaged. And recovery would not be rapid.

Response to treatment

Since anorexia nervosa usually comes from psychic tension, psychotherapy relieves most patients who truly desire to be helped. Should you become the victim of a seriously depressed appetite, your first step should be the same as for all suspected psychosomatic disorders: consult your physician.

At the same time, however, you should conduct a self inventory, endeavoring to discover if you have serious psychic tensions that might be responsible. Your physician can no doubt advise you if you need psychotherapy. Only an insight into the relationship between phychic tension and poor appetite can clear up the problem, however, if it is of psychic origin.

STRIKE A HAPPY MEDIUM

One will be far better off if he is neither fat nor too lean. To walk this middle road, eat adequate but not excessive quantities of well-balanced foods, lead an interesting and productive life so that eating does not become your chief concern. For neither obesity nor underweight has any place in a well ordered life.

nine

How to pump new life into
your glands

One reason why we do not all have good
health is . . . we lack will.
                    Elbert Hubbard (1856-1915)

It became clear many years ago that the glands of the body
are generally divided into two great groups. One group forms
secretions that are poured into the body tracts, particularly the
digestive tract. All of them, as the salivary glands, those in the
walls of the stomach and intestines, sweat glands, and the liver,
have one common characteristic: they possess tubes or ducts
through which the substances they manufacture are emptied into
the region where they do their work. The second group, known as
the endocrine glands or glands of internal secretion, have no ducts.
Instead, these ductless glands pour their products, complicated
chemical compounds called hormones, directly into the blood
stream for transportation to the various parts of the body. They
include the pituitary gland, the adrenal glands, the thyroid and
parathyroid glands, the sex glands and others. The pancreas is both
a gland of external secretion and a gland of internal secretion.

We have previously seen, in the chapter about stress, how
those important glands of internal secretion—the pituitary and
adrenal glands—valiantly defend the body against the effects of
severe stress, be it physical or psychic. We have also seen how the
defensive reaction sometimes goes askew with the result that
hormones are released in seriously unbalanced quantities. Thus,
too much aldosterone may be poured into the blood stream and a

disabling disease such as rheumatoid arthritis starts its joint destroying inroads. This sort of ailment is not caused directly by the stress but, rather, by the body's maladaptation to stress. In the vast majority of instances the acute stresses that Dr. Hans Selye describes do. no damage at all because the body successfully neutralizes them.

The body reacts directly to tension

On some occasions, however, the glands of internal secretion react directly to psychic tension by secreting too little or too much of a given hormone. This sort of error in hormone secretion does not result from the gland's attempt to defend the body; rather the gland's secretory activity is simply thrown out of kilter by disturbing nerve impulses reaching the gland as a result of storms riding out on the wires of the autonomic nervous system. The exact route varies somewhat depending upon which gland is involved. Likewise, the disorders that result depend upon the endocrine gland affected. But since physical changes result from psychic disturbances, the ailments represent psychosomatic disease.

THE DEPRESSED PITUITARY

You will recall that the pituitary gland stores or secretes a constellation of highly important hormones. Indeed, it is often called the "master gland" because all other endocrine glands— thyroid and adrenals, for example—depend upon its secretions for stimulation. One of these hormones, the human growth hormone, or HGH, controls the growth of virtually all the tissues of the body. It is an especially exciting hormone because it is the only one known to affect *every* tissue and cell of the body. Other hormones, important as they are, seem to single out certain specific target organs to influence but HGH is everywhere in the body cells.

When too much HGH is secreted because of a tumor or overgrowth of the pituitary gland, the victim becomes a giant. Probably most of the giants of history have suffered from disease of the pituitary. But if too little of the hormone is secreted as a result of destruction of part of the gland, dwarfism results. As in the case of twins, whom we shall call Jennifer and John, psychic effects can also block secretion of normal amounts of HGH and produce the same effect.

An example of psychosomatic dwarfism

Jennifer and John developed normally and at about the same rate until they reached the age of 18 months. Shortly thereafter, both were given a careful physical examination. Jennifer was found to weigh two pounds less than her twin; moreover, both her skin and her hair seemed to be extremely dry, certainly an abnormal condition.

By the age of three years, Jennifer had fallen still further behind her twin. At that time, because not only her physical growth but her motor and speech development were obviously retarded, Jennifer was studied in a hospital. The findings were most disturbing! Jennifer weighed only 19 pounds and was less than 30 inches tall. Her bone development was less than for normal children of her age. A disorder of the pituitary gland was suspected but no attempt was made to explore the matter further, nor was any treatment given. Instead, continued observation to see what would develop was the recommendation.

Six months later Jennifer's weight had dropped to 14½ pounds. In all respects Jennifer continued to drop further and further behind her brother. At the age of six she was refused admittance to school because of her short stature and retarded mental development. At the age of seven and a half, her intelligence quotient (I.Q.) was measured as 65, indicating serious mental impairment. Now her parents were successful in having her admitted to a class for handicapped children.

Better times for Jennifer

The choice of school was particularly fortunate for it was staffed by teachers and nurses intensely dedicated to the welfare of their little charges. Jennifer's progress during the first year in school was little short of miraculous: she grew 5 inches and gained 18 pounds. Her I.Q. was rechecked and found to be 93! Still more amazing was the change in her personality. From an unhappy, morose, inactive little girl she became cheerful, active and cooperative. She enjoyed school so much that she cried when the term ended in June.

But that first year was only the beginning. Her rapid rate of growth—really catching up—continued. Her learning ability improved, too. After only two years in the class for handicapped children she was believed able to undertake the studies of the regular third grade. They turned out to be just a little beyond her so she returned to the school for the handicapped for an additional year.

All continued to go well for Jennifer. When she and John were 13 years of age both were reexamined. Both were found to be normal in every respect. Jennifer was 55½ inches tall and weighed 76 pounds. John was 58 inches tall and weighed 80 pounds. But in maturity of bone and of sexual development Jennifer exceeded John.

In retrospect

When physicians and social workers reviewed the past history of Jennifer they discovered that shortly after the end of the first year of life an abnormal antagonism had, for reasons unclear, developed between Jennifer and her mother. Mutual hostility had increased over the years. But hostility on the part of the mother gave way to depression when the mother concluded that the child was destined to be a mentally retarded dwarf. Then Jennifer started at the school. Here the conscientious efforts of teacher and nurse caused her to blossom and make truly remarkable progress.

Thoughtful consideration of the child's history and results of physical and laboratory examinations led to the conclusion that her failure to grow and develop normally stemmed from the suppressive effects of psychic tension on the child's pituitary gland. The remedy, which in a sense occurred almost accidentally, consisted of her attendance at a school where she received the affection, attention and acceptance that every child craves and deserves.

Synthesis of HGH—an outstanding achievement

Even in this day of extensive research, a true "breakthrough" is a rarity. But there is one on the records of 1971—the artificial laboratory production of the human growth hormone. To the average person this may seem to be of little significance, but to the entire medical and scientific world it was cause for rejoicing. And for Dr. Choh Hao Li of San Francisco, it was the culmination of a 32-year career devoted to delving into the secrets of the pituitary gland. Dr. Li's discovery makes it possible for researchers to have a greater supply of HGH, formerly obtained only from human cadavers. And from their research could come giant advances in man's long fight against such diseases as cancer, rheumatoid arthritis, and hardening of the arteries.

It is known that HGH is a factor in not only these diseases but in obesity, male and female sexual function, and numerous other areas. A sufficient supply of the synthesized product can open new doors of investigation. And when the role of HGH is related to physical problems, the psychosomatic aspects will also become apparent. Dr. Li's discovery is, indeed, an outstanding achievement.

Other pituitary hormones

Disturbing emotions have a harmful effect on the production of the other hormones secreted by the pituitary as well as on HGH. One of these hormones resists excessive loss of water, and helps to maintain that constant balance of salt and other minerals in our body fluids that is so essential to life. Another is important in childbirth; still another in the function of female milk glands. Others exert a control over the activity of other endocrine glands. Psychic tension, for example, is an important factor in many instances of thyroid gland malfunctioning.

TENSION AND THE THYROID GLAND

The significance of the thyroid gland was dramatically highlighted by Christopher Morley when he described New York as "the nation's thyroid gland." Located in the front of the neck, the thyroid gland regulates the metabolic or chemical reaction rate of all the tissues and organs of the body. It does this through several hormones, chief of which is called thyroxin. Nevertheless, it receives its instruction from the executive gland—the pituitary.

As part of its overall function, the thyroid gland contributes to growth and development and helps maintain the proper level of that essential mineral, calcium, in the blood stream. Under the potent influence of thyroxin, at least 13 different chemical activators or enzymes are produced in the precise quantities necessary for the chemical reactions to take place, without respite, within the myriad body cells. Every body system—heart and blood vessels, nervous system, and digestive system, as examples—march to the muffled drums of the thyroid.

When the thyroid gland pours increased quantities of its hormones into the blood stream, either because of excessive goading from the pituitary gland, or excessive production of thyroid hormones because of disorders within the thyroid, serious illness develops. The chemical factories of the body work at a furious pace, perhaps doubling their rate of activity.

Like a Model T Ford with a Cadillac engine

The patient with increased thyroid activity may react somewhat like a Model T Ford powered by a Cadillac engine. He becomes jittery, tremulous, apprehensive; he feels as if he would like to "jump out of his skin." The heart rate speeds up with the heart thumping against the chest walls so furiously that the patient can feel each beat. All body activities are correspondingly accelerated. The excessive action of the gland, known as hyperthyroidism, imposes enormous wear and tear on the patient. The increased rate of body chemical reactions can lead to early aging and degeneration; it may even play a role in causing senility.

Hyperthyroidism is usually accompanied by a swelling or goiter in front of the neck. This may become so large as to be unsightly. (Goiter can, however, occur with normal or depressed thyroid secretion.) Some persons with hyperthyroidism suffer from protrusion of the eyeballs, a disfiguring and distressing symptom. Blindness can result. Unfortunately, the protrusion does not always disappear after the hyperthyroidism is corrected; the exact cause of the protrusion remains a mystery.

The importance of tension

While the cause of many instances of hyperthyroidism cannot be definitely determined, the disorder is often closely related to psychic tension. Crucial events in patients' lives have often been associated with the onset of the disease: leaving home, becoming involved in a demanding job, marital problems, childbearing, family disappointments, and excessively ambitious undertakings have all appeared to touch off the malady.

But hints from life situations are not enough to establish psychosomatic relationship to hyperthyroidism, or to any other disease for that matter. Therefore, we rely upon numerous studies and personal observation for the support of our assertions. In one group of 159 patients, forty-five stated that their thyroid hyper-activity began with an emotional upset. One hundred eighty-eight of a group of 200 had suffered psychic injury shortly before the thyroid disorder started. Another series of patients with excessive thyroid activity were compared with persons who did not have the ailment: pronounced differences were found in family history, in early development, and in sexual and marital adjustments.

One investigator writes in detail about her examinations of patients, employing both physical and psychological methods. She began with a careful check of the exact time and sequence of the appearance of symptoms of hyperthyroidism. This was followed by a review of the family situation. A constant watch was kept for signs of unexplained emotion and particular attention was given to any alteration in any situation that occurred prior to the onset of symptoms.

During the examinations, she frequently noted reddening or flushing of the neck and lower face. The degree of blushing was directly related to physical alterations, such as basal metabolic rate, and to the severity of the incident recalled. The blushing extended from the upper chest to the middle of the cheeks and sometimes to the forehead, with the neck veins standing out and obvious pulsations in the neck increasing in violence, so that in extreme cases the thyroid gland itself appeared to increase in size.

This reddening was noted when specific sensitivity of the individual to an emotional experience had been stimulated. Not only did these examinations point out the relationship between psychic tension and increased thyroid activity, but they led the way to treatment of those patients examined. For once the emotional conflict became apparent, relief was within their reach.

Like so many psychosomatic diseases, a vicious circle is here again set in motion: psychic tension starts off thyroid hyperactivity; thyroid hyperactivity stimulates more psychic tension; tension adds more fuel to the fires of the disease, and so on. Therefore, the quicker the disease is discovered and treatment begun, the more chance there is of interrupting the reciprocal process.

Shadow symptoms

Shadow symptoms of hyperthyroidism include jitteriness, sweating of the palms, rapid heart rate, difficulty in sleeping, excessive appetite with simultaneous loss of weight. Diarrhea might also be present. The appearance of these symptoms should alert the person to seek medical help, including laboratory tests specifically designed to detect hyperthyroidism.

A dreadful series of tragedies

The case of a patient we shall call Doris illustrates the sort of background emotional experience that can precipitate hyperthyroidism. Fortunately, few of us are exposed to the sort of terrifying events that befell Doris.

She had suffered through extreme poverty as a child, had been treated harshly by her stepfather. And when she was only four she had seen a woman burn to death. At the age of eight she had the unforgettable experience of seeing a coffin tipped over by accident and the corpse of a three-year-old friend thrown out on the floor. And if all of this was not enough, she later witnessed the suicide of her grandfather and the death of her grandmother. The horror of these events never left her; indeed, it's surprising that she even kept her sanity. It was at the age of 32, shortly after her husband had died, that she developed hyperthyroidism.

Suspecting that the death of her husband might be the guilty factor in causing her illness, her doctor took a considerable amount of time searching out her personal history. Shocked at the series of tragedies that she described, he was most sympathetic and explained how such memories could cause her trouble. Since she had come to him when she first recognized symptoms—extreme jitteriness, pounding heart, and abnormal loss of weight—it was possible to restore her health without prolonged treatment or surgery. Wise counsel, in combination with medication, brought full relief and to this date, she has had no recurrence.

How about thyroid underactivity?

Some physicians believe that underactivity of the thyroid gland, called hypothyroidism, can stem from psychic tension. The patient with hypothyroidism is slow moving and lethargic, puts on weight, has a peculiar type of skin swelling known as myxedema, develops dryness of skin and hair, and undergoes profound changes in personality. Development of hypothyroidism may represent a defense designed to protect the patient from over-whelming emotions and situations. The general inactivity of the state permits the patient to retreat in the face of unmanageable pressures.

THOSE POWERFUL ADRENALS

We have seen how the adrenal glands can be a party to diseases of maladaptation to stress. Now we shall enquire as to how they can cause psychosomatic disorders by reacting directly to psychic tension by abnormal secretion of hormones. Each of our adrenal glands is curled comfortably over the top of a kidney. And as we noted previously, the outer portion or cortex of the adrenals produces anti-inflammatory hormones—cortisol is an example—and pro-inflammatory hormones—aldosterone is an example. The internal portion of the adrenal glands secretes quite a different hormone, epinephrine, perhaps the most stimulating of all hormones. Indeed, the secretion of epinephrine establishes the close relationship between hormones and the autonomic nervous system, since the latter employs epinephrine to stimulate muscles, glands, and blood vessels. The effects produced by epinephrine are identical with those caused when the sympathetic division of the autonomic nervous system becomes activated.

Studies of persons under emotional pressure have revealed that production of the various adrenal hormones is increased. One special group of men with a high percentage of coronary artery disease, who were quite ambitious and often forced to meet deadlines under pressure, secreted increased quantities of epinephrine during working hours. Placid subjects were found to secrete significantly less. One result of increased outpouring of epinephrine by the adrenal glands would be narrowing of the tiny blood vessels of the kidneys. This could well represent the first step leading later to high blood pressure.

Shadow symptoms

Shadow symptoms of disease caused by excessive stimulation of the adrenals by psychic tension are indeed shadowy. The first indication might be dizziness or headache caused by elevated blood pressure. Or, the first indication might be the finding of an elevated blood pressure at a routine physical examination since high blood pressure is not always accompanied by symptoms.

HOW THE PANCREAS BECOMES INVOLVED

The blood level of a carbohydrate called glucose regulates the secretion of the chief hormone of the pancreas, called insulin. This hormone keeps the blood glucose at the right level by promoting use of glucose by the cells and tissues of the body, by causing glucose to be stored in the liver, and by helping form fat from glucose. When the amount of insulin secreted by the pancreas is inadequate or when its quality is impaired, the patient develops an ailment called diabetes mellitus, which means literally "a flowing through of honey."

Since in diabetes the body cells find themselves unable to utilize glucose for energy, the level of glucose in the blood rises two or three times normal. Large quantities of glucose pass out in the urine, giving the urine the consistency and appearance of water mixed with honey. Not only is glucose lost from the body but water, minerals and protein as well are contained in the urine. Not receiving the energy normally received from the breakdown of food and unable to manufacture body proteins, the patient weakens and loses weight. Although he may have a ravenous appetite and may eat voraciously he receives little nourishment.

Can tension contribute to diabetes?

General agreement does not exist on the impact of psychic tension on the development of diabetes mellitus, sometimes called sugar diabetes. Certainly there is an inherited tendency, although persons often develop diabetes when there is no history of the disease among ancestors or close, even distant, relatives. But we believe that psychic tension and emotions can play a role in the diabetes of some persons. Certainly the history of Jeannie, described in Chapter Three, bears this out. And Jeannie is not the only person we have seen who was able to completely discontinue medication without recurring symptoms.

It is quite certain that diabetes that is already established can be worsened by psychic tension; when patients encounter unpleasant events the blood glucose rises and the urine shows increased amounts of glucose. Such events can also favor the development of acidity of the blood, known as acidosis, caused by the improper metabolism of fats when insulin is not performing its assigned task. Moreover, circumstances that provoke feelings of frustration, loneliness, or dejection may be accompanied by a marked increase in the need for insulin. And when these conflicts have been resolved, the state of the disease improves, as shown by a decreased blood glucose level, less glucose in the urine and lowering of the need for insulin. These findings have been supported by laboratory experiments on animals as well as on humans. A classic test revealed that fear and anxiety can cause an increase in the urine glucose of the normal cat. In other studies, sugar was found in the urine of football players after an exciting game and in students after a grueling examination.

Sugar diabetes in children

Diabetes mellitus also occurs in childhood. It is frequently associated with stressful conditions and, in turn, the diabetes can cause even greater stress within the family circle. In one study of a group of 21 diabetic children, a third of the cases had developed the diabetes at the time of a disturbance in family relationship such as boarding out with relatives, divorce, deaths in the family. Less than a third of the children had suffered infection preceding the onset of their diabetes. But even more important than the psychic factors that might have precipitated the disease was the emotional turmoil in the household following the discovery that the child was suffering from diabetes. The first reaction was generally one of great emotional disturbance and bewilderment. Then followed dejection and depression. The child was constantly reminded of his condition. Frequently the mothers were responsible for cheating on the dietary limitations because they could not bear to see the child deprived. In other instances, the mothers were cold and impatient toward their children's natural desires for rich foods. Only in those homes where there was understanding, harmony, and security was the child's adjustment good and his personality development normal. In these homes, the diabetes was controlled with a minimum of difficulty.

Influence of unhappy life events on Ronald's diabetes

The case of a 17-year-old boy named Ronald suggests the possiblity that unhappy life events can open the door for diabetes, and spells out in bold letters the impact of continual emotional conflict on the course of diabetes. Ronald's mother had died when he was two and he lived thereafter either with relatives, his alcoholic father, or in institutions, never enjoying the security of a stable home. His diabetes was discovered at the age of 13 while he was living in a school for delinquent boys and where he was most unhappy. In the four years that followed the onset of diabetes he was hospitalized 19 different times because of the severity of the acidosis that he developed in spite of a large insulin dosage each day (110 units).

Then, for an interval of nine months, he was removed from his dreaded environment and placed in a more permissive foster home where he was encouraged to express himself more. He was treated with respect and even his "big-shot" strivings were accepted. During that nine months, Ronald developed no symptoms of acidosis and his requirement for insulin was reduced. For reasons never fully understood by either Ronald or his foster parents, he was suddenly required to return to his former environment—the home for delinquent youths—and within 24 hours he was admitted to the hospital with severe acidosis. Unfortunately, it appeared doubtful that Ronald would ever fully control his ailment.

Unconscious emotional conflicts pose problems

So psychic tension can undoubtedly make established diabetes worse and can probably, although indisputable evidence is not yet available, contribute to the appearance of diabetes in susceptible persons. Perhaps prolonged or repeated tension will only cause diabetes in those persons whose body mechanisms for metabolizing glucose are already shaky or where predisposition exists. For if a person is indeed healthy, he probably enjoys a fair share of emotional stability as well. He would not be a likely candidate for psychosomatic diabetes.

It appears that psychic insults shower the pancreas with damaging impulses, via the autonomic division of the sympathetic nervous system, thus impairing the production of insulin and producing diabetes. Indeed, the way in which diabetes comes on often suggests psychic factors. Depression, anxiety, fatigue and psychic trauma precede the start of the disease in many patients. Some have been suffering from a compulsive desire to eat, intensified during periods of loneliness, depression or stress. Flanders Dunbar found that a frequent pattern in diabetics was a steady grind of fatigue and deprivation with an increasingly passive personality. Resentment was frequently called into play by daily life situations.

Shadow symptoms

What are the shadow symptoms of inadequate secretion of insulin? One, of course, is the finding of glucose in the urine during a period of stress or infection. Repeated tests should be made and if the finding continues, immediate control should be effected by medication. A more serious symptom is excessive urination over a period of a week or more. Failure of infections to heal promptly, loss of weight and malnutrition are signs that diabetes may already be present. Extreme fatigue is generally associated with diabetes. Any of these symptoms are a signal for medical attention, particularly if there is a history of diabetes in the family. And even if there is no such inherited tendency, a physical examination is advisable. Some persons regularly test their urine with small strips of chemically treated paper that will turn a certain color if glucose is present in the urine. This is a wise practice and will eliminate a degree of anxiety in many persons.

Too much insulin

Psychic tension can, in some persons, stimulate the production of excessive insulin. This produces a bothersome lowering of the level of glucose in the blood known as hypoglycemia or low blood sugar. The shadow symptoms include fatigue between meals immediately relieved by eating something sweet; the need for food in the middle of the night; and a desperate craving for orange juice on awakening. Anxiety, irritability, excitement, confusion, and finally complete loss of consciousness (coma) can result from low blood sugar. And these symptoms may or may not occur in persons subject to psychic tension. In an impressive number of cases, however, symptoms have been relieved when the patient was given wise psychological counsel and was taught to "enjoy life" and achieve a healthy state of mind.

WHEN THE PSYCHE CAUSES HORMONAL
IMBALANCES . . .

Hormonal or endocrine imbalances caused by psychic tension are particularly insidious, since the symptoms of hormonal imbalances are unfamiliar to most persons. Moreover, the psychic tension may occur in the unconscious, with the patient unaware of the emotional civil war raging beneath the level of his conscious mind.

Psychosomatic symptoms in most organ systems are not often difficult to recognize: a "jumpy" heart, overbreathing, pain in the pit of the stomach, an itchy rash, for example, are quite obvious. But not so, the majority of symptoms resulting from the impact of the autonomic nervous system on endocrine glands. When hormones become involved in the psychosomatic complex resulting ailments are less simple. Abraham Myerson phrased the complexity well in *Speaking of Man* when he said, ". . . Somehow there is a constant and shifting balance of forces in which hormones, ferments, enzymes, memories, ideas, emotions, and moods all play a part; and all of this is an unexplainable transit from conception to that catalytic dispersal, perhaps reassemblage, called death."

Still, the basic steps for psychosomatic disease of endocrine origin is much like that for all such diseases: See your doctor and if organic factors are eliminated, then work to also eliminate the psychic factors. In many cases, emotional problems result from not enough to do, no purpose or direction to living, and, in short, being bored. In other persons, the problem is just the opposite— too much to do, too much pressure. But in either case, you must take definite action to achieve greater happiness. If you're bored, do something different. Volunteer work in hospitals or nursing homes helps many to feel useful. And when they're busy helping others, they forget to be bored. Their secret is forgetting themselves.

The secret for those persons suffering from pressure, particularly related to their jobs, is to consider themselves more. No job is worth the sacrifice of one's health. If the situation cannot be relieved, perhaps it would be wise to look elsewhere. In all too many unhappy persons, however, the problem cannot be avoided or eliminated. In these cases, shrewd mental diversion may be possible. Some such methods are discussed in the last chapter of this book.

The importance of employing tactics designed to improve your emotional outlook on life become clear when we recognize the important interrelationship between our glands, our health, and our state of mind. The possible rewards make our efforts worthwhile.

ten

Amazing "x factor" can
rejuvenate your sense organs

> Our senses perceive no extreme. Too much
> sound deafens us; too much light dazzles us;
> too great distance or proximity hinders our
> view. Too great length and too great brevity
> of discourse tend to obscurity; too much
> truth is paralyzing.
>
> Blaise Pascal (1623-1662)
> *Pensees*

Our sense organs enable us to enjoy the blueness of the sky, the warmth of the sun, the fragrance of a rose, the trill of a song sparrow, the taste of a strawberry, or the tenderness of a kiss. But this is only the beginning of their usefulness, for without sense organs we would be more helpless than a newborn baby and quite unable to survive for more than a few black and silent days. We would be unaware that our stomach was empty, or that a tooth was aching, or even that we were too hot or too cold. We would have no warning at all of sickness or danger; we would be incapable of learning, for even the deaf, mute, and blind retain their sense of touch by which they are taught.

Man is traditionally credited with having five senses: *vision*, detected by light-sensitive cells in the eye; *hearing*, detected by tiny hair cells of the inner ear; *smell*, detected through cells embedded in the moist lining of the upper cavities of the nose; *taste*, originating in onion-shaped buds below the surface of the tongue; *touch*, including the sensations of warmth, cold, and pain, felt through special organs and nerve endings in and below the skin.

But we now know that there are other senses as well. *Equilibrium,* a sense of balance or position and bodily motion, is detected by certain hairs in the inner ear but can in no wise be lumped together with hearing. Sensations of touch, as felt by the skin, are rightly separated from those felt by our internal organs, such as the lining of the stomach or intestines. These internal responses are attributed to a seventh sense known as *organic sensitivity.* Still another sense is *muscle sensitivity,* which denotes sensations in the muscle, tendons, and joints. In time, it is not unlikely that additional senses will be discovered.

Memories are made of sensations

When a sense organ is acted upon by some form of stimulus, as light, sound, or pressure, we experience a sensation. Each sensory experience leaves some sort of deposit in the nervous system—a unique image or feeling—so that when the experience is repeated, we recognize it. Indeed, we can recall certain images or feelings or "re-live" certain experiences in the absence of the original stimulus. Our memories, in fact, are made up of countless sensations that have left their marks upon our minds.

You have no doubt wondered on occasion why a certain experience or situation aroused feelings of pleasure or displeasure, tension or calmness with no apparent provocation. The answer is that some time in the past your sense organs recorded your reaction to a similar experience; some sensory stimulus has brought the past experience to mind and you are reliving the sensations felt before. These memories may be in your conscious mind or they may be chucked away in some dark corner of your unconscious mind but they are always on call, as we mentioned in Chapter Three.

Varying degrees of sensitivity

Sense organs vary in sensitivity. Organs of taste can respond to only four chemical substances—sweet, bitter, sour, and salty. The eyes, however, are sensitive to more than half a million differences in stimuli. And there is a tremendous range of intensity in sound, light, odor, and other stimuli. A sound may be so low that it cannot be heard, a light so dim that it cannot be seen. The sense of smell is particularly remarkable because such a small amount of substance is needed to stimulate the nerve endings in the nose and produce a sensation. Some substances can be detected if as little as one thirty-billionth part is present in a given weight of air.

The various senses work in close alignment. Smell and taste are frequently confused because much of the so-called taste of many foods is really an aroma, or smell. Touch is also involved as well as vision. For example, when you eat an apple you first see it and recognize it as an apple, thus preparing your taste buds to expect a certain taste. You bite into it and the pressure and touch are significant. The sweet taste buds of the tongue are stimulated at the same time that a distinct odor reaches the organs of smell. And the different sensations are fused so that you are not aware of them individually, you simply enjoy the "taste" of an apple. Test this sometime by having someone offer you a food substance (dry coffee is particularly interesting) while you close your eyes and hold your nostrils together. Taste is almost non-existent in many cases when the sense of smell is hampered. This explains why food does not "taste" right when you have a cold or nasal congestion.

Muted sensations

Modern man has lost much of the sensory input of bygone days. Frequent bathing and deodorants decrease or eliminate most body odors. Modern plumbing has rendered the bathroom virtually odorless. If you were suddenly transported through time and space to a medieval village you would probably find the odors overpowering. And the medievalist transported by time machine to our time and place might possibly miss the redolent aromas of his former home. Travelers to Japan who leave the cities and drive through the countryside find themselves overwhelmed by the almost indescribable beauty of the Land of the Cherry Blossoms; they are equally overwhelmed by the pungent and sometimes nauseating odors that frequently assail their western nostrils.

Because of our disuse of smell it is a relatively weak sense for us. The Australian aborigine, on the other hand, has cultivated his sense of smell over the ages as an important aid in hunting game and detecting the approach of enemies. Indeed, all the aborigine senses are sharpened to razor edge acuity. They make outstanding trackers of fugitives, using their acute senses to detect tiny clues that would escape our dulled perceptiveness.

Similarly, when a person loses the use of one or more senses, he frequently develops an amazing degree of sensitivity in the remaining sense organs. A person who is blind, for example, can often detect sounds that escape another's ears. Blind persons' sense of touch may be greatly improved so that they can "see" by touching the petals of a rose or brushing their fingers lightly over Braille print.

A school for the senses

Recognizing that sensitivity can be increased, modern social scientists are making considerable effort in this direction. At California's Esalen Institute, 35 miles south of Carmel in the Big Sur country, psychologists have been engaged in the new technique of sensitivity training. An instructor may begin by dangling a sheet of paper between his fingers, instructing the student to imagine that he is that paper. The student concentrates—imagines himself thin, flexible, fragile. Then the teacher suddenly crumples the paper into a wad. The student winces, having become sensitized. Such sensitivity training has as its goal helping business executives, doctors, lawyers, clergymen, and others to become more aware of themselves and of their relationships with those about them through sensory rather than verbal experience.

It remains to be seen just how useful sensitivity training will ultimately prove. Its merits, however, lie in the theory that modern man hides his feelings and emotions to his own detriment, and fails to utilize his senses for greater satisfaction and fulfillment. The emotional involvement of the senses is recognized and stressed. For instance, a group of 20 businessmen attended a two-day workshop at Esalen in which they played "blindman's buff," one man with eyes open leading another who shut his eyes and contacted his surroundings through touch and smell, all the while encouraged by a trained psychologist to relate his tense emotions and "hang-ups" to particular sensations. On another occasion a public school teacher was encouraged toward greater creativity by being made aware of the sense of pressure that restrained her: she was told to go through the arduous motions of taking off her girdle while she concentrated on the restrictive emotions responsible for her inhibitions.

Such sensitivity training, certainly no far-out cultist fad, is suddenly in vogue across the nation: over 350 officials of the State Department, including ambassadors, have taken sensitivity classes at Washington's NTL Institute for Applied Behavioral Science. And Ford Foundation's Fund for the Advancement of Education recently gave Esalen a $21,000 grant to train five public school teachers who will then try some of its techniques in their classrooms.

Emotions play a part in sensory deprivation of aged

Psychic tension and senses are intimately intertwined. Our sense organs bring us the messages from the environment that cause tension and unhappiness; the tension thus produced sometimes appears to "seek revenge" on the sense organs by producing malfunction and even disease. The sensory deprivation of the aged, although caused largely by organic changes due to aging, might well stem in part from a dim outlook on life and the hopeless feeling of having outlived one's usefulness.

A passage from Ecclesiastes 12 portrays in beautiful but sad language this great trial of the aged: "Remember thy Creator in the days of thy youth, before the time of affliction come, and the years draw near of which thou shalt say: 'They please me not' . . . before the sun, and the light, and the moon, and the stars be darkened . . . and they that look through the holes shall be darkened . . . and they shall shut the doors in the street, when the grinder's voice shall be low [the person hardly hears the sound of his own teeth] . . ." Although couched in the allegorical language so frequently used in the Old Testament of the Bible, the passage quoted clearly refers to decreasing sharpness of the senses, to the failure of vision, to deafness.

Shocked recognition of former theatrical director

It is difficult to say how much of the sensory deprivation of older persons could have been avoided, or could even be reversed, if a positive, purposeful mental attitude existed. One writer tells the story of his visit to a home for the aged in southern California. He was shocked to recognize a man he had known some years before, a talented theatrical director. But the man who sat slumped over in a large cane chair bore little resemblance to the person he had known. His hands trembled, his hair was disheveled, he mumbled in a low raspy tone, cupping his hand around his ear to indicate he could hardly hear what was being said to him. And his eyesight was obviously failing.

After leaving the home, the writer checked into the old man's past to see when he had left the theatrical business and what had transpired in the years following. It developed that the man had been released from his job although he was still extremely capable, because he had reached retirement age. Unable to find other work, without a family, and with no sense of meaningfulness left in his life, the old man sank into a state of depression, secluded from the world about him, until he was moved to the home for the aged.

Having been an ardent admirer of the man's work while in theatrical business, the writer wondered if rehabilitation would be possible. He was strongly discouraged by the supervisors of the home, told that the man had not responded in several years. But determined at least to make an effort, the writer began taking the old man with him several evenings a week to practice sessions of a small community drama group that presented plays several times each year. The immediate response was encouraging, the old man sat erect and absorbed every movement on the stage. After several sessions, he began to make suggestions in his almost inaudible voice. Gradually, his voice became stronger; his hearing was obviously improved as he seldom missed a word spoken by the actors.

Inspired by the wisdom of the old man's suggestions, the group decided to hire him as a "consulting director." The improvement in his health was almost miraculous. He continued to live at the home and members of the cast would pick him up for each rehearsal. But it was a different man they picked up now—hair combed and dressed in a new suit he had bought with the money they paid him. Having found a reason to live, he became an inspiration to others in the home, indeed to everyone who met him. This one small change in his life—call it the "X factor," or what you will—made all the difference. The "X factor" had restored his youth!

To be sure, much of the sensory deprivation that this man suffered was no doubt voluntary and may not have involved true physical changes. But the psychosomatic element was undeniable in relation to his vision. For when he had his eyes checked by the same physician who had prescribed his lenses the previous year, his vision had improved markedly and the strength of his new lenses was notably reduced.

Preventing the degenerative process of aging

The above example of decreased acuity of the sense organs only underlines a fact that we have long known, that much of the degenerative process of aging is due to lack of love and purposefulness and that great wonders can be wrought in the constructive atmospheres of many homes for the elderly. The growing number of senior citizen activities and housing complexes being built for persons over 65 that include planned social functions is encouraging.

Indeed, in disorders of old age, no less than any other psychosomatic problem, prevention is far better and more effective than cure. The child who is taught to be sociable, adaptable and resourceful will usually continue so in adult life and even in old age. But education must not stop in childhood. Adult education is being looked upon with increasing interest and classes are being offered in all realms of study. Hobbies, as well as new forms of recreation, can be discovered, not to mention instruction in many subjects which contribute to intellectual improvement.

The old phrase, "You can't teach an old dog new tricks," has done great harm, for as a result many older people admit defeat before trying and opportunities for learning are suppressed. Studies reveal that once this resistance to adult learning is overcome the capacity to learn is only slightly diminished by aging. Grandma Moses started her art career in her eighties; the great French entomologist J. Henri Fabre came into his own professionally during his eighth decade! It would be far better to say, "It is never too late to learn." This has a considerable bearing upon the psychosomatic problems of aging. Our bodies naturally deteriorate with age but emotional well-being and a healthy mental attitude will go far toward extending our use of such essential organs as the organs of sense.

SENSE OF VISION

It has been said that the eye doctor is in a position to see a great many symptoms that are due to emotional conflict. Memories, which are made up of sensory experiences, are behind most of our emotional upsets. And since the eye receives innumerable sensations hour after hour, day after day, it is not unexpected that it would be subject to the backlash of unpleasant, hostile, or guilty memories. Much that is forbidden is apprehended by the eye. The eye is most important in learning the secrets of sex; if sexual problems exist, either consciously or unconsciously, it is not uncommon for a disturbance to occur in the organ whereby the person comes in contact with so much that is forbidden. Magic and allurement seem to emanate from the eye, providing additional reasons why, in the unconscious, the organ is closely related to sexuality. Persons who are harboring guilt, hate, self-condemnation or fear related to sex might react by squinting, watering of the eyes, and actual physical malfunction of the eye when viewing something that they consider to be improper.

Freud—the lust of the eye

As Freud expressed it in one of his early papers, "If the sexual instinct which makes use of sight—the sexual 'lust of the eye'—has drawn down upon itself, through its exorbitant demands, some retaliatory measure from the side of the ego-instincts, so that the ideas which represent the content of its strivings are subjected to repression and withheld from consciousness, the general relation of the eye and the faculty of vision to the ego and the consciousness is radically disturbed." Or, as he later states in the same paper, it is as if an accusing voice had reared up within the person concerned, saying, "Because you have chosen to use your organ of sight for evil indulgence of the senses, it serves you quite right if you can see nothing at all now." Of course, sex is not the only source of damaging emotions that can affect the proper functioning of the eyes.

Hysteria is not psychosomatic

We must differentiate here, as we did in the first chapter, between the occurrences of true psychosomatic disease and hysteria, for hysterical blindness is often erroneously referred to as a psychosomatic ailment. Recall that a primary difference is that hysteria solves a problem for the affected person, whereas psychosomatic illness only complicates the problem. Moreover, psychosomatic disease is accompanied by actual physical changes while hysteria represents a central nervous system disturbance *without* organic changes. From outward appearances, they might appear quite similar but a thorough investigation will reveal whether an ailment is hysterical in origin or whether it is truly psychosomatic.

Hysterical blindness (deafness or loss of voice might also be hysterical) occurs most frequently in military circles or in prisons where serious symptoms can relieve an unpleasant situation or remove the person from an undesirable environment. It is a serious problem but should be handled by a psychiatrist, not a general physician and definitely not by an untrained, self-appointed "psychotherapist." All too often, when the crutch of physical symptoms is irresponsibly yanked out from under the person suffering from hysteria, he feels his only resort is suicide.

Visual disturbances

The improved vision of the aged theatrical man, referred to earlier, illustrates that actual visual disturbances can be improved or even corrected by a better mental state. But this sort of visual improvement is by no means limited to the elderly. A person may have several changes made in the strength of his lenses during a period when he is under intense emotional strain. When that strain eases, his eyesight may become stronger or even improve to the extent that glasses are no longer necessary.

Nearsightedness

The effect of emotional tension upon certain vision problems has been explained by the fact that tension causes intracranial pressure, meaning pressure within the head. Such pressure can push the eyeball forward causing actual nearsightedness. If, by changing the emotional atmosphere or through successful psychotherapy, the tension can be eased and emotional well-being restored, nearsightedness might be decreased or even eliminated.

One ophthalmologist has stated that he has seen many a patient suffering from certain visual disturbances who needed "a change in his outlook upon life rather than a change of his lenses."

Eyestrain

The term "eyestrain" is frequently misused. It properly refers to those cases in which visual discomforts are brought on by prolonged close work, limited strictly to the eyes, which promptly disappears when close work is discontinued. More often, however, we refer to eyestrain as including not only a strained feeling in the eyes but also an overall feeling of fatigue and vague pains, headache, and perhaps even dizziness. When all of these symptoms are present, the "eyestrain" probably is more psychic than physical. It is the pressure of the close work, and not the work itself, that causes the difficulty. And although glasses might relieve the symptoms, it may well be through the "power of suggestion" rather than through the improved eyesight.

Glaucoma

Glaucoma is a fairly common disorder caused by increased pressure within the eyeball. It is associated with such symptoms as headaches, blurred vision and eye pain and might require surgery to relieve the pressure. Glaucoma can be caused by heredity, tumors, or other factors but a large percentage of the cases appear to also be related to emotional upsets. Worry over ill health, financial losses, death of a member of the family or of a close friend, or similarly tense situations have frequently preceded an attack of glaucoma.

Much evidence has been gathered to show the close relationship between blood pressure within the eye, the secretion of fluids within the eye, and the autonomic nervous system. An emotional shock sends out its damaging impulses over the wires of the autonomic nervous system; among the numerous responses is an increase in inner eye pressure. In the case of a forty-four year old woman who had undergone an operation for glaucoma, intense anxiety was striking. Following the surgery on one eye, psychotherapy was begun and precise charts kept to record both the physical and psychic responses. A definite relationship was found between inner eye tension and emotional tension; the inner eye pressure rose whenever aggressive, hostile feelings were great and fell during periods of relative freedom from anxiety.

Because of the potential severity of glaucoma, prevention of anxiety is extremely important in those persons who are known to have a predisposition to glaucoma. Certainly, frequent tests for glaucoma are advisable. If trouble is detected, an emotional evaluation should accompany needed physical measures.

Correcting visual problems of psychosomatic origin

Those eye specialists who are well versed in the psychosomatic aspects of visual disturbances point out that the best treatment, once the exact diagnosis is known, is to carefully, simply, but frankly explain the trouble to the patient. Relief, then, depends largely on the patient's own efforts.

Discomfort from eye pain stems more from habit than from anything else. It is well known that pain in any area can become a habit, and as the eyes are used constantly during our waking hours, "habit pain" repeats itself frequently. Basically, the use of the eyes is a subconscious function. It is only when we are conscious of them that we notice discomfort. Hence, the only way to avoid this discomfort is to get the eyes back to the subconscious level. To accomplish this, the patient should be encouraged to use the eyes, not to rest them, regardless of pain; even when the eyes feel especially uncomfortable they should be used. Such discipline will usually effect a cure if the person has competent guidance by a physician and if he simultaneously seeks out and corrects any contributing emotional problems. It is unwise, even dangerous, for a person with psychosomatic eye pain to rest his eyes rather than to use and exercise them. Many a sensitive person has been made hypersensitive by the prescription of rest and dark glasses; the potential vision problem becomes an actual one. The aim, again, should be prevention, to nip the disturbance in the bud.

SENSE OF HEARING

Ringing in the ears, ticking, throbbing, and roaring can all result from psychic strain. Even loss of hearing and deafness can stem from psychic factors. There are those who *seem* to have a loss of hearing although tests demonstrate that the ear is functioning properly; in true psychosomatic hearing problems, on the other hand, there is a real change in the hearing mechanism, precipitated by an emotional disturbance. This occurs primarily because of an interruption of blood flow through the tiny hair cells in the inner ear, producing transient or even permanent impairment of hearing. In many instances, the hair cells are destroyed and no amount of therapy can reverse the condition; drugs and sensible psychotherapy can only prevent further attacks and deterioration.

If the problem is detected soon enough, control or relief can be obtained through strong reassurance, discussion of the emotional factors involved, and elimination of the cause of the mental stress. Medication will help to regulate blood flow within the hair cells of the inner ear but cannot continue indefinitely and does not cure the underlying source of the problem.

In a severe case of psychosomatic hearing loss, the patient is admitted to the hospital for medical treatment. Recovery, however, seems to depend more on hospitalization than on treatment received, for when the patient is again exposed to the psychologic stresses of his home environment, a relapse often occurs. Counseling and understanding can often help a patient ignore the stressful situations or avoid them. Guidance along these paths is given in our last chapter.

Noise pollution

Our sense of hearing nas made the headlines lately as we recognize "noise pollution" as a serious and ever-increasing problem. The sound intensity of noise in our throbbing cities of today has increased a thousandfold since 1939, creating a plague loaded with threats to our health. And because "noise" is defined as "meaningless sound," this becomes an emotional as well as an environmental problem.

Our autonomic nervous system begins to react when noise reaches a degree equivalent to traffic on a relatively quiet city street (technically rated at 70 decibels of sound). At that level, narrowing of the arteries occurs, raising the diastolic blood pressure and also lessening the supply of blood to the heart. As the sound becomes louder, the effects grow stronger: dilation of the pupils, drying of the mouth and tongue, loss of skin color, contraction of leg, abdomen and chest muscles, sudden excessive production of adrenaline, stoppage of the flow of gastric juices, and excitation of the heart. The toxic force of noise not only affects our sense of hearing but can cause emotional damage, loss of sleep, and have detrimental, even fatal, effects upon sufferers from diseases such as heart trouble, asthma, ulcers, and intestinal spasms.

Heart patients are particularly vulnerable to loud noises; the bursting of a paper bag close to the ear, the backfire of a truck, or the blast of an auto horn may spur an autonomic response that could bring on a seizure.

A doctor and former chancellor of U.C.L.A., Dr. Vern Knudsen provides a classic example of the effect of noise on ulcer patients. While in the hospital undergoing treatment for stomach ulcers, he began to experience a strangely recurrent pain. Through the process of elimination, Dr. Knudsen traced the cause of the pain to a series of noisy trucks that passed by his hospital window regularly, shocking his ulcer into activity. (In self defense, he invented an earplug that has since been used by millions of military personnel to protect their hearing.)

Some 18 million Americans suffer from some degree of hearing loss, more than suffer from all other disabilities combined. Approximately two out of three working males are victims of work-connected perceptive deafness, caused by the continuous impact of loud sounds on our highly sensitive hearing mechanism. And nearly 34 million Americans are exposed daily to such sounds. It has been predicted that more than fifty per cent of them will suffer hearing loss after ten years . . . and such loss is not reversible.

Emotional damage from noise

Dr. Hans Selye defined the last stage of our reaction to stress as the "stage of exhaustion." Similarly, noise seems to push us, emotionally, beyond our ability to resist. During the Korean war, for instance, a favorite means used by the North Koreans to weaken the resistance of prisoners was to put metal buckets over their heads and bang the buckets with a stick. This clanging torture, a combination of noise, fright, and anxiety, broke human spirits more rapidly than did starvation, cold, or the ceaseless third degree.

Noise alone causes mental aggravation but would not normally unhinge a well-adjusted person. But combined with other stress factors—financial, marital, or health—it can be the trigger for gross emotional as well as organic reactions. Then, it is undeniably a psychosomatic ailment.

Loss of sleep because of noise

Noise does not relax its grip even when you're sleeping. It has been demonstrated that bursts of sound, mild enough not to awaken the sleeper, stimulate the brain causing the same autonomic nervous system responses experienced during the waking hours. The result is loss of sleep or disturbed slumber which can have harmful effects, particularly on aged or ailing persons.

Is treatment possible?

Noise is, indeed, a spiraling national health problem and immediate steps *must* be taken by governmental agencies to establish realistic noise limitations, and to enforce them. Likewise, private corporations should make every effort to reduce their noise output as well as the noise output of their products. It will mean redesigning both machinery and equipment with added cost both to manufacturer and consumer. But as an anti-noise law states: "Public health is above any economic consideration."

In the meantime we can, to a degree, help ourselves by adjusting our temperaments and evaluating our emotional responses to certain noises that assail us. Noting that the meaninglessness of a sound causes it to be classified as noise, we might try to be more understanding. The roar of a sports car revving its motor or a rock group twanging at electric guitars can either be informative and gratifying, or a giant earache, depending on how you are "tuned in." We cannot necessarily learn to enjoy such sounds but we might become more tolerant, easing the pressure on our emotional well-being.

SENSE OF SMELL

Although seriously deteriorated by disuse, our sense of smell is still of enormous importance. Much of the enjoyment of eating is related to our sense of smell; part of the lack of appetite that is such a prevalent symptom of old age arises from a fading sense of smell.

Linked with sexuality

The sense of smell has also been linked with sexual development, identity, and function. Certain fragrances have long been advertised as being erotic, stimulating, and enticing or alluring to members of the opposite sex. Other odors are most repulsive and cause a sudden aversion to certain persons. Recent experiments suggest that the sense of smell is actually related to the degree of sexual excitement that might be achieved. Women, for example, have a much greater sensitivity at the time of ovulation—100 to 100,000 times that present during menstruation. Women whose ovaries have been removed were 100 to 1000 times less sensitive to odors than other women. But treatment with certain hormones restored normal sensitivity.

Odors can be reminiscent

Encountering a certain odor may, quite unconsciously, recall a past experience. We can become greatly disturbed if the experience unconsciously recalled was unpleasant, and we will be totally unaware of why we are disturbed.

One of the authors, after attending a small college for two years, enrolled in a large university. He signed up for a course in general chemistry. But when he attended the lectures in the course he found himself extremely nervous and edgy, to the extent that it was difficult for him to grasp the lecturer's message. This continued for some weeks until the reason suddenly became clear: the lecture hall smelled strongly of chemicals that brought forth familiar sensations. During two years of playing college football, the subject had received pre-game pep talks for home games in a former chemical laboratory. These periods were characterized by high tension, criticism, and apprehension. When the subject smelled that same aroma of chemicals, nervousness and dread came over him. But when the cause of the unhappy emotions was recognized, the nervousness at the lectures ceased. It was succeeded by a great wave of relief and an eventual "A" in the course.

Other impairments in the nasal passages that can disrupt or hinder the sense of smell include such respiratory ailments as asthma, sinusitis, and allergy, discussed at length in a previous chapter.

SENSE OF TASTE

Since taste is closely associated with the sense of smell, the psychosomatic possibilities are similar. We all know the feeling of temporarily losing our sense of taste following an emotional upheaval. Death of a loved one frequently causes such a reaction; then everything has the bland taste and unappealing texture of "cardboard" or "newspaper," as many have described the lack of sensitivity. Despair and loss of the will to live in older persons contributes to their decreased sense of taste, frequently leading to severe malnutrition.

Like a reminiscent odor, taste can bring back memories long since tucked away in the unconscious. Here again, however, it is difficult to say whether taste or odor is responsible.

If serious psychosomatic disorders develop because of disturbed sense of taste, the solution is to try to eliminate the emotional stimulus, provide greater impetus for living, or retrieve the old memory from the attic of the unconscious and examine it, thus rendering it impotent. The choice of treatment depends upon the individual problem.

SENSE OF TOUCH

The relationship of touch sense to skin disorders will be discussed in another chapter. But here we should emphasize the importance of the sense of touch in developing a healthy emotional attitude and in demonstrating affection to those we love. Often we fail to use the sense of touch to our best advantage. We shrink from revealing our feelings, as if they were a sign of weakness or shame. But how comforting is the handclasp of a friend in the time of need, or the warm embrace of a loved one when we are feeling blue or "up tight." Parents frequently shy away from embracing their children as much as they should, relying upon frail words or implications to express their love. No doubt many a child, even teenagers and young adults, have felt a twinge of neglect or rejection that might have been avoided so easily with the warm, assuring touch of a loving parent. The sense of touch, then, can be either a part of the problem or a part of the solution of psychosomatic disease.

SENSE OF EQUILIBRIUM

The organs of equilibrium, or balance and position, are frequently disturbed by psychic tension. The inadequacy of our language makes it difficult to differentiate the many degrees of what is called, in a sweeping manner, dizziness. A drink makes one dizzy. Altitude makes one dizzy. A crowd makes one dizzy. The sea makes one dizzy. Falling in love makes one dizzy. But do all of these statements signify the same sensation and experience, differing only in degree, or are they different in kind?

Vertigo is the form of dizziness caused by dysfunction of the organs of equilibrium; its symptoms range from a fleeting feeling of spinning around to a sensation of rotation so violent that the victim is thrown to the ground. It is essential, when a person suffers from dizziness, for him to seek immediate medical attention. The physician can then secure an accurate description of the sensations that the patient has experienced, a detailed statement of associated symptoms, and such personal information as conflicts or conditions that seem to precede the "dizziness."

Only when all the facts are known can a physician evaluate the significance of dizziness, for it can be a symptom of numerous physical ailments, or it may signify psychosomatic illness. Dizziness must never be treated lightly and as of little moment, even when physical diseases are eliminated from the diagnosis, because it is still a sign of sensory disorientation—an important danger signal. The earlier the correct diagnosis is made, the sooner appropriate therapy can be instituted, and the more satisfactory will be the results.

Psychosomatic vertigo

The medical records of a twenty-nine-year-old lady whom we will call Linda tell the story of a case of psychosomatic vertigo that existed for ten years before it was accurately diagnosed. When admitted to the hospital, Linda complained of dizziness and nausea, pain in the right ear and in the right side of the head, pain in the right arm and right leg, and an occasional pain in the right side. During examination she explained that she was well until the birth of her first child ten years before. Shortly after that she noticed a tendency to fall to the left as though she was "sinking into the ground." At times she felt as if her surroundings were revolving and at other times as if she herself was revolving.

During the past ten years she had been to "so many physicians I can't remember them all." For the past eight years she had practically been an invalid, afraid an attack would occur while she was out on the street. She felt unable to do her housework because of the fear that she would "fall and be forced to lie there totally helpless." At one time the pains in her right side had become so severe that an appendectomy was performed. Two years after that she had a tonsillectomy in an effort to alleviate her dizziness. She even had a lift built for her left foot, but nothing helped.

Now the physician ordered an exhaustive physical examination, including X-rays of the head, spine, and pelvis and a thorough neurological check-up. A test of equilibrium indicated a definite disturbance but further examination failed to show evidence of physical disease. The answer to her problem appeared to be in her personal history.

Linda was the third of seven children, her father a laborer, not cruel or unkind but at the same time not at all close to his children. Her mother was a rather average person; Linda said she was never on particularly good terms with her mother. She described herself as a lonely, sensitive child—a day dreamer. During her second year in high school she ran away to get married. She said she wanted a little freedom but in less than a year her first child was born, and soon after that her illness began. She became depressed, cried a lot, and became sexually frigid. Her trek from clinic to clinic in search of medical help had created a serious financial crisis. And it appeared that there was little hope for her marriage.

Recognizing the vertigo as a symptom of psychic tension, the physician prescribed psychotherapy for Linda, along with counseling for her husband so that he would understand her problem and learn how to best assist her in recovery. Convinced that she would conquer her illness, Linda secured a job and began a steady climb toward emotional stability. Fortunately, her dizziness was still in the shadow symptom stage. Others have not been so lucky. Emotional tension causes decreased blood flow through the tiny hairs in the inner ear that control our sense of balance. Such continual disruption can eventually lead to damaged or deteriorated cells and irreversible disease. But for Linda, the "X factor" had come through, and restored her health to what it had been ten years before.

PROTECTING OUR SENSE ORGANS

Because of the imminent role that our sense organs play in our very existence, it is imperative that we offer them the best possible protection. Happy emotions are the most dependable guarantee we can have that psychosomatic disease will not decrease or disrupt the normal functioning of any of our organs of sense.

eleven

How to have a clear, youthful-looking skin

> ...so I am allotted months of emptiness, and nights of misery are apportioned to me...my skin hardens, then breaks out afresh.
>
> The Book of Job

Just as the eyes are said to be the mirror of the soul, the skin can be regarded as the mirror of the internal state of the body, including the psyche. Like the eye, the skin is an organ of expression. It reflects emotions, as indicated by the expressions "crimson with rage," "white with fear," and "pale as a ghost." But beyond these obvious reactions, emotional factors can also be responsible for various skin problems, some of which are quite serious, loathsome, or disfiguring. Even Job, who suffered much affliction, seemed to recognize the association between "nights of misery" and skin eruptions.

The skin is a great deal more than an inert, though protective, covering of the body. It is the largest organ of the body as well as being the most versatile; it possesses numerous important functions. Acting as a mechanical barrier, the skin prevents invasion of germs and protects the delicate tissues below from physical injury. A waterproof covering, the skin makes it possible for the body to retain the water it requires even when the air outside is dry. Without our waterproof exterior, we would be unable to swim in fresh water without becoming swollen or in salt water without becoming shrunken.

The skin also plays an important role in regulating body temperature. It contains numerous sweat glands, important in one mechanism for cooling the body. Evaporation of sweat from the body surface helps dispell body heat when the outside temperature becomes too hot. The skin plays a role in yet another mechanism for controlling body temperature. Thus, blood brought to the skin loses heat through the process of radiation.

The skin is also an unusually efficient sense organ. It contains nerve endings that transmit such sensations as hot and cold, smooth and rough, sharp and blunt. It responds to varying degrees of pain. Touch is important in the normal development of children for the infant receives many of his earliest sensations through the skin. Studies have revealed that children will not develop normally unless they have frequent intimate contacts with others involving the skin. The sensitivity of the skin can be observed by anesthesia, or lack of feeling; paresthesia, a feeling of pins and needles; and hyperesthesia, or abnormal sensitivity.

Waste products are excreted by the skin. Sweat contains not only water, but various minerals. Vitamin D is formed in the skin by the action of the ultraviolet rays in sunlight. The skin, therefore, covers, cushions, excretes, insulates, weatherproofs, and manufactures. And, it responds to emotional disturbances.

The skin's response to emotions

Certain emotional states go along with specific forms of skin troubles. Generalized itching, for example, reflects aggression. Sexuality is associated with itching of the genital and anal region. Anxiety causes excessive sweating. Shame leads to the flushing skin rash known as rosacea. Anger produces hives. A longing for love is associated with the skin rash known as neurodermatitis. Every one of these skin disorders can have purely organic causes, but psychic tension often contributes, if it is not the chief cause.

The organic causes of skin disorders include hereditary or familial disease; infection with any of a wide variety of micro-organisms; allergic sensitivity either to food or other substances taken internally or to substances that contact the skin directly; drug reactions; and physical agents, such as X-ray, sunlight, wind, or irritating materials.

Various systemic ailments, of unknown cause, can be accompanied by skin rashes, which provide the doctor with invaluable diagnostic clues. Often a psychologic and an organic cause combine to produce a skin disorder. Psychic tension, for example, can impair the skin circulation until the skin becomes wrinkled or pale or even purplish. If the circulation is impaired sufficiently, death of a patch of skin may take place. Or, psychic tension can cause psychosomatic reactions that can complicate or worsen a physical disorder.

Sweating complicates fungus infection

A fungus infection, for example, is greatly affected by excessive perspiration. And perspiration is increased during periods of emotional turmoil or stress.

Why Henry suffered foot fungus

Henry, a handsome young Marine, spent much time in military hospitals because of a severe, recurrent fungus on his feet. When medical treatment failed to control the problem, a complete personality study was conducted. This revealed that Henry had extremely low self-esteem, frequent periods of depression and anxiety, and an unmistakable feminine trend in job preference. This latter discovery seemed to provide the answer to why he was anxious and depressed and why he had such a low opinion of himself. During discussions, he admitted to homosexual desires. Apparently the strain of constant stimulation and threat of exposure kept him in a state of anxiety. This caused excessive sweating of the hands and feet, and the presence of constant moisture prevented the fungus infection from responding to treatment. His problem, then, was psychosomatic even though the physical ailment did not originate in the psyche.

Mental perturbance can lead to warm or cold hands, blushing or blanching, and to tingling of the skin. Indeed, psychic tension can induce eczema, acne, hives, and probably even warts.

Most persons with skin disorders stemming from psychic tension exhibit intense and restless ambition. They may be bitterly dissatisfied with their environment or their accomplishments. Perhaps they harbor deep gnawing regrets for past actions, inactions, or decisions. All too often, changing the skin condition to one of health means changing the personality of its owner.

REVELATIONS FROM A NAZI CONCENTRATION CAMP

Between the years 1958 and 1965, some 1943 persons with various skin disorders were examined in the Department of Dermatology, Hadassah University Hospital, in Israel, under the supervision of Dr. Jacob Shanon. Particularly interesting was the finding that 476 of these patients had formerly been imprisoned in Nazi concentration camps. The remaining 1467 patients had not been subjected to the inhuman treatment and severe emotional trauma of the Nazi prisons.

As the staff examined and treated these patients with skin diseases they observed that the former concentration camp inmates had a far higher percentage of skin disorders caused by psychosomatic factors than did the non-concentration camp patients. Thus, of the former concentration camp inmates 27 per cent had skin disorders caused by psychosomatic disease; of the non-camp patients only 10 per cent had skin disease of a psychosomatic origin. This finding confirmed the concept that severe emotional trauma causes psychosomatic disorders. And the skin is a likely target.

Another revealing finding was that among the men from the concentration camps, 33 per cent of the skin disorders were psychosomatic while among the women, only 22 per cent of the disorders were of psychic origin. This suggested to the investigators that the more active, more aggressive men reacted more vigorously under the dreadful circumstances of life in the prisons. The women, more passive, more patient, more submissive by nature, were better able to endure suffering and to adapt themselves to unpleasant situations.

PSYCHOSOMATIC SKIN DISORDERS

Sweating

We have mentioned that perspiration increases under emotional stimulation. Such psychic disturbances as fear, rage and prolonged tension can increase sweat secretion, chiefly on the palms of the hands, soles of the feet and under the armpits. Perspiration may drip from the armpits, unabated by anti-perspirants; beads of sweat may stand out on the forehead and chin. The palms and soles may be continually moist and clammy. Some persons, particularly adolescents, perspire in the palms of their hands until they become cold and blue. With excessive sweating from prolonged tension, various skin disorders can develop, including rashes, blisters and infection.

The warmer the climate the greater the harmful effects to the skin from excessive sweating. In the tropics prolonged excessive sweating can lead to a reddened raised rash that spreads over all skin surfaces coming in contact with the sweat. After the passage of a few days or weeks the patient appears to develop an allergic sensitivity to his own skin rash. Then the rash spreads even more extensively and the patient is made miserable day and night with a burning, sticking, intolerably itching skin. Sleep for more than brief periods becomes impossible. Despite skin lotions, repeated cold showers and various medications many such patients do not recover until they are returned to a cooler climate. Even then, they are prone to develop a recurrence of the rash with the onset of hot weather. And although there is definitely a physical element involved, unless the psychic stimulus has been dealt with adequately, the rash may continue for a long time. Unfortunately, such irritated skins are particularly susceptible to skin infections such as boils, furuncles and the horrid skin sores known as impetigo, sometimes called improperly, infantigo.

Causes of rosacea

The skin condition known as rosacea represents a sort of permanent blush. More common in women than in men, it usually occurs during the thirties and forties. First there is an increase in the filling of the blood vessels. Then small raised bumps appear on the blush area of the face and upper chest. Sufferers from rosacea show increasing sensitivity to heat, hot drinks, spiced foods, hurried meals, and, of course, psychic tension. Sometimes rosacea is associated with life situations leading to shame.

Closely related to rosacea are blushing and pallor. These are normal under many life situations, but they are abnormal when they occur frequently and on slight provocation. The necks and faces of some persons develop a mottled pink color when they try to control their emotions. But there is no sharp dividing line between normal and abnormal.

Hives (wheals or urticaria)

Hives are not at all uncommon and can vary both in severity and duration. Allergic factors are at times clearly evident but at other times obscure. It is the chronic, puzzling cases to which psychic tension is most frequently related.

Suppressed weeping may well cause an attack of hives, for many persons with the disorder cannot cry easily. Indeed, attacks of hives are often suddenly ended by a crying spell. Again, it is not particularly abnormal for a person to suffer an occasional attack of hives, perhaps three or four times in a lifetime, when he is the central figure in an intense, emotion-charged situation. But when the attacks occur more frequently, and with no apparent allergic aggravation, it is wise to seek out the underlying element, which may well be psychologic.

Conditions of stress

A group of thirty persons was studied to determine if there was any relation between a stressful life situation and their repeated attacks of hives. And the researchers found little or no relationship between exposure to allergens and the attacks of the disease. On the contrary, the skin eruptions were found to be strongly correlated with an emotional disturbance. Hostility and resentment were the dominant emotions; the victim felt he had received unjust treatment or had been wrongly accused or had not received his just deserts. But he carefully repressed his feelings.

The cause of Rosannah's food "allergy"

Even hives that are apparently associated with food allergy might have psychologic overtones. Rosannah, for example, always broke out in hives when she ate lobster. But upon examination, she admitted that the first time she had suffered from such an attack was when her husband had walked into an out-of-the-way restaurant where she and a secret lover were enjoying a lobster dinner. He did not see her, in fact he never knew of the affair which quickly dissolved, but her guilty conscience punished her each time she dined on lobster thereafter; she had eaten it many times before and had never been sensitive to it.

Hives can be bothersome, even unbearable. They call for continued scratching, and this leads to changes in the delicate structure of the skin, making the sensory endings more sensitive. Such sensitivity, of course, increases the itching and the scratching, and we have another vicious circle of psychosomatic disease. It is of obvious benefit to the victim to seek out the underlying cause or causes as quickly as possible.

Neurodermatitis

Neurodermatitis really refers to a skin rash caused by nervous or psychic influences. Sometimes, however, allergy appears to contribute. Loss of love has apparently brought on some cases of neurodermatitis. Other patients with the condition felt they had not received their fair share of affection as children. Neurodermatitis sometimes occurs as a result of repressed hostility in persons described as driving, ambitious perfectionists.

The cause of Lillian's annoying skin rash

Lillian, who was in her early fifties, had suffered for fifteen years with an annoying skin rash behind the ears and the back of the neck, sometimes extending to the arms. She had been studied in many excellent clinics and the diagnosis of neurodermatitis was firmly established. Dermatologic and allergic treatments, however, had failed to help her. When psychotherapy was begun, she made rapid improvement; multiple causes were found as well as additional psychosomatic manifestations. Indeed, her story encompasses many of the sort of conflicts that we recognize as dangerous in regard to psychosomatic disease.

Born and reared in a small town in Illinois, Lillian had always been rather quiet and frail. Her mother was extremely nervous and overprotective, her father was strong and dominating. They were moderately wealthy and Lillian's father was known throughout the town as a benevolent "tyrant."

Lillian had developed severe migraine headaches shortly after her menstrual periods had begun; her menstruation was irregular and painful. During high school she had suffered from "anemia" and profound fatigue until the fatigue became so oppressive that she gave up school in her third year. Later, the migraines disappeared only to be replaced by the skin ailment, as well as asthma and hypertension.

At the age of twenty-seven she married a man she had known for four years. (Her father had forbidden her to marry until her older sister married.) Her husband had much difficulty in holding a job and never made a satisfactory living. He was inattentive and restrained in his relationship with Lillian. Indeed, their marital relations were far from adequate. There had been three pregnancies but only one child. Lillian had always been frigid but during the last ten years or so her husband had become increasingly impotent. She suspected that he was being unfaithful and in an unguarded moment blurted out her suspicions, shouting that she "hated him."

Further complicating her life was a family feud that had developed shortly after her parents' deaths, only a little more than a year apart. Her two brothers quarreled so bitterly over the settlement of the estate that they haven't spoken to each other since and Lillian played a buffer role between them. Her sympathy was always with a younger brother, who was frail like herself and suffered from a heart ailment, whom she felt was cheated out of his fair share of the estate. Living in a small community, she could not escape embarrassment and was constantly reminded of the family quarrel.

How Lillian's condition was healed

It seemed more than obvious, when she was examined by a psychosomatically-minded physician, that her life situation was the source of her neurodermatitis, as well as being a contributing factor in her asthma, and hypertension. Psychotherapy was directed toward giving her strength and complacency to live with an inadequate husband, the highly-charged tension of the family schism, and related problems. She was encouraged to express her feelings more openly and "to carry on in spite of symptoms." This meant more work, such as sewing, housework, and cooking, which not only kept her mind occupied but also kept her hands busy so that she scratched her skin less. She was told to go out more socially in spite of "the appearance of the skin." And she began to take more care in her personal appearance; she lost twenty pounds of excess weight and bought new clothes. In effect, she came out of her shell and learned to live, perhaps for the first time in her life. Gradually, her skin condition improved and, coincidentally, her marriage seemed to be more congenial and satisfying. A check-up two years later revealed complete elimination of the neurodermatitis.

Allergic dermatitis

Allergic dermatitis represents a skin rash apparently caused primarily by allergy either to foods or to substances that contact the skin directly. It can be quite difficult to differentiate allergic dermatitis from neurodermatitis, which can also be partly caused by allergy. For frequently, psychic tension and allergy team up to cause an individual misery. Some allergic patients whose symptoms have been controlled for long periods of time develop mild or even severe skin rashes without any apparent cause. Sometimes such persons develop "anniversary reactions," with the rash appearing on the anniversary of some emotional upset, such as the death of a loved one.

Some clues to psychic skin disorders

Certain clues indicate that psychic factors are involved in what are apparently allergic skin rashes: First, the rash may be limited to one area—for example, a rash confined to one finger only. Perhaps the rash covers only one hand or one foot. Second, the nature of the rash may be unusual. Or, the onset of the rash may be connected with an emotionally potent event, such as the loss of employment, a violent argument, or an upsetting conflict. If the rash occurs only in the evening, when the patient returns from work, or only on weekends, this might indicate psychic involvement. And, of course, emotionally tense persons are more prone to have rashes from tension than are others who take upsets in their stride.

Rachel, a thirty-year-old bride, developed a rash on her ring finger when she discovered shortly after her marriage that her husband was a salesman and not a wealthy industrialist as she had assumed. When he lost his job, the rash became much worse and extended to both hands. Then, after he accepted a highly remunerative position, both hands cleared rapidly.

A similar case of "ring finger dermatitis" involved a middle-aged housewife whose husband's business required considerable travel. She was informed by "friends" that her husband had been seen entertaining women in distant cities, and promptly developed a rash, on the ring finger only. When she would leave the wedding ring off for a few days, the rash would clear.

Acne

Acne vulgaris, the common pimples that plague so many teenagers, can result from psychic tension. The very fact that the disorder is so prevalent in adolescence suggests that it is related to the increased psychosexual development during this period. One female and eight male medical students with acne were studied before, during and after an eight-hour examination. During the period of the examination, their acne became significantly worse. The acne was associated with increased acid production on the skin surface.

Doctors now have several medications that can help to alleviate the problem of acne. And, of course, the most important bit of advice is not to irritate or "pick" the pimples. But equally as important might be the suggestion that the sufferer look deeply into his personal life and try to eliminate as many problems as possible. During the period of adolescence, this is no easy assignment for there appears to be a formidable mountain of obstacles that must be "changed" and a deep chasm of "outmoded precepts" that must be hurdled by the rapidly maturing generation. And acne represents only one manifestation of the emotional volcano that boils beneath.

THE ROAD TO RELIEF

The skin is a symbol of the whole self. And skin problems, possibly more than any other affliction, tend to destroy or damage one's self-esteem and morale. This deterioration makes it all the more difficult for the sufferer to face up to his real problem, his underlying emotional disturbance, much less to overcome it. But that is precisely what he must do in order to travel the road to relief.

The first step, of course, is a thorough examination by a general practitioner or a skin specialist. If the skin disorder is not explained by organic findings, then it is necessary to delve into the inner person—his unfulfilled desires or ambitions, his resentments and hostilities, his frustrations, his loves, and his lack of love. One skin patient has said what so many others have felt, "I guess what I need more than anything else in the world is to be loved." Because of his loss of self-esteem, the person with skin ailments needs to be bolstered as much as possible. But he must not allow himself to wallow in self-pity. Hopefully, much help can be attained by reading the last chapter. We have there tried to summarize our precepts and to grasp the hand of the one afflicted by psychosomatic disease, whatever the specific ailment, and lead him along the road to relief.

twelve

The secret of a happy
and harmonious sex life

> There is no man or woman who does not
> face in his or her lifetime the concerns of
> sexual tensions.
>
> William H. Masters and
> Virginia E. Johnson
> *Human Sexual Response*

Perhaps no aspect of living is more heavily charged with potential tensions than are matters pertaining to sex. Every living person, at one time or another in his life, faces sexual problems. These may be minor and merely bothersome, or they may be major and quite devastating.

The sexual organs, both male and female, are well supplied with nerve connections from the autonomic nervous system. They are also, to an important extent, under the control of the pituitary gland, which itself receives commands from the autonomic nervous system via that part of the brain just above the pituitary, the hypothalamus. It is easy to see, then, how psychic factors can cause disturbances affecting the sexual organs.

FRIGIDITY AND IMPOTENCE

Frigidity, which affects females, and *impotence,* which sometimes plagues males, occur all too frequently. In past years, it was usually the male who consulted a doctor when he could not experience orgasm. Today, however, attitudes toward women have changed and more and more women feel free to visit the doctor with the complaint that they are unable to achieve sexual satisfaction. It has been estimated that more than 50 per cent of adult women are unable to have orgasm and hence are left unfulfilled in their sex life. The percentage of men affected by impotence is considerably less.

Although frigidity and impotence occur in different sexes, the two conditions have much in common. Both affect the family. Either can lead to a broken marriage. And most persons who suffer from these ailments have psychologic problems at the base of their trouble. All too frequently, doctors are frustrated in their attempts to expose the problem. Perhaps part of this frustration may be due to the doctor's own feeling of self-consciousness in discussing the intimate aspects of the patient's sex life. For this reason, he may fail to obtain the entire story. Or he may be too blunt, causing the patient to bristle and become withdrawn. One young lady, for example, who had been married only a few months consulted her doctor about her inability to enjoy sexual intercourse. Quite bluntly he asked, "Do you love your husband?" "Of course!" she replied. When the doctor appeared unconvinced, she became greatly disturbed and refused to answer any further questions. Her problem was not her feelings toward her husband but, rather, inexperience. Consulted six months later, she beamed that she was "extremely happy."

The bases of frigidity

Frigidity represents a state in which the woman can neither initiate nor maintain the heterosexual arousal pattern. Many persons mistakenly believe that a woman is frigid if she cannot reach orgasm during intercourse. This is not the case. The absence of orgasm does not necessarily mean that the woman is discontented or unsatisfied, nor does orgasm automatically imply complete happiness and fulfillment.

Frigidity, like all psychosomatic complaints, can be caused by organic conditions. Generalized body disease can put the damper on sexual feelings. The body changes which come on during the menopause can contribute to an increase in anxiety or depression and a decrease in sexual desire. Other women, however, may find renewed or increased sexual interest with the onset of menopause. Narcotics can cause frigidity. Alcohol can act as a sedative rather than as a stimulant. *But there are many psychologic tensions that contribute to frigidity.* They include fear, hostility, and conflicting love.

Many types of fear may be involved in frigidity. There may be the fear of injury; fear of pregnancy and of the pain of childbirth; fear that an attractive figure may be changed; fear of rejection; or fear of unfavorable attitudes on the part of the husband.

In some women, hostility can be responsible for frigidity. They may be hostile toward the husband, or toward men in general. Some women envy the masculine role and resent having to submit in the feminine role. The hostile woman may be unable to allow the envied male the satisfaction of successful intercourse.

The effect of conflicting love

Conflicting love can be responsible for frigidity. Perhaps the woman loves or desires another man. More often, however, the conflicting love is buried in the unconscious mind. A strong attachment to some man with whom she had been closely related during her developing years can play an important role in a woman's ability to enjoy sexual activity with her husband. This is most often the father but may be a brother, uncle, or family friend. She has never realized the sexual element of this emotional bond and feels that she is in love with her husband until the sex relationship reveals the emotional barrier between them. Other women are filled with such great self-love that they have little emotion left with which to love a husband. Still others have unrecognized homosexual conflicts.

Some women, because of their upbringing, question the propriety of the sexual act. They may have been led to view it as something that was "not nice," dirty, disgusting, shameful, or dangerous. Enlightened sex education in the schools will hopefully improve this misconcept of an act that is not only natural but beautiful and essential between a man and wife. Wise and understanding parental guidance can do even more to keep attitudes toward sex in the proper perspective and to eliminate inhibitions that so frequently cause frigidity in married women.

Clearly, for correction of frigidity, physical factors must first be ruled out. This must be particularly emphasized if painful intercourse is involved. Then the woman must have a thorough psychological inventory, preferably under the guidance of a person skilled in psychotherapy. The male partner should be brought into the counseling for he may be an important part of the problem. Many men pay too little attention to achievement of orgasm in the female, thus depriving her of much of the pleasure of intercourse. There is no human relationship in which so much can be shared, so much of emotional and spiritual value given to each other, as in a well-adapted sexual relationship between a man and wife who are devoted to making each other happy. Indeed, a complete lack of selfish desire has been set forth as the key to effecting a pleasurable response in one's partner in sexual intercourse, after psychological barriers have been removed.

The bases of impotence

Impotence can be defined as a state in which the male can neither obtain nor maintain a satisfactory erection for heterosexual intercourse. The condition occurs fairly frequently and is particularly distressing for the young adult. For the male to function sexually in a satisfactory manner, both psychic and bodily factors must be in harmony. The sex act falls under the influence of many factors, including conflicts, conscious and unconscious; psychic illness; the state of both the nervous system and the endocrine glands; age; and such social and cultural considerations as income, education, and the man's sexual attitude toward women. When any one of these elements is disrupted, impotence can occur.

Naturally, organic conditions must first be ruled out before it is concluded that impotence is psychic. Physical disease can cause weakness and thus interfere both with the sex drive and sexual arousal. Particularly important are such ailments as diabetes mellitus (sugar diabetes), underfunctioning of the thyroid gland, shortages of red blood cells, and malnutrition. Age, too, is important. Perhaps 77 per cent of men are impotent at the age of 80.

At one time impotence was believed to be caused by inflammation of the lower part of the urinary tract. For this reason, the area was painted with a strong solution. But recent studies have revealed that men with gonorrhea, which involves severe inflammation of the urinary tract, are anything but impotent. Indeed, if they were impotent, gonorrhea would be far less of a public health problem than it is. Apparently, the overwhelming majority of men with impotence are suffering from psychologic problems.

Effects of psychic tension

Impotence due to psychic tension may occur in one situation but not another. The man, for example, might be impotent with his wife but not with other women. In such cases, the explanation may lie in development of hostile feelings subsequent to marriage. Or, he may be impotent with his mistress but not with his wife. He may be impotent with his wife and women of her social class but not with prostitutes. In some cases, a man idolizes his wife as a mother figure. Then incest prevents him from having normal intercourse with her. For the man who is potent with prostitutes but not with his wife, love and sex may be separate and psychologically incompatible. Some men are impotent with women but are quite able to obtain erection, orgasm, and ejaculation with masturbation.

Impotence may be associated with sexual deviation. The homosexual male may find it quite impossible to carry out heterosexual coitus, although he is quite capable when the relationship is with another male. His impotence, of course, may simply be due to a lack of interest in females.

Impotence may be caused by inexperience. The boy may suffer from a feeling of inadequacy; fear of hurting the girl; feelings of guilt; an inability to both love the girl and have intercourse with her; or fear of pregnancy. Impotence caused by inexperience may afflict a bridegroom on his honeymoon; impotence from guilt also interferes with successful erection for the bridegroom.

Regardless of the cause, impotence represents a blow to the male image of masculinity, and the afflicted male may try to hide his condition by avoiding sexual relations. He may claim he is too tired or that his mind is elsewhere or that he has physical problems. His impotence can be worsened by such fears. A man who cannot maintain an erection on occasion dreads the repetition of the failure later. If the wife is critical, she will probably make the problem worse. Or, she may fear that her husband is "over the hill" and will therefore become less aggressive herself. Either attitude can perpetuate the problem.

Premature ejaculation

Closely related to the problem of impotence is that of premature ejaculation. The male suffering from this condition arrives at orgasm and ejaculation before he wishes to do so. He loses erection before the sexual partner has reached orgasm. Sometimes improper techniques of lovemaking can cause premature ejaculation. Since man is more easily aroused sexually, he may be less sensitive to the finer techniques of lovemaking and less considerate of the psychologic and physiologic aspects of the techniques of arousal. Premature ejaculation, which may represent a significant marital problem in itself, develops in men who are not properly sensitive to their wives' needs.

Certainly proper diagnosis of the cause both of frigidity and impotence requires a complete and thorough psychologic inventory. In either case, both partners of the sexual act must be involved. In the case of impotence, when an erection occurs at any time of day or under any circumstances, this is adequate proof that erection is possible. One can then conclude that the cause of the impotence is psychogenic. The physician or psychotherapist must inquire quite carefully into attitudes toward parental love; affection; the degree of sex education; religious views about sex; and guilt feelings subsequent to masturbation. Other aspects of the marriage should be explored. Sometimes husband and wife have serious interpersonal conflicts not related to sex.

Mike's impotence threatened his marriage

Michael was 25 years old when he married Joan, age 18. He had an excellent job as a graduate engineer in the heavy construction industry. At first, all went well with the marriage. Wedded bliss impressed Mike as all it was said to be. Joan, too, was happy. Then Mike began having trouble with impotence. He just couldn't perform successfully in the sexual act, and the more he tried the worse his performance seemed to get. And Joan wasn't of much help. She became impatient and critical, forcing matters almost nightly. An apparently ideal marriage was no longer ideal; indeed, it was in serious trouble.

Wisely, Mike and Joan sought professional help, in this case a psychosomatically-minded physician with considerable experience in marital problems. He met several times with the couple and twice with each of them separately. Careful study convinced him that the source of the trouble was Joan's over-aggressiveness. She was simply too affectionate, and that was, in effect, turning Mike off. As Mike's performance became less satisfactory, Joan's efforts had increased and the impotence became more pronounced.

The physician revealed his conclusions to Joan and urged a somewhat more restrained and passive role. He reassured Mike and confidently predicted all would be well. Shortly thereafter, it became apparent that Joan's new tactics were working. Mike's impotence rapidly disappeared. With each intercourse, the situation improved more and more; a six-months' check showed that the problem was no more.

Potential for sexual feeling always present

Every normal man and woman has the possibility of sexual feelings, but these feelings are not going to be experienced unless the correct ideas concerning such relations have developed during the growth of the individual. Normal sexual feelings will be inhibited when natural feelings have been curtailed by fear, restrained by guilt, smothered by shame, or made impossible by a feeling of disgust. If the individual experiences such inhibitions during adolescence, he can only grow up fearing or hating matters sexual. Certainly frigidity in a female and impotence in a male represent large problems in human adjustment. Nearly half, perhaps more, of adult women do not enjoy complete sexual satisfaction when first married. But relief can be afforded to more than 80 per cent of this group by proper treatment. But therapy may not be easy. A girl cannot have fear and hatred of sexual relations instilled for 15 or 20 years and then suddenly begin to love and enjoy such a relationship.

PSYCHOSOMATIC PROBLEMS AS LIMITED TO WOMEN

Even though the menstrual flow falls under careful physiologic control, nevertheless emotions can influence it just as they can influence the secretion of sweat, tears, saliva, or intestinal digestive juices. The word hysteria means "wandering of the uterus," indicating the close kinship existing between psychic disturbances and the sexual organs in women. This kinship is widely recognized. Probably half of the patients who consult a gynecologist have no organic disease; their complaints are of psychologic origin.

Menstrual disorders

Psychic tension can either delay or hasten the onset of the menstrual period, may make it irregular, or may cause it to be accompanied by severe cramps. A delay in the start of a menstrual period can occur in an unmarried woman who fears conception and in a married woman who does not want to become pregnant. Indeed, fear of an unwanted pregnancy can prevent menstruation for a month or more. Psychic tension may at first delay menstruation and later cause the periods to be abnormally frequent and the flow to be excessively profuse. Some of these effects can be caused by irregularity of endocrine secretion. Fortunately, even though the endocrine dysfunction is caused by psychic factors, administration of the proper hormones can help correct the problem. Various other organic problems, such as nutritional disorders and shortage of red blood cells, can prevent menstruation. Even a profound desire to be pregnant can cause lack of menstruation and distention of the abdomen.

Menstruation may be accompanied by cramps, low back pain, irritability, and melancholy appearing a day or two before the onset of the period and disappearing after a few days. In some women, such symptoms appear as much as ten days before the period starts and last for several days afterward. Although physical disease can cause such symptoms, they are often the result of emotional turmoil and distress; they clearly can involve far more than the patient's pelvic organs.

Severe and prolonged pain with discharge of blood clots can also accompany menstruation. Menstrual colic, so-called, is associated with pain in the abdomen, nausea, vomiting, headache, rapid heartbeat, anxiety attacks, and fainting spells. Many patients who suffer from painful menstruation also have fatigue, backache, digestive disorders, and violent mood swings. And although outwardly the woman can appear to be the soul of tranquility, a fierce emotional civil war may be raging in the depths of her subconscious.

The psychic cause of some painful menstruation may stem from the fact that the woman is reluctant to accept the stereotyped role of femininity; she resents being a woman. If a child has developed a strong sense of repressed guilt and anxiety during his toilet training, eliminative orifices may be viewed in later life as shameful and dirty, and menstruation may be placed in the same category. Many women are convinced that menstruation is a "curse" placed upon them and thus expect discomfort and difficulty; their very expectations bring on the afflictions.

Painful intercourse

Pain or difficulty in sexual intercourse, which may include involuntary spasms of the muscles of the vagina (termed vaginismus), differ somewhat from frigidity. Nevertheless, the underlying psychic causes may be the same. Fear, hostility, or guilt can result in sexual avoidance, displeasure, aversion, plus pain and discomfort. Although painful intercourse occurs less frequently than does frigidity, it poses a distressing obstacle to pleasurable relationships when it does occur.

The solution, again, lies in the person's capacity to explore her own emotions, her possible guilt reactions, her repressed disapproval of sexual activities, her conflicting loves. Consciously she is consenting to participate in intercourse but unconsciously she may be trying to prohibit it. Genuine efforts to overcome such psychological barriers to the achievement of sexual fulfillment are usually rewarded with success.

Sterility

Female sterility frequently rests on psychic factors. The endocrine glands in general and those of the reproductive system in particular are highly sensitive not only to physiologic but to psychic impulses. The smooth muscles of the female sexual tract can readily go into spasm as a result of emotional tension. Proof that sterility can be psychologic in origin lies in the observation that conception often occurs after an apparently sterile couple has adopted a child. This sudden ability to conceive may result from improved relations between the husband and wife or from relief of anxiety over childbearing, diminished conflict about motherhood, or a generally increased sense of well-being following the adoption.

Of course, fear of becoming pregnant can be crucial in preventing conception. Although voicing the desire to bear children, a woman may unconsciously or silently fear the pains of childbirth, or she may be reluctant to surrender the father-daughter relationship she enjoys with her husband. She dislikes the idea of competing with a child for his affection. Or, hostility toward the male can result in an inability to conceive.

The treatment of infertility of the female involves a thorough physical and psychological survey of the woman and of relationships between husband and wife. The woman's feeling of frustration over their incompatibility must be investigated. Naturally, the man should be examined to see whether he might be the sterile party.

A woman's fear of being childless, therefore empty and unfulfilled, can be similar to the man's dread of impotence. If she has this self-image of herself, it can make emotional tensions worse and thus decrease the chance of impregnation. Such simple measures as reassurance, sedation, or vacation might help. Sometimes apparent sterility and frigidity are relieved at the same time. And, of course, the husband's attitude is enormously important.

How adoption "cured" a family's sterility problem

Alberta, a 28-year-old housewife, was married to Bill, a 30-year-old farmer. Bill was industrious and successful. They had a splendid farm in the rolling hills of central Ohio and could hardly wait until they had children to share their country life. But no children were born to the couple. Careful physical examination by a local specialist revealed no organic problems in either Alberta or Bill. But no psychologic analysis was carried out.

Finally, after considerable discussion, they decided to adopt a child. They added their name to the list of prospective parents at an adoption agency. Some two years later they were delighted to be permitted to adopt a healthy, two-month-old boy. He was a joy in every respect. The marriage, which had apparently been a good one, now reached new heights of happiness. But the couple began longing for a little brother or sister for their son. Before they could make application for adoption of another child, however, Alberta became pregnant! Within another year two little sets of feet were pattering about the house and enjoying the broad lawn and lush meadows of the farm. Apparently the psychologic dam was broken, for Alberta continued to have children, nearly one a year for three years, at which time she and Bill decided they had family enough.

What "cured" Alberta's sterility? Probably the adopted child so enriched her life that unconscious inhibitions and strong desires were resolved and conception made possible. Experiences of this kind are not at all unusual. Conception may even occur before adoption, when permission has been granted and the couple is awaiting the arrival of their designated child.

The effect of the menopause

Most women have, at one time or another, heard alarming tales concerning the menopause. Such tales may cause a woman to fear that she will be less attractive to her spouse as a woman, that she will be incapable of sexual participation or of enjoying sensual pleasures. Perhaps she fears that she will be abandoned, old, and purposeless. These attitudes can contribute to her irritability, hypersensitivity, complaining, or cause her to experience various psychosomatic symptoms. There are, of course, definite physical alterations and uncomfortable manifestations that occur during the "change of life" but these are usually worsened by psychic tension.

An enlightened explanation of the menopause can be enormously helpful to many women prior to its onset. Some physicians administer various sex hormones that, in effect, prevent the woman from going into the menopause. She may even continue to menstruate, depending on the system of hormone therapy used. Physicians who advocate such therapy regard the menopause as a deficiency disease and report in glowing terms the results attained with some, but by no means all, women who accept this therapy.

But regardless of medication or other physical therapy, an invaluable adjunct to uncomplicated menopause is mental preparation. Some women who were psychologically prepared and strongly determined to ride out the waves with as little turbulence as possible report that they were through the worst of the storm almost before they knew it was upon them. Individual reactions will vary, of course, but the mental state appears to be a vital factor.

STEPS TO TAKE FOR ANALYSIS OF SEXUAL DISORDERS

We have mentioned several steps that can be taken to avoid or correct many of the psychosomatic sexual disorders that can occur. A thorough physical and psychic study both of the man and the woman is vital, regardless of which is experiencing distress. Often education or re-education concerning the sexual functions is required. After all physical and organic factors have been carefully considered and needed education has been given, the psychologic problems should be attacked directly, with emphasis not only on the sexual aspects of the matter but on the overall relationships between the couple.

Both parties should also undertake an honest, unvarnished self-inventory. This might include such questions as:

When did you first learn about sex?
How did you regard sexual matters during your teen years?

Did your parents apparently enjoy a happy sex life?

Do you harbor guilt feelings because of promiscuity?

Do you have an abnormal love for someone other than your spouse (father, mother, brother, or another)?

Are you jealous or envious of your spouse in any way?

Do you fear disfigurement or discomfort from sex?

Do you fear an unwanted pregnancy?

Is your method of contraception satisfactory?

Do you love or desire another person other than your spouse?

Are there other conflicts between you and your mate?

If you can detect possible trouble from your answers to any of these questions, don't just accept the accompanying sexual difficulties as merely inevitable consequences. Make an all out effort to achieve a more tranquil and meaningful relationship; work toward deleting the problem. The rewards will be worthy of the endeavor.

A happy healthy sexual atmosphere in a home represents one of the strongest powers existent; countless psychosomatic ailments hark back to an unsatisfactory attitude or experience with sex. Indeed, all members of the family will benefit to some degree from a congenial home life, which depends heavily upon satisfactory sex relations between man and wife. Whether sex is bane or blessing depends upon the individual—few obstacles are truly insurmountable.

thirteen

How to banish insomnia and
get rid of painful headaches

> "I'm very brave generally," he went on in a
> low voice, "only today I happen to have a
> headache."
>
> Lewis Carroll
> *Through the Looking Glass*

Hardly a person lives who has not suffered from headache at one time or another. Perhaps as many as 42 million Americans experience chronic, severe headaches. Indeed, headaches have become so important that a private headache clinic has been set up in Chicago. The importance of headaches is also evidenced by the abundance of television commercials promoting a host of diverse remedies for headache and nervous tension. So it should come as no surprise that we consider psychic tension to be a major factor in many instances of headache; it is an important psychosomatic disease.

Headaches can stem from organic causes

Headaches can arise from all sorts of causes—from general body infections; from tumors within the skull; from infections within the brain or its lining; from head injuries; from arteriosclerosis of the brain blood vessels; from severe high blood pressure; from lack of oxygen in the brain; from diseases of the eye, nose, throat, and ear. Headaches can result from pressure or traction on any of a great number of structures of the head that are sensitive to pain—for example, the tissues covering the skull; nerves of the brain and of the upper spinal cord; large blood vessels of the brain; and the heavy brain covering at the base of the skull. Allergies to food or to pollens or to chemicals or dust can cause headache.

Types of migraine headaches

All the headaches we have mentioned thus far stem chiefly, if not entirely, from organic causes. But there are many headaches to which psychic factors make an important, sometimes the entire, contribution. These include the type of headache known as migraine.

Migraine headaches are not uncommon; perhaps as many as 10 million Americans suffer from them. The usual attack of migraine comes on suddenly, is accompanied by nausea and vomiting, and ends in a desire to sleep. The pain is characteristically on one side of the head. Galen, an early physician (A.D. 131-201) was possibly the first to use the term hemicrania, meaning half-skull, in reference to the typical one-sided migraine headache. The word was successively changed to hemigranea, emigranea, migrainea, and migraine.

Migraine attacks can come two or three times a week, or only once a year, and generally occur in persons who are in good health between attacks. They may be initiated when the victim suppresses rage or hostility. The great physiologist Cannon stated that the blood flow to the brain is increased in states of violent emotion. When rage is restrained, with muscle action blocked and no increase of blood flow to the muscle and a decrease of blood flow to the abdominal area, blood flow to the brain increases even more. It may be such increase in blood flow that contributes to attacks of migraine.

Persons most susceptible to migraine attacks

Migraine, sometimes called familial headache because of the hereditary factors, usually strikes persons between the ages of 15 and 35. The migraine sufferer is likely to be a trim, neatly dressed woman of above average intelligence who has an inclination to speak quickly. She is usually slow-moving in the morning but has a peak of energy in the evening.

But men can also get migraine. The typical man who suffers from migraine is likely to be a perfectionist who demands perfection not only in himself but in others as well. He is ambitious and has an exaggerated sense of responsibility. He may have difficulty in delegating responsibility to others.

In general, migraine sufferers usually have a history of headaches in their family and have a tendency to worry. They often possess rigid standards and exhibit a strong need for approval. They are sensitive to criticism and tend to feel a sense of frustration about life. Migraine sufferers react actively to emotional influences and are sensitive to all sorts of stimuli. Sometimes they stay up too late and fail to get adequate rest. Often there is unhappiness, family squabbles, or sexual incompatibility. Sometimes migraine sufferers develop attacks when they face a task beyond their ability. In women, migraine often occurs just before the onset of the monthly menstrual periods and may completely disappear after menopause.

The pattern of a typical migraine attack

In the typical attack of migraine, pain comes from a change in the size of blood vessels around the brain. At first, the blood vessels become smaller. About 20 to 45 minutes before the onset of pain, the eyes may feel hot and painful, and the lids begin to droop with a feeling of heaviness. The patient often sees flashing lights, bright spots, and zigzag bright lines in front of the eye opposite the side of the head where the migraine is usually felt. The visual fields shrink. There may be dizziness, with ringing in the ears, strange odors, and taste disturbances. Sometimes there is soreness of the scalp and a numbness or tingling feeling in one or more of the limbs. The patient with a classic migraine can tell quite accurately when the headache is about to appear.

The pain of migraine comes when the blood vessels around the brain begin to dilate. As they expand beyond their normal size, they cause intense pain, usually only on one side of the head. The pain may last four to six hours and is often accompanied by nausea, loss of appetite, and vomiting. Migraine may involve a change in the level of a substance called serotonin in the brain. This causes blood vessels around the brain to dilate, creating the pain of the headache. Once a migraine headache has started, slamming of a door, street noises, or glaring lights may greatly increase the pain.

Emotional background of a migraine sufferer

Shirley was thirty-two-years old and had suffered from migraine headaches for at least ten years. She came from a fairly congenial family with no more than the normal tension that occurs in a home. During her adolescent years she was slim, quite pretty, and did not want for fashionable clothes. She was popular in high school and was chosen cheerleader in both her junior and senior years. She married a school sweetheart with whom she had quarreled incessantly but always seemed to achieve reconciliation. He was both nervous and extremely demanding of her time and affections. And he insisted upon three full meals on the table daily, on time. In fact, he was almost addicted to food and seemed to overcome emotional problems with eating. After a few years, Shirley also turned to food for relief of tension and together they became quite obese.

During her examination for migraine headaches, Shirley seemed to exhibit no other organic ailments but did appear quite nervous and apprehensive. She was particularly conscious of her weight. It finally became evident that her migraines occurred within 24 hours of a clash with her husband or after she had suffered embarrassment because of her obesity. In fact, it developed that her first attack had occurred shortly before her high school class was to celebrate their five-year reunion. She was ashamed to face her classmates but felt compelled to attend the reunion. Shortly before time to leave for the affair, however, she developed a sickening headache, blinding in intensity, and accompanied by vomiting. After the pain had lessened she drifted into a deep sleep and awakened the next morning, much too late to attend the reunion. She expressed much despair at having missed it but inwardly was thankful for the reprieve, no matter how painful.

The doctor counseled for some time with Shirley and tried to explain the mechanism of migraines and the role that unhappy emotions play in triggering the attacks. He prescribed a medication that would ease her pain to some extent but advised her that *only a change in her emotional responses could bring an end to her suffering.* He also suggested that she lose weight to regain her self-esteem. But Shirley was unable to stand up to her husband and regardless of her efforts, her migraines continued although not quite as often. At the last check-up she had lost six pounds but was still considerably overweight. She appeared destined to experience migraines for some time to come.

Headaches that are not classified as migraine

Headaches that do not exhibit the classical symptoms of migraine can also come from psychic disturbances. Fatigue and psychic tension of all kinds can cause headache, which may consist of dull pain, a feeling of pressure, or a feeling of pulsation, as in a throbbing headache. Unrecognized depression, too, can cause headache. Or, a headache can develop when an individual reaches the limit of his capacity to repress or suppress anger.

Some patients develop severe headaches from substances to which they are allergic. One man developed a headache at least once a week following meals taken in a Chinese restaurant. His headache stemmed from a toxic reaction to the monosodium glutamate in soy sauce, which caused a dilation of the blood vessels around the brain. A woman developed headache from working in a munitions plant. Nitrite, a chemical commonly used in munitions, was causing dilation of the blood vessels of her head and giving her a severe headache. But emotional factors are important in combining with allergens in producing headache. Thus, an individual might develop an allergic headache, perhaps to a food to which he was sensitive, if he was emotionally upset but not if he was in good spirits.

Tension headaches

Another type of headache due largely to psychic factors is tension headache, consisting of tautness in muscles at the back of the neck. Muscular contraction causes a patient to have periodic recurring headaches varying in frequency and severity. They may persist for hours or days. The headache usually follows a tense situation. When the patient is examined at the time of the headache, one finds excessive muscular contraction. The person may complain of tenderness in the neck. Tenseness and emotional tension cause tightening of the scalp and neck muscles and prolonged muscular contraction. Patients with this sort of headache are the victims of chronic anxiety. They are usually apprehensive and sensitive to the opinions of others. They are easily embarrassed and worried. They often have sleep problems, are irritable and restless. They have occasional outbursts of aggression and fits of weeping.

Relief from nervous tension can be achieved through self-directed relaxation. One man has said that when he gets a "nervous headache" he promptly imagines himself as a burlap bag of potatoes, then he cuts the string at the bottom of the bag and lets all the potatoes tumble out. This, he says, through strong concentration will effect profound relief from tension and "up-tightness." Dr. David Harold Fink has written a book entitled *Release from Nervous Tension* that also offers some concrete suggestions for relaxing. Such methods can be far more effective than aspirin because they eliminate the underlying factor and don't just treat the physical symptoms.

Constipation headaches

Some headaches appear to be due to constipation. While many doctors do not believe that constipation causes headaches because many persons who are chronically constipated do not suffer simultaneous headaches, yet patients who have found such an association to exist for years are convinced that there is a causal relationship. Even in such instances we cannot deny the emotional factors, particularly when a headache disappears magically just as soon as the bowels move—too soon for a physiological mechanism to be responsible.

Headaches due to head injuries

Some headaches occur in persons who have previously suffered a head injury or an illness in which head pain was a prominent component. When they remember such past experiences, the headache can recur. In 1940, one of the authors treated a patient who had acquired his headache when a beam fell on him during the San Francisco earthquake of 1906. There were no anatomical reasons for the prolonged headache; it appeared to wax and wane with the occurrence of fatigue and emotional stress.

"Sinus headaches"

Some persons complain of "sinus headache." Again, we can recognize the prominence of this complaint by its prevalence in television commercials. In the so-called sinus headache, the nose is obstructed, burning, and perhaps running. The nasal membranes may be swollen, and the patient experiences a tight sensation in the nose. Indeed, so common is this conception that patients habitually state that their "sinus" is troubling them again, instead of saying "I have a headache" or a "post-nasal drip."

A true sinus headache is limited to one small region and is accompanied by tenderness over that region. It is periodic in character, occurring at intervals during certain times of the day. If the headache is vague and not localized, and if sinusitis cannot be demonstrated by X-ray, the headache may well be of psychic origin—which does not mean that it is any less painful. There has been some indication that atmospheric pressures, represented by changes on a barometer, can cause dilation of the cranial blood vessels causing headache. Others argue that such headaches are the result of allergy in combination with psychic tension.

But regardless of what the cause of your headache is, there are few who will argue with the old English proverb that "when the head aches, all the body is the worse." Definite steps should be taken to relieve the ailment, and aspirins do not necessarily represent the ideal approach.

STEPS TO TAKE FOR TREATMENT OF HEADACHE

Certainly the first step in the treatment of a headache is to have a thorough physical and laboratory examination to determine if the headache stems from organic causes. If the host of physical conditions that can cause headache are ruled out, then the possibility that the headache may be psychosomatic should be seriously considered. The diagnosis of migraine rests on the characteristic symptoms. If the headache fits these symptoms, then a diagnosis of migraine is justified.

Migraine

Sometimes mild attacks of migraine are helped by eating a small amount of food, drinking a glass of hot milk, or by taking a cathartic or a hot enema. The pain of migraine can frequently be reduced by drugs that cause narrowing of the blood vessels. Compounds of ergot are commonly used for this purpose. Sometimes hormones are useful, particularly in women who experience migraine with the beginning of their menstrual periods. Certain antihistaminic drugs may be successful in relieving the pain of migraine. But such treatment must take place considerably before the onset of the migraine attack. If the migraine process is not interrupted quickly, medication may be ineffective.

Headache cures based on removing causes of tensions and irritations

But ultimately, the struggle against migraine is a personal, as well as a medical, one. The person must come to grips with the life situation and, one way or another, remove sources of tension and irritation. Sometimes moving a mother-in-law out of the house cures migraine, for example. Many a husband could help his afflicted wife if he would show her more affection and consideration or stop drinking, gambling, or spending too much time away from home. But all too often, avoidance is not practicable.

Then, the patient with migraine should be taught to avoid mental, nervous, and physical fatigue. He should thoroughly regulate his habits of life, should normalize his mode of living. He should do everything possible to develop a harmonious, peaceful, and happy frame of mind, "even in the presence of his enemies." He should, as much as possible, avoid worry, fatigue, and anxiety.

Perhaps he can apply Alfred Tennyson's precept, "I must lose myself in action lest I wither in despair." Too much leisure to think about oneself is harmful, not only for the migraine sufferer but for all of us. Yet we should not get so involved in activities as to allow no time to just let go, relax, and replenish our spirits. Indeed, moderation in all things is sound advice.

Migraine sufferers should be encouraged to talk about their attacks and the events in their lives that occurred during the 24 hour period preceding the attacks. They should also learn to ventilate their emotions, thus dispelling tension, relieving anxiety, and dissipating the effects of frustration and resentment. The migraine patient, like all victims of psychosomatic disease, faces the problem of how to handle hostility in a socially acceptable fashion. Unleashing it upon himself can lead to illness, and viciously directing it upon others disrupts society. If, indeed, the anger is justified, there is enough evil existing in our society to furnish sufficient avenues for channeling it effectively.

Gimmicks to release causes of headaches

Some persons employ gimmicks to release strong emotions without causing a disturbance or creating a scene. They might stand in front of a mirror or just sit alone in a room and "confront" the object of their hostility, cursing him freely until all has been said. Once the anger is vented aloud, it often becomes much less important, perhaps even a little ridiculous and unworthy of the trouble it could cause. Others might write a letter to the offender, expressing as strongly as possible their hostile feelings and resentments. They read it over several times, then carefully and deliberately tear it to tiny bits and toss it in the waste container. Under no circumstances, however, should you show your "poison pen" letter to anyone or leave it lying about to be seen. By destroying it, you can also dispose of your feelings in a symbolic fashion. Also, after you have lashed out at the object of your hostility, then take an equal amount of time to enumerate his good points and his attractive qualities. There is good to be found in every man. And no virtue exists in simply being able to express resentment, then stopping there. Maturity demands a larger perspective.

Overcoming the common headache

Persons with headache caused in part or entirely by psychic tension should, like the patient with migraine, reorder their lives, learn to live less stressful, less hectic, more meaningful lives. Sometimes psychotherapy will permit recognition of conflicts and reveal the connection between such conflicts or repressions and headaches. Simple drugs, as aspirin or acetylminophen, are helpful; tranquilizers, however, can be dangerous due to unrecognized depression, for they may make the depression worse.

Patients with headaches due to allergy, which are often conditioned by psychic tension, should not only endeavor to avoid eating foods or being exposed to allergens that cause a headache, they should also learn to reduce the tension in their lives. Some patients experience combined headaches—that is, headaches with several causes. These can be particularly difficult, both from the standpoint of diagnosis and of treatment.

How Martin got relief from a tension headache

A patient whom we shall call Martin was a third-year student at a state university. He had always been a good student, had participated actively in athletics in high school but did not have time to do so at the university. He did not smoke, drank only in moderation, and was conscientious about eating a good diet. But at the end of every quarter, when final examinations came up, Martin inevitably developed a splitting headache. No doubt, lack of sleep on nights before examinations and the general state of tension produced by the examinations themselves contributed to Martin's headaches. He felt that constipation might also be a factor.

During this third year, Martin determined that instead of steeling himself against the inevitable headache at the end of each quarter, he would, if it was humanly possible, rid himself of the miserable experience of suffering the headaches. So, first of all, he saw to it that he studied enough during the quarter so that he would not have to cram at the last minute. Next, he convinced himself that since he had never flunked a course in his three years at the university, he need not worry on this account. (Power of positive thinking!) These measures made it possible for him to get adequate sleep. He drank plenty of water and ate wisely. Much to his relief, he sailed through the final examination period with no trace of a headache. Martin had learned how to avoid tension headaches at final examination time. And his efforts can provide a lesson for all who have similar distress, whether at exam time or prior to business meetings that are notoriously tense or when the children disrupt the household with "constant bickering" or whatever might be your particular problem.

How a child's headache problem was overcome

A ten-year-old child whom we shall call Mary Ann had an attractive older sister whom she loved but of whom she was quite jealous. Whenever the older sister received compliments or any preferential treatment at all, Mary Ann would react by developing a violent headache. She was hospitalized and studied thoroughly, but no physical basis could be found for the headaches. Then the psychologic situation was carefully investigated, and the basis for the headaches was discovered.

The jealously actually stemmed from experiences when Mary Ann was only two years old. The grandparents had frequently taken the older sister shopping, to the show, or to stay overnight although they showed no such interest in Mary Ann. They explained, quite sincerely, that the older sister was old enough to be self-sufficient and that when Mary Ann was older she would receive the same privileges. But that time never came. So eight years later, the resentment still smoldered in her heart.

When the parents, and grandparents, became aware of the problem they carefully avoided showing undue preference to the older sister and made special efforts to let Mary Ann know that she was loved and wanted. The incidence of the headaches decreased greatly, although it must be admitted that they did not entirely disappear.

Yogurt's conception of headaches

William Schwenck Yogurt had this to say of headaches in Iolanthe, Act II: "When you are lying awake with a dismal headache, and repose is taboo'd by anxiety, I conceive you may use any language you choose to indulge in, without impropriety." Certainly a throbbing, pounding, splitting headache can be one of the most unpleasant ailments to which the flesh is heir. You will find your personal efforts to rid yourself of headaches well worthwhile, particularly if they are successful.

SLEEPLESSNESS (INSOMNIA)

> What probing deep
> has ever solved the mystery of sleep?
> Thomas Bailey Aldrich (1836-1907)
> *Quatrains*

Despite all our vaunted scientific and medical advances we really don't know much more today about sleep than did Aldrich around the turn of the century. We do know, as did scientists then, that sleep represents a mysterious and complicated state of changed consciousness. Four separate states characterize it and in these stages sleep depth, sensory activity, motor activity and the responsiveness of the sleeping person are all different.

Sleep can be deep, continuous and refreshing on the one hand or shallow, interrupted and exhausting on the other. It may be dreamless or laced with nightmares. A mother sleeping deeply may ignore loud noises yet awaken promptly with the soft whimpering of her infant. Just as mysterious is the way many of us can awaken at a specific time—on the minute—without recourse to an alarm clock. Inability to sleep is called insomnia; all of us experience it, to some extent, at one time or another.

The amount of sleep needed by each of us varies. Some will get along on five or six hours nightly but they sleep soundly and awake refreshed. Others require as much as eight or ten hours to avoid early fatigue during the following day. A victim of insomnia, and we refer to chronic sufferers and not to those who have infrequent or temporary loss of sleep because of unusually tense events or irregular arrangements, as sleeping in a different bed or where there are unfamiliar noises, usually has difficulty in going to sleep. He sleeps only a short time and then awakens early. Or, he may wake up frequently during the night, toss about restlessly, have disturbing dreams, and awaken unrefreshed and too fatigued to do his work.

Sleep normally comes within 15 minutes after we settle down, relaxed for sleep. When a person has difficulty in falling asleep, there is thought to be an inability of the normal sleep mechanism of the body to inhibit sufficiently a hyperactive arousal system. Thus, a person in a state of anxiety is unable to fall asleep at his usual bedtime as a result of continued cortical activity (rapid heart rate). Anxiety also produces increased muscular tension that stimulates the brain and causes continued activity rather than the relaxation compatible with sleep. Drugs, notably stimulants, can thus cause insomnia. Even drugs that sedate some individuals keep others bright-eyed and awake. Coffee stimulates some people enough to prevent sleeping. It is interesting to note, however, that laboratory studies of persons suffering from insomnia reveal that almost without exception, the victims underestimate the amount of sleep obtained and overestimate their sleep disturbance.

Psychic tension is frequently a contributor to sleeplessness. After what may have been a harrowing day, the patient pleasantly anticipates falling asleep. When bedtime comes, however, the idea of permitting consciousness to escape terrifies him. He doesn't want to surrender to the domination of his subconscious life. He fears that sleep will bring horrible dreams and he may stay awake until sheer exhaustion forces him to slumber.

Persons with irregular bedtime habits may have difficulty in sleeping. Worry over unsolved problems, intensive mental concentration, a stimulating discussion, or a memorable experience can all cause sleeplessness. Even severe fatigue, simply being too tired, can prevent sleep, perhaps because of the production of stimulating chemical by-products of muscle exertion. But when difficulty in sleeping occurs frequently, it should be taken seriously and relief should be sought. Such relief is generally of a psychological nature.

WHAT TO DO IF YOU SUFFER FROM INSOMNIA

Although not a specific psychosomatic disease, insomnia is a symptom that crops up frequently in the medical histories of persons with psychosomatic ailments. Clearly, the first step to take is to determine if you really have insomnia. As mentioned, many persons who think they are losing sleep are actually sleeping far more than they imagine. But if your insomnia is real, serious mental ailments and organic disease should be ruled out.

Let us suppose that it becomes clear that your sleeplessness is on a psychic basis: Here are some steps you can take to conquer the problem. They are recommended by the American psychiatrist, Dr. William S. Sadler, a student of Sigmund Freud. We have added editorial comment.

1) Don't go to bed until you are really *physically* tired.
2) Arise at the same hour each morning, even though you do feel tired.
3) Don't take an afternoon nap unless your physician prescribes it.
4) Get by with as little sleep as possible rather than trying to see how much you can sleep. (Don't be like the old gentleman from Missouri who, when asked how he slept, responded, "I sleep fine of a night and of a morning but afternoons I jest toss and toss.")
5) Leave your work problems at work.
6) When you go to bed, relax. If you don't go to sleep right away then turn the light on and read awhile. Not mystery books, but rather soothing, pleasant reading.
7) Don't engage in active mental work before retiring. And keep thoughts of hate and revenge from your mind before going to bed.
8) Have your sleeping room dark, well-ventilated and as quiet as possible.
9) A hot bath, hot drink, or a little food just before retiring may help sleep.
10) Don't eat a hearty meal just before retiring. An alcoholic drink helps some persons sleep, stimulates others. Avoid drinking too much water just before bedtime, for obvious reasons.
11) It may help to exercise vigorously, breathe deep, or do sitting up exercises just before retiring.
12) Sedative medications have their place. But one should avoid becoming dependent upon them.

If the person who suffers from insomnia of a psychosomatic origin will conscientiously employ these measures, he should find at least partial, if not full, relief. The emotional background of the insomniac is, of course, of primary importance and should be considered. But if a person is sincerely determined to overcome his problem, he will soon see an improvement in the insomnia. And additional benefits might also accrue, as sleeplessness is a factor in numerous other psychosomatic ailments.

fourteen

A healthy youthful life
is no accident

> Carriages without horses shall go,
> And accidents fill the world with woe.
> Prophecy Attributed to
> Mother Shipton (17th Century)

The black cloud of misfortune that seems to accompany so many people wherever they go is frequently referred to in humor. Richard, for example, had suffered three disabling injuries and numerous others less severe during the past five years. All of his mishaps had been classified as accidents. His friends joked a lot about his "personal raincloud" that seemed to hover over him but Richard did not find the increasing regularity of his "accidents" humorous. If, indeed, he was "accident prone," was it possible that he was, in some way, responsible for his misfortunes? And were there any steps he could take to prevent future mishaps from occurring?

There is overwhelming evidence that certain persons are accident prone, either because of ingrained personality traits, or because of prolonged psychic tension. This condition deserves to be called a psychosomatic disease for its results include organic harm, including death.

THE SHOCKING TOLL OF ACCIDENTS

Accidents are seldom considered a disease, hence they are all too frequently ignored as a factor in public health. Yet they cause an appalling amount of human pain, suffering and disability. They also form a substantial part of the work load of the medical and nursing professions. To be more specific, injuries from accidents represent the chief killer of persons between the ages of 1 and 37; they represent the number one cause of disability. They most frequently strike the young, thus killing and disabling many who would otherwise have contributed much to society.

The toll from accidents is discouraging and grisly: each year 740 of every 10,000 people in the country are hurt so as to be kept from work for a full day or more. Twenty-six of this group suffer permanently impaired function. Accidents are exceeded as killers only by heart disease, cancer or brain hemorrhage. As one would expect they kill more males than females, more males between the ages of 2 and 38 than any illness. In our allegedly peaceful United States, a citizen who falls either at home or at work is six times as likely to be permanently injured as a soldier wounded in battle.

Although the country's workers account for less than a third of our total population, accidents kill or injure four million each year. And even though most of these accidents are not connected with the job, the loss in man days exceeds that from strikes, even in a year of major industrial disputes. Also startling is the fact that auto accidents don't take the greatest toll in death and disabling. In one year, motor vehicle crashes killed 33,500; home accidents 34,000; industrial accidents, aircraft crashes, railroad collisions and all other types of accident 32,500. Falls caused twice as many accidents as the auto collisions.

Most distressing is the fact that, although gratifying progress has been achieved in controlling most diseases, the annual death rate from accidents appears locked at the 1900 rate: 88 for every 100,000 persons.

THE EVIDENCE FOR ACCIDENT PRONENESS

Ambrose Bierce in his clever *Devil's Dictionary* defined an accident as "an inevitable occurrence, the action of immutable natural laws." If accidents were truly inevitable we could do nothing to prevent them. Fortunately, the picture is not so gloomy: many accidents are quite preventable, since they by no means result from blind chance. *Many appear to be preplanned, engineered, however unintentionally.* Often we can discover the precise causes and the background of those causes. If this were not the case we could not speak of accident patterns; and accidents often do fall into patterns, so definite that accidents can often be predicted both by type and number.

We must conclude, then, that accidents are often not accidents at all, in the strict meaning of the word. *A person usually causes them by his behavior or his emotional attitude.* Such occurrences fail to meet the definition of an accident, which is an event beyond an individual's control. What, then, is an accident? A golf ball striking a person walking past a golf course would be an accident, provided the victim received no verbal warning such as "fore!" If an innocent passerby was struck by a bullet in a bank robbery, that would be an accident. If lightning struck a tree causing it to fall on your house or your car while you were inside, that would be an accident.

But most mishaps in the home, at work and on the streets differ sharply from these true accidents: *The victim has a role in causing the accident!* It's easy to assume that the person hurt or killed was clumsy, tired, absent-minded or thoughtless. Scientific examination reveals, however, that certain people have accidents not because they are clumsy or absent-minded but because of their personality structure. That structure is lacking in qualities far more basic than slow reaction time or lack of intelligence.

Discovery of the "ailment" of being accident prone

Back in the Turbulent Twenties, 1926 to be precise, a German psychologist named Marbe observed that a person who had had one accident is more likely to have another than the accident-free individual. His findings were supported by statistical studies of large companies that revealed that accidents are by no means evenly distributed among the workers. Might this be because employees having accidents have the more hazardous jobs? No! It became clear that the people who have the most accidents in one type of job also have the most accidents on other jobs. And the same persons who had accidents at work had them on the way to and from work and at home.

Consistently, when the accidents of any type of group are reviewed it is found that a small fraction of the group cause a disproportionately large fraction of the accidents. A study of motor vehicle accidents in Connecticut showed that 3.9 per cent of the drivers had 36.9 per cent of the accidents. Another report is still more revealing: A public utility company that operated a large fleet of trucks became seriously disturbed by the accident rate. Accidents involving the company's vehicles, which were traveling some 2,900,000 miles a year in the aggregate, were eating seriously into net profits. Under orders from top management, company managers ordered tests of every factor from weather to reaction times of employees. Drivers received intensive truck operation courses. Those who had accidents and survived had severe penalties imposed. But the accident rate continued to mount.

Having failed with sophisticated approaches to remedy the problem, the company tried a simple, common sense tactic: men with bad driving records were shifted to other work. In less than four years the accident rate dropped to one-fifth the previous rate. Insurance premiums fell. But the picture was not all sunny for the men taken off the trucks had not lost the accident habit. Now, instead of smashing up their trucks they were smashing up themselves on the job and outside of working hours. The finding bore out a conclusion of the National Research Council: ". . . analysis of the records of more than 2,000 drivers . . . showed that their automobile accidents and their personal injuries [in non-auto accidents] tend to accumulate side by side."

PROFILE OF THE ACCIDENT PRONE

Granted, then, that some persons are more prone than others to have accidents, what qualities of personality are responsible? Alexandra Adler of Vienna in 1934 suggested that an unknown factor in the human personality lay behind the curious repetition of accidents for the prone group. But before we examine these traits a word of caution: We cannot be certain that a given person is accident prone simply because he has had repeated accidents. In some instances a series of accidents involving one person can occur by chance—"accidentally," we might say. Even unloaded dice now and then turn up a string of sevens.

So before indicting a person we should consider all the facts. An individual may have more auto accidents because his work demands that he drive a great many thousands of miles each year, thus having had more exposure to the possibility of accidents. A boy living in a rough neighborhood may have more accidents than a girl in a sedate neighborhood because of the social differences, and because boys play rougher games than girls. Indeed, boys in general have more accidents than girls because they are boys and not because they are necessarily accident prone. Nevertheless, there are definite character traits that set apart the genuinely accident prone person. A leading physician made some basic discoveries in this area quite "accidentally."

Dr. Dunbar discovers personality factors in being accident prone

Flanders Dunbar, M.D., wanted to know how the personality factors in heart and diabetic patients could be said to characterize the diseases and how the personalities of these patients differed from those of healthy persons. But healthy people do not frequent hospitals, nor do healthy persons take kindly to exhaustive psychologic testing. So, acting on the assumption that accidents can happen to anyone, Dr. Dunbar and her colleagues decided to use the patients in the hospital fracture ward as representative of healthy people. But as they began to study the individuals with broken bones they found that they were by no means psychologically normal (whatever "normal" might mean). Rather, they were accident prone, victims of accidentitis and they had broken bones *largely because of their personality profile.*

Further analysis of the group showed that the fracture patients had an average of 14 times as many disabling mishaps as did the other patients in the hospital. Thus, 80 per cent of the fracture patients had had two or more accidents; in no other group of patients did more than 14 per cent have two or more accidents. Over half the fracture patients had had three or more accidents; none of the other patients had had so many. The data from this

single study offers convincing evidence in favor of an accident
prone personality.

Specific traits

Additional studies provide more specific information as to
the traits and background of the accident prone. Persons with
records of repeated automobile accidents showed these traits:
hostility, self-centeredness and disregard for the rights of others.
Some daydreamed; many feared loss of affection and friendship.
As a group they tended to be resentful, sometimes even bellig-
erent. Their tolerance for tension was lower than that for the
non-accident prone. They were also less conventional and more
poorly adjusted.

Other studies have contributed to the group image of the
accident prone. They appear to be impulsive, resentful of authority, easily frustrated, quick to take action—any action—when faced
by a problem or when frustrated. Many appear to be under
tension, appearing restless, although not constantly so. They are
prone to plunge headlong into foolish activities. They seem to
have accidents particularly when their aggressiveness is aroused or
when pressures from authority figures become too great. (As we
shall shortly see, those "authority figures" are enormously important to the accident prone.) Tensions stemming from a long period
out of work or pressure from a spouse to get a better job can cause
some accident prone persons to suffer injury.

But the accident prone have some favorable traits: They
have, in general, a low illness rate—aside from broken bones. They
are self-reliant. They are usually regarded as good fellows by their
agemates. The rate of venereal disease is low and unwanted
pregnancies are avoided.

General background of accident prone persons

Many accident prone persons have described their upbringing
as strict. This may well account for the fact that the accident
prone usually show extreme resentment of authority, whether that

authority is represented by parents, guardians, spouse, relatives, church, or employer. Inquiry into the childhoods of the accident prone showed that many had been sleep walkers and sleep talkers and had persisted in lying, stealing and truancy. Later these actions disappeared, apparently replaced by the accident habit.

Listen to the impulsiveness of the accident-prone as they speak to Dr. Dunbar:

> I always like to keep working and can't stand around doing nothing. Adventure and excitement appeal to me.
>
> When I find a way to do a thing, I always stick to it; if I don't, I do something anyway and take a chance.
>
> I like to finish what I'm doing but sometimes I like to do something else first, so I jump up and do it."

Overall, the response pattern of the accident prone matches in several respects that of the juvenile delinquent and of the adult criminal. The persistent breaker of bones and the persistent breaker of laws have much in common. One has an accident, the other commits a crime. In both there is a story of poor adjustment in childhood to a strict authority in home or school. Parental rejection is common. But the lawbreaker carries his early record of lying, stealing, and truancy to criminal activity and the other hurts himself instead of the community. In this the accident prone deserves a measure of credit!

Case history of Marie, an accident "victim"

Let us examine the case history of one of Dr. Dunbar's patients, typical of the accident prone. We shall call her Marie. At age twenty she was admitted to a hospital emergency room for treatment of an old injury to her left arm. The doctor who took her history discovered the following: Marie had broken her arm six months before when she worked in a factory. It had never really healed and finally, after months of pain, she impulsively went to the hospital. She was one of ten children of a strict but quick-tempered father and a pleasant mother. Marie took vitamins and tonics, had always watched her health carefully. She spent much time outside and was fond of athletics. She had many friends including a steady beau. But she had been somewhat lonely since her accident because the injury curtailed her social activities. She revealed much of herself when she said, "I'm pretty fast to make my mind up, like other people would be scared to undergo an operation and I just made up my mind like that [she had demanded an operation on her arm in the emergency room]. Same way when I go some place."

Psychologic examination revealed that Marie always focused on the goals of the moment; long-term objectives were not for her. She had strong attachments to people but no intellectual interests. She was originally trained to be a secretary but she lost her job and went to work in a factory. She worked on machines for a while then was transferred to work not involving machines. One Monday, after returning jubilant from a happy weekend a girl had fainted at her machine. Although unfamiliar with the machine, Marie had volunteered to take the girl's place. Shortly after starting on the machine Marie's glove caught in the gears and drew her arm into the mechanism. A serious injury resulted, including a fracture of the arm and considerable injury to muscles and skin. Marie looked on the accident as just punishment. She said, "I didn't like the work and I was always complaining to my mother. I wanted to rest and now I've got a good long rest—too long." Perhaps Marie's complaints about her factory job were indirect criticism of her father. The accident was probably set off by feelings of over-confidence combined with guilt.

With her background of a strict upbringing, deep resentments with childhood roots, impulsiveness and lack of forethought, Marie's case is fairly typical of the accident prone person.

Hidden emotional conflicts as causes of accidents

Inquiry into the circumstances leading to accidents will often reveal hidden conflicts responsible; accidents are the means that many persons use to atone for guilt, hostility or frustration. It must be repeated, however, that these mental processes that lead to an act of seeming self-destruction are not conscious. The individual feels tension only in terms of working it off by muscular action, but this impulsive burst often gets him into trouble. Or, lacking a healthy outlet for strong emotions, the accident prone person may use a self-destructive mishap as a way of avoiding confrontations, of getting care and attention, of expressing hostility, and as punishment for sexual guilt.

Cases of emotional conflicts causing accidents

Take the case of *X*, who was on the way to apply for a new job, all the while dreading the tearful scene to which he would be subjected if he had to tell his wife he didn't obtain employment. Brooding over the unpleasant possibility, he slipped on the ice and broke his leg.

Y, a young Catholic housewife, was on her way to confession. She had been using contraceptives against the laws of the Church and was deeply concerned lest the priest demand that she promise to give them up. Thinking about this she slipped and fell down the steps of her home, breaking her leg.

Q had been ordered to work Sunday morning. Incensed that he had to arise at 6:30 a.m. instead of lying in bed until 10:00 a.m., he slipped on the floor, fell and broke his leg.

M took part in a sandlot football game because he was angry. Over the years he had found that he could dissipate rage by vigorous exercise but in this game he broke his leg.

F was returning from an enjoyable dance. But on the way home her mind dwelt on her irritation at the necessity of working in her father's hated business instead of getting a job she liked. As she entered the house she fell and broke her arm.

L was hurrying home to get supper when she passed the Catholic church she attended. She recalled that she had not made her usual daily visit to the altar. As she crossed the street her mind was on this omission; she was struck by a car and seriously injured.

P, a 17-year-old girl, fell off a sled. She had been worried because she was disobeying her parents in going sledding that afternoon. Her ankle was badly sprained. Years before, she had sprained her ankle under closely similar circumstances.

In all these accidents a serious emotional conflict precipitated the mishap. Every one of the conflicts involved the person's relationship with authority, in different instances a wife, the church, the boss, parents. Resentment of authority and inability to do anything about it is a hallmark of the accident prone. In every case cited the worry of the moment was not really important, but it was a symptom of the basic conflict. In these mishaps there is more than a suspicion of unconscious intention; the underlying conflict, even the surface tension, may not be so readily apparent in other instances.

Accidents may well represent errors of everyday life such as those described by the famous psychiatrist Sigmund Freud. He pointed out that misplacing an object, forgetting to mail a letter, misspelling or mispronouncing a word are not always accidental: they may be unconsciously intended. A person who carries a letter in his pocket for ten days without mailing it must have an unconscious reason for neglecting to mail it.

Accident-prone adolescents

Teachers were quizzed concerning a group of adolescents with a high auto-accident record, asked for opinions of the students quite apart from the accident incidence. The attitudes of the group of students toward authority was distinctly inferior to that of other students. The accident prone group showed far less consideration for the rights of others than did the students without high accident records. Both the work habits and the sense of responsibility of the accident prone were poorer. From the social, emotional and moral standpoints the teachers regarded the group as inferior to the students as a whole.

Even children can be accident prone

The fact that even children can be accident prone further emphasizes the importance of inherited traits. Accident prone children are often more active not only after birth but in the uterus. They appear anxious, become emotionally disturbed quite readily, but on the positive side reveal earlier motor development and superior physical coordination. Parents of accident prone children, on the other hand, give the impression of anxiety, insecurity and lack of assertiveness. They tend not to spend a great deal of time with their children.

One type of accident prone child apparently copes with fear arising from the subconscious by exposing themselves to the very hazard they dread. Such children are often tense and edgy; they reveal an inner urge to keep active. These children take dares, plunge headlong into situations without thinking of the risks involved.

Today's protesters against the conventional standards

Many of the protesters of the radical left share qualities with the accident prone. Consider: both are impulsive, ready to act on the spur of the moment; both like excitement and adventure but do not plan for the future (protesting and rioting can be far more exciting than drab classroom work). Both are people of action, however ill-considered. Both show an inability to discipline themselves, are non-analytic. Unable to express their emotions and feelings appropriately, the protesters take to the streets and campuses to vent their anger. But unlike the accident prone, their destruction is not usually directed at themselves.

The need for penance as a causative factor

Some persons have accidents because they are trying to do penance by self-imposed punishment. For there exists in our society a deeply-ingrained attitude that suffering makes up for guilt. When a child does something wrong he expects to be punished. After the whipping he feels he has attoned for his guilt and can once again deserve and receive the love of his parents. A person convicted of a crime serves his sentence and can then return to his community (although he may not receive a hearty welcome or a readily available job). As a general principle, suffering tends to relieve the pangs of guilt and to restore inner peace.

Young Charles, for example, was told by his mother that he could not go out on a certain Monday night. But he decided to go out anyway, got involved in a wrestling match, and broke his arm. Shortly after arriving at the emergency room at the hospital, he commented, "I guess Mother's sorry now that she's so strict with me." Not only had he inflicted a self-punishment, but he had also managed to gain more attention, care, and sympathy and, in his own mind at least, he had brought a share of guilt upon his mother. These are rather typical actions of the accident prone.

In another incident, Alan was driving his mother on a shopping tour. As they sped down the highway he asked her to let him use the car the next day for a fishing trip. She refused. He snorted, then impetuously jammed down the accelerator, plunging the car into the ditch and injuring both his mother and himself. While he had punished his mother, he had also punished himself. His emotions after the mishap were a curious mixture of the gleeful and the penitent.

CAN PERSONS WHO ARE ACCIDENT PRONE TAKE STEPS TO PREVENT FUTURE MISHAPS?

The crucial question in this chapter is obvious: Can we use the insights here presented to *prevent* accidents? The results of a two-year study at a large metropolitan department store indicate that simple recognition of accident proneness is a vital first step in prevention. For in this particular study, when word got around that a psychiatrist was interviewing all accident victims, the store's accident rate dropped drastically: during the study, the number of days lost because of accidents dropped 33 per cent. By contrast, a program of accident-prevention measures that had been instituted in the previous two years had succeeded in bringing the figure down only 14 per cent.

If you have recently suffered a series of accidents, don't resign yourself to the fact that "a black cloud" hangs over your head and your accident trend cannot be broken. Instead, analyze what happened during the day that preceded an accident. Go over every event until you can pinpoint the incident, or incidents, that caused a strong emotional response. It could be something as simple as a sharp word from a friend, a boss, a husband or wife; or it could be guilt or hostility developing from social contacts. If you can thus expose the event, you may be able to recognize the reason for the accident.

The accident prone persons should remember, as should those who suffer from any form of psychosomatic ailment, that you *cannot* pull yourselves up by your own bootstraps; you cannot separate yourself from society in an effort to find relief and achieve satisfactory, lasting results. So seek out a friend or relative and talk out the most recent accident with them. Friendly conversation and simply telling your troubles aloud to one who is concerned is one of the best remedies we can recommend. (Remember, too, the value of *your* listening ear when others come to you for solace and understanding.)

For many persons, the recognition and prevention of an accident pattern—particularly where accidents result in serious injury—may require a careful psychologic inventory conducted by an expert who can extract the pertinent facts from the patient's life story. Examination of the childhood events rates special emphasis: the accident habit develops early in life and reveals itself in the young by frequent physical injuries, major and minor. The skilled psychotherapist can ferret out these important roots of the accident prone problem.

"Accidentitis" or accident proneness is not a matter to be lightly dismissed. Death or serious injury can be the result, not only for the accident prone person but for persons innocently involved. But the cure of accidentitis demands a deep understanding of the underlying causes of the ailment. If the accident prone person is to avoid serious mishaps, measures must be directed toward the person. It is far less satisfactory to remove such a person from an occupation that is potentially dangerous—although this is a wise precaution—than it is to change the person.

If you are even suspicious that you might be accident prone, conduct a careful inventory of your personality and life situation. This might prove a wise, even a life-saving, step.

Dr. Karl Menninger, a founder of the famed Menninger Clinic in Topeka, Kansas, summarized his approach to preventing what he called "purposive accidents": "The sum of the whole matter is that our intelligence and our affections are our most dependable bulwarks against self-destruction. To recognize the existence of such a force within us is the first step toward its control."

fifteen

How to escape
from the "terrible traps"
that cause sickness

> The Mind in its own place, and in itself can
> make a Heaven of Hell, and Hell of Heaven.
> John Milton
> Paradise Lost I

Fear is an emotion from which none of us are exempt. Generally, however, it is short-lived. We fear a coming event, an encounter, a medical diagnosis. And when the object of our concern is past, our fear retreats—at least until another foreboding obstacle emerges. But for many unfortunate persons, this is not true. They either cannot or will not resolve the situational trap that ensnares them. In many instances, they are truly unaware that it even exists.

Countless patients have trekked from clinic to clinic searching for relief from a peptic ulcer, from arthritis, from ulcerative colitis, from bronchial asthma, from migraine, but to no avail. Physicians, under the pressures of overcrowded waiting rooms, all too often focus on the illness and ignore the situational traps that might be causing it. The patient is caught in a sort of vicious cycle, unable to take even halting steps toward better health until the bond between trap and illness is recognized. Even then, improvement depends in large part on eliminating the trap and, in many cases, there is no escape compatible with what the patient considers honor or kindness or love.

A few of life's terrible traps

Some years ago a wise and understanding physician, Dr. Walter Alvarez, wrote a timeless article for the medical profession that made starkly clear the terrible traps of life that can produce psychosomatic illness. He told of a patient trapped by the need to care for an aging father; a girl trapped by a psychopathic mother; another trapped by a cruel father; of persons trapped by unhappy marriages, or no marriage at all, by years of boredom, by alcoholism, by marital triangles, and even by religious convictions.

Occasionally Dr. Alvarez was able to spring the traps, release the captive patients, and effect a cure. More often, he could only offer a new understanding of the situation and help the patient to find some peace and better health through acceptance. Several of the following case histories were reported by Dr. Alvarez in his article. Others are from our own experiences.

. . . Tension at work

A fifty-five-year-old man had worked in a small manufacturing company for some twenty years. He had earned impressive seniority rights and was looking forward to retirement with a generous pension. Then a fateful juggling of personnel placed him under the direct supervision of a bitter rival. They spoke to one another only when absolutely necessary but the ever-present tension could be felt even by fellow employees. Suppressed emotions, probably a combination of anger, hate, anxiety, and perhaps even guilt, eventually took their toll and the result was the development of a peptic ulcer.

This man was well aware of his problem but refused to request a transfer to another department for fear of showing weakness. This would seem a small price to pay in order to escape a wretched life of strict diets, milk and crackers, and antacid medications. But he preferred to take his punishment.

. . . Inability to break home ties

A youthful, sad-eyed Irish girl suffered from a cluster of ailments including intense headaches, backache, abdominal pain, insomnia, and a profound sense of fatigue. A physical examination failed to reveal any cause for her complaints. Then, quite by accident, it was learned that the girl not only supported her mother and an irresponsible, drinking father, but had recently made a most painful decision. She had been engaged to be married when her fiance realized that she had no intentions of leaving her parents. He knew that on his moderate salary he could not hope to support four adults and shuddered at the prospects of such a marriage. He pleaded with her to consider their rights to a future together, a family and a home of their own.

Torn between love for her fiance and a sense of responsibility for her parents, she chose the latter. The doctor explained that there was no medication to cure her illness. Her only consolation was that someday she would be free and with some hope, life could become bearable. Although she had the key to her own trap, she could not bring herself to use it.

. . . Repressed desires

Puzzling, indeed, was the case of a respected civic leader, president of the town's largest department store, who suffered from violent attacks of abdominal pain, accompanied by bloating and vomiting. His ailment was diagnosed as intestinal obstruction and he underwent exploratory surgery on four separate occasions. The results were negative. There appeared to be no logical explanation for his repeated attacks.

Finally, however, a casual conversation with his wife shed the first ray of light on the mystery and the pieces gradually seemed to fall into place. She recalled that when he was much younger he had the soul of an artist and a burning desire to prepare himself for a career in musical composition. He enrolled in college and was in his second year when his plans met with an abrupt reversal. Due to the untimely death of his father, he was called home and compelled to manage the family business. He shouldered the responsibility without murmur although pangs of hatred welled up inside of him anytime he dared to remember his shattered dreams.

Now, many years later, it appeared that he was releasing this smoldering resentment upon his employees, whom he would reprimand unmercifully at the slightest provocation. During such upbraidings he would work himself into a violent rage that sometimes ended in one of his acute abdominal attacks.

In this case, when the source of the distress was brought out into the open, the man was so determined to achieve full recovery that he took definite steps to curb his temper and learned to exert a firmer control over his emotions. It took considerable practice but the end result was a much happier, healthier man.

. . . Regretted decision

A young lady suffered from complete lack of appetite and vomiting and had lost a considerable amount of weight when she appeared at the doctor's office. He discovered with little difficulty that she had trapped herself by entering a convent and a life for which she was not adapted. She admitted her mistake but feared that she would offend God if she were to go back into the world. A consultation with her wise and understanding Mother Superior soon convinced the girl that God would understand and that there was no disgrace in leaving the Order if she was truly unsuited to the life. With great relief the young lady went back into the world, quickly regained her health, married, and is living a normal, happy life.

. . . An unhappy marriage

Another woman, frail and quite nervous, had been treated for some time for tuberculosis because she suffered from a chronic fever. At last, after several thorough studies, it was concluded that she did not have the disease. But the fever continued so she sought another physician.

After much testing and questioning it gradually became apparent that the lady's illness had begun the week after she realized she had trapped herself in a stupid marriage. A highly intelligent woman of 37, with a fine position in a bank, she had married a handsome young man of 30, a salesman in a grocery store, without even a high school education. She had determined to teach him evenings and help him better his position. But within a few weeks she could see that he did not have the mental capacity to learn; he bored her, and she wanted to leave him but could not summon up enough courage. Her energy waned and she became so weak she was instructed to get as much bedrest as possible. Her job soon terminated. Her problems were only compounded then as both had to exist on his small salary.

But he nursed her so tenderly that she hadn't the heart to leave him. And even when the source of her illness was explained to her, she refused to pull herself together and start life again so that she remained an invalid in her self-erected trap.

... An unwelcome house "guest"

There appears to be no limit to the list of ailments that can result from emotional stress. Perhaps most unusual was the recent case of a lady who consulted her physician concerning a maddening anal itching. It had begun some nine months before and was now so severe that she hesitated to go out in public. A thorough examination proved futile in locating the cause of the problem but the physician was able to elicit bits of information that revealed the source of her distress.

It seemed that the ailment had started shortly after her husband's brother had come to make his home with them. He was no bother at all and was even a pleasant sort, but merely his presence in her home and the invasion of the family's privacy disturbed her immensely. She had not considered, however, that this might be even remotely connected with her embarrassing problem. Arrangements were made as tactfully as possible for the brother to live elsewhere and the itching promptly disappeared.

... Inconsolable grief

One final case history concerns a man who had worked hard for seven years to accumulate enough money that he felt he could afford to marry and support his wife in the manner he thought she deserved. His lovely young fiance had been waiting patiently and it appeared to everyone that theirs was, indeed, a perfect union. But after only one year of marriage, the cherished wife developed a severe lung infection that was both rare and fatal. Her husband's grief was inconsolable.

It was only with enormous difficulty that he was able to continue his work. Then, after about six months, he developed severe arthritis. Medical treatment brought only limited relief although there was little doubt in the doctor's mind that the tragedy had induced the arthritis. The past could not be undone, however, nor could the bereaved widower find another to fill the loathsome vacuum in his life.

The biblical Job spoke an ageless truth

When Job said, "Man is born of woman, his days are few and full of trouble," he spoke an ageless truth that helps explain much about psychosomatic illness. Although some persons are not affected physically by the little unpleasantries, even the tragedies, of life, others, through the mechanics of their autonomic nervous systems, develop real physical diseases.

Several groups of researchers have pointed out that men are more likely than women to suffer from the ill effects of pent-up emotions because they are trained to bottle up their feelings. It is considered "unmanly" to complain, or cry, or express pain so they turn all their feelings of rejection, disappointment, rage, or jealousy inward. The result is often manifested as hypertension, with an elevation in blood pressure that, if prolonged, can cause damage to both the blood vessels and the heart.

A vicious circle of psychosomatic illnesses

Not only are we often caught in a vicious circle of life traps, but one psychosomatic ailment often begets another, and still another. A vicious circle might be defined as a self-perpetuating series of harmful events that tend to become progressively more serious. And there is probably no field of medicine in which the vicious circle is more important than in that of psychosomatic disease.

Consider: psychic tension, from whatever cause, produces shadow symptoms. With time, these vague symptoms can develop into a psychosomatic ailment. The ailment itself may worry the patient, thus adding to his psychic tension. If the individual is too ill to work, he may worry over the actual or possible loss of his job and income, adding still more tension. The mounting tension causes the psychosomatic disease to get worse, which, in turn, further increases psychic tension. And so on, around and around the circle.

How the vicious circle operates

Suppose a person is undergoing severe psychic tension, as from the pressures of an extremely difficult job. Messages passing out over the autonomic division of the nervous stsyem cause the tubular gastric glands of the stomach to secrete too much acid and perhaps not enough of the mucus that forms a protective lining in the duodenum. The acid eats into the duodenum, forming a peptic ulcer. The ulcer makes the individual miserable, forces him to go on a special diet, and perhaps causes him to lose considerable work, even to lose his job. All of this contributes to additional psychic tension, which, then, tends to make the ulcer worse.

Or, take the case of high blood pressure. Because of psychic tension, autonomic messages cause a narrowing of the blood vessels of the kidneys. Next, a chain of chemical events causes excessive production of a hormone called aldosterone, which can produce high blood pressure. The high blood pressure causes dizziness, roaring in the ears, and perhaps headache. The ailment is bound to cause worry, which represents additional psychic tension. In response to the tension, the kidney produces more and more aldosterone, resulting in a still higher blood pressure. If the vicious circle continues, the high blood pressure may progress to the point where a stroke occurs. The individual may be severely incapacitated, further contributing to his troubles.

A person suffering from hyperventilation, or overbreathing, caused by psychic concern suffers additional psychic stress when he worries over his condition or when it prevents him from working at a job or associating with other people. The worry tends to increase the hyperventilation, and so the vicious circle continues.

The patient with asthma, sometimes partly caused by psychic tension, naturally worries about his asthma—particularly if he has the vicious episodes known as status asthmaticus. The tensions generated by worrying over the disease produce more disease.

Thyroid malfunction can be caused by psychic tension. Hyperthyroidism itself is a cause of extreme tension. The rapid heart rate, rapid breathing, sweating, and difficulty in sleeping associated with hyperthyroidism are all sources of additional psychic tension, which itself can further accentuate the hyperthyroidism.

Rheumatoid arthritis, often a disease of maladaptation to stress, is frequently incapacitating. The incapacitation represents additional stress. If this stress is met with further maladaptation, then the disease worsens.

Melancholy, or depression, is usually the result of long-continued tension. Depression can seriously handicap an individual in doing his work, even in living an adequate life. The slowing down process naturally causes additional tension, and the additional tension causes further melancholy.

Painful menstruation, resulting from psychic tension, is naturally a cause of worry, additional tension, and, in turn, increased pain.

Disease of the coronary arteries, a familiar heart condition, can result from prolonged emotional upset. If the individual survives the heart attack that results from this condition, he may well be incapacitated, or at least restricted in his activities. Restrictions in his work and the worry of additional attacks cause more psychic tension, which can well cause repeated heart attacks.

How the vicious circle can be broken

There is scarcely a psychosomatic ailment that cannot become involved in a vicious circle, an increasingly severe series of harmful events. Obviously, interrupting the circle is important, and the sooner the better. If the circle can be broken early, when only shadow symptoms are present, full relief is almost assured. But the old adage, "better late than never," holds. If psychosomatic disease has occurred, then both treatment of the organic disease and concentrated attention on the psychic events or life situations that brought it about are needed.

Only when the connection between the physical ailment and the emotional problem is recognized can relief be procured. It is vital, therefore, that we tell the doctor our whole story, not just the physical symptoms that we experience. As the old English proverb states, "A disease known is half-cured." And only then can life's terrible traps be sprung and the vicious circle of psychosomatic disease be broken.

sixteen

How to prevent
your "health battery"
from running down

> If there be a hell upon earth, it is to be
> found in a melancholy man's heart.
> > Robert Burton

> Never give way to melancholy; resist it
> steadily, for the habit will encroach.
> > Sidney Smith

The state of melancholy, or depression, is probably the chief disorder affecting the mind. Most doctors will see at least one depressed patient every day. Indeed, since the beginning of history melancholy has been recognized as an important ailment. The 1st and 2nd century Roman, Plutarch, wrote of it. In the 17th century, Robert Burton wrote an entire book on the subject, and Miguel de Servantes, William Shakespeare, and John Ford all spoke of it in their writings. In the 18th century, Voltaire, Samuel Johnson, Thomas Gray, and Tobias Smollett covered various aspects of depression.

WHAT IS DEPRESSION?

Depression has many faces. In a nutshell, the term can be taken to mean low spirits, unhappy mood, and dejection. Some depression represents part of a serious mental disease called manic-depressive psychosis. Discussion of this ailment is beyond the purpose of this chapter, so we shall confine ourselves to the sort of depression that afflicts people who have simply endured more psychic tension of one sort or another than they can stand. Usually a period of anxiety precedes depression. Depression leads to a general slowing down both of physical and mental functions, hence can ultimately result in disease of an organic nature. It is, therefore, properly regarded as a psychosomatic ailment.

Symptoms of depression

Many depressed individuals who seek medical help have a considerable number and variety of symptoms. They may suffer from intense fatigue, which sometimes comes on suddenly and is not relieved by sleep or rest. Other symptoms might be lethargy, or difficulty in getting moving; loss of appetite; difficulty in sleeping; indigestion; headache; rapid heart rate; symptoms of the lower gastrointestinal tract, chiefly constipation; recent loss of weight; pain or tightness of the chest; loss of the sexual urge; generalized mild pain; frequency or pain in urination. Especially important are difficulty in sleeping and in eating.

Persons suffering from depression tend to be self-critical and disparaging, expressing an extremely low opinion of their own worth. They report loss of interest in life and vague, unhappy feelings. Their muscular and intellectual processes may slow down; speech and action become sluggish, thinking is difficult. Those thoughts that do emerge usually relate to the patient himself—his aches and pains, his sins and afflictions, his unworthiness. Such persons may withdraw and become increasingly dependent on others. As Dr. Francis J. Braceland said, "Depressed individuals suffer deeply, much more so than in any other medical condition."

If depression progresses far enough, the individual seeks a way out of his misery—and one way out is suicide. Indeed, suicide is a constant hazard in depression: fifty times as many depressed people commit suicide as do members of the general population. This danger is greatest when the patient enters or emerges from a depression.

WHAT CAUSES DEPRESSION?

Here again, we must distinguish between manic-depressive psychosis, which apparently stems from a basic problem of unknown origin within the personality, and the sort of depression not really representing mental disease that afflicts so many people. The latter type can properly be called *reactive depression,* because it represents a reaction of a susceptible individual to certain events in his life.

We have all heard—and probably used—the slang expressions "down in the dumps" and "the blues." Indeed, we have all been down in the dumps or had the blues. These expressions refer, of course, to mild depression, such as might be experienced on Monday morning or following some disappointment. In a sense, reactive depression represents a severe case of the blues that refuses to go away. Therefore, it must be regarded as an illness. The onset of a depression means that the individual has passed his breaking point. Everyone has a breaking point, given adequate psychic tension or injury. All of us have different inheritances and have led different lives. Hence, we may react in different ways to similar threatening situations.

Death of a husband or wife, a parent, a child, even a close friend, is accepted in varying degrees by different people. But how do we distinguish between normal, profound grief and reactive depression? Everyone finds it both difficult and painful to carry on after a deep loss, but most individuals have the ability to do just this. They continue to work, to love, and to avoid withdrawal. And after a period of time they are able to resume their normal activities. Gradually, they find new objects of affection and concern, giving some credence to the statement that "time heals all wounds." But when grief continues in a severity and for a period that is beyond the normal expectation, depression is quite possibly present. Near the end of his life, Sigmund Freud was visited by a woman deeply depressed after the death of her husband. Freud listened carefully to her story and then told her, "Madam, you do not have a [depression], you have a misfortune." Freud was a wise psychiatrist and he could intuitively distinguish between normal grief and depression.

IS THERE A DEPRESSION-PRONE PERSONALITY TYPE?

Some authorities believe that reactive depression chiefly afflicts persons who might be said to be rigid; who try to achieve perfection in everything they do; who are overconscientious, extremely neat and orderly. A good term for them might be "worrywarts." The housewife who keeps her house immaculate, who never leaves dishes in the sink or beds unmade, who must have everything in its place is a good example of a worrywart. The typical male worrywart keeps precise business records, always tries to clean his desk off before leaving at night, and maintains his office in a state of extreme orderliness (making it almost look as if he never does any work). He works as long and as hard as is necessary to get a given job done, and he may well be harder on himself than his boss is.

The tightly organized type

But what is it about the perfectionist's personality that makes him prone to develop depression? Clearly, the perfectionist has an enormous need to please. This may result from a quite unconscious fear of rejection, from deep feelings of inadequacy or inferiority, from underlying feelings of guilt, or from a combination of the three.

Reactive depression may come on suddenly, or it may come on gradually—insidiously. It depends to some extent on the individual's tolerance. The perfectionist usually keeps going at an active pace. He treats his body somewhat like the man who always uses the bright lights, the air conditioner, the radio, and the electric windows in his car, causing a constant drain on the battery. If he leaves the ignition key on for a few hours, the battery will run down since its reserves have been constantly used up. Similarly, some unusually traumatic event, such as loss of a loved one, failure in business, loss of position, or some other tragedy, can bring on a reactive depression in the perfectionist. In a sense, his "battery" could not handle the traumatic event since it had been continuously drained in everyday activity.

The loosely organized type

The easy-going individual, on the other hand, is like a man who seldom uses the bright lights, has no air conditioner, doesn't play the radio, and who has manually operated windows in his car. If he leaves the ignition key on, the battery does not run down for it has a sufficient reserve to handle the added stress. However, if stresses are repeated, the battery gradually becomes drained of its reserve and finally can withstand no more unusual demands. Similarly, the easy-going individual is able to cope with occasional difficulties with no ill effects. But repeated stresses can gradually overcome him and he, too, might succumb to depression.

Miscellaneous types

So we see that there is a depression-prone personality type. When individuals do not fit this description, the doctor is prompted to search further for possible organic causes of the presenting complaint. Let us consider, for example, the case of a bachelor dentist who reported to his doctor with what appeared to be a typical reactive depression. The dentist enjoyed an excellent practice, and he didn't have any particular history of psychic tension or anxiety to explain the depression. Likewise, he was not at all the worrywart type. His personal habits were not meticulous; he was, in fact, quite lackadaisical. The physician, recognizing that this man did not have the typical personality for reactive depression, decided to look further for an organic cause. When he gave the man a careful neurologic examination, he discovered findings that eventually led to the diagnosis of a tumor of the brain. The tumor was removed by surgery and the dentist made a full recovery with complete relief of the depression.

Chain of events leading to depression

The chain of events resulting in depression varies from person to person. Frequently the onset of the depression follows months of concern or worry over a real problem or over a series of problems. Ill health, financial reverses, a wayward child, a sick relative—all can contribute to the psychic erosion that terminates in a depression.

Frequently, anxiety is the prelude to depression. Anxiety, which results from tension, has been said to be fear's first cousin. Like fear, it is accompanied by autonomic nervous system effects, particularly when it is severe. But there are differences between actual fear and anxiety. Fear focuses sharply on real danger; anxiety anticipates future danger or difficulties. Anxiety has its useful functions, though. It can cause people to be alert for danger and to take steps to avoid it. It can drive them to perform difficult tasks successfully. On the other hand, it can prevent well-prepared students from getting good grades on examinations.

Anxieties as a psychic response

Anxiety really represents our psychic response to troubles that are anticipated, whether they are real or imagined, dimly or accurately seen. Timid, inexperienced, or excessively conscientious persons frequently concern themselves over trivial matters. Other persons seem unaffected by the same concerns. Most persons are anxious when they think they might have a dangerous or even fatal disease or if they are threatened by real danger, as in a battle. Indeed, anyone can develop disabling anxiety if the stimulus is sufficiently great.

One's resistance to anxiety varies with his physical condition. When we are tired, sick, or injured, we are more easily overcome than when we are fresh. Persons whose mental powers to analyze and discriminate are deficient may develop unjustified anxiety. Thus, immature persons, elderly persons, or the person with brain damage may become unjustifiably anxious.

We may become anxious in daily life when we are forced to make difficult decisions. Upon these decisions may rest financial or social success. Or, the decision may produce an unexpected response in an inconsistent, unpredictable boss. This sort of situation was illustrated by the great Russian physiologist, Pavlov, in experiments with dogs. By giving them food, he trained dogs to respond to the picture of a circle. If, on the other hand, they responded to a picture of an elipse, they got no food. Then he simply compressed the elipse so that it resembled a circle more and more, which made the discrimination between circle and elipse more and more difficult. The dogs showed a violent emotional response, becoming ferocious when put in harness for the experiment. They snapped at their restraints, barked wildly, and refused to participate.

As anxiety develops, one first has an inner feeling of tension, dread, and apprehension. Then his intellectual powers become disturbed. He can't think clearly, use proper judgment, learn efficiently, or remember accurately. When anxiety is severe, various internal organic changes cause such symptoms as shakiness of the fingers, rapid heart rate, high blood pressure, increased perspiration, dilation of the pupils of the eye, and reduced secretion of saliva and stomach juices. These all result from increased activity of the sympathetic division of the involuntary nervous system and of the adrenal glands.

Anxiety states occur in combat areas

Front line soldiers often display anxiety states. The infantry-man, for example, is always threatened with death and mutilation and he cannot tell when it is coming. He must go sleepless and hungry and is exposed to the weather. He usually doesn't know what is taking place in surrounding areas. Gunfire continuously frightens him. He is distressed by the death of companions. Should he be exposed to this situation long enough, he will develop a persisting anxiety state, which has been called battle fatigue.

The soldier with battle fatigue is tense and easily startled. His judgment is poor, so he can't be an effective soldier. He may suffer from headache, lack of appetite, or diarrhea. He usually is convinced that he is about to die. Almost all men will develop such an anxiety state if they are exposed to battle long enough. The average man in the United States Army reaches this point after 85 days in combat. So, in his resistance to crippling anxiety, even the bravest man has a breaking point. He doesn't run from the enemy, but he does become less efficient in protecting himself; he runs a high risk of being killed as a result of his anxiety.

Prolonged anxiety can lead to depression

Some persons may have a single anxiety attack, which represents a reaction to an acute threat. Others have repeated attacks, which gradually lead into a chronic state of tension. The periods of tension can vary in severity from mild apprehension to actual panic. Sometimes attacks occur at night. In the absence of daytime distractions, apprehensions take over the thoughts of the individual, and he develops the internal responses to fear. He can't think, nor can he sleep. His heart pounds. He has tightness in his chest, and he may respond to this sensation by deep and sighing respirations. Thus, he develops the overbreathing syndrome, as described in the chapter on respiratory diseases.

Anxiety can—and frequently does—merge insidiously into depression. Then the individual becomes sad and miserable. He has a loss of interest and decreased capacity for enjoyment or for productive work. He feels lonely and may be tearful. He may have difficulty sleeping plus all the other symptoms of depression. In many depressed patients, the mood is blackest in the morning. One may wake up with a leaden heart and a dread of facing the day. He may even wish he could pull the covers over his head and go back to sleep forever. But ironically, the depressed individual is often so "blue" that he cannot sleep. Gradually, as the day wears on, the depression lightens somewhat.

Evidence, which is by no means final, has been accumulating to indicate that chemical changes gradually occur as a depression develops. They appear to be a result, not the cause, of the depression. The exact nature of the chemicals involved is not yet known with certainty. These chemical alterations may perpetuate a depression after the environmental causes have disappeared. They may be in part responsible for the woeful morning depression experienced by so many depressed persons. Some victims of depression, however, are fairly cheerful in the morning and gradually become more depressed as the day passes.

Why Agnes could not find peace of mind at the seashore

Persons who are more or less naturally pessimistic tend to develop depression following relatively minor events. Agnes, who was precipitated into acute episodes quite readily, took a trip to the seashore in an attempt to improve her mental and emotional state. She arrived about dusk on a windy, gray day. A heavy cloud cover hung overhead, conveying a feeling of oppression even to an emotionally healthy person. The ocean, so often bright and sparkling, was leaden in the twilight. As Agnes stepped from her car, the mournful sounds of a local amateur band practicing on the beach reached her ears. Crows circling overhead screamed their depressing "caw, caw, caw!" The montage of pictures and sounds shattered what equanimity Agnes still possessed. Her spirits dropped to the lowest point they had reached for months. Even after two days of sunshine her peace of mind was only partially restored.

How a futile triangle of love led to depression

Let's examine another true case history, with non-essentials altered and all names changed: Jon had worshipped schoolmate Julie from afar throughout four years of high school. Not until they became freshmen at the university did he get up the nerve to ask her for a date. She accepted with alacrity. Now followed a whirlwind courtship, followed by Julie's accepting Jon's proposal of marriage. Jon could hardly believe his apparent good fortune. But Julie proved to be as shallow as she was beautiful, and she by no means loved Jon as he loved her. She made this cruelly clear when she told him, just after the honeymoon, that she reserved the right to go out with other men when and where she pleased. A series of battles ensued; then, the inevitable divorce.

On the rebound from the divorce Jon married Lorraine, a girl with real depth of character though not blessed with Julie's beauty. Still, Jon could not forget Julie. Looking forward to a lifetime with Lorraine, whom he respected but did not love, Jon became disconsolate; his unhappiness became worse with each passing month. Then, when he failed to get a desired promotion at work, largely because of his half-hearted work performance, Jon went into a reactive depression. He became morose, his work suffered still more, he found little joy in life. He consulted a physician whose prescription of medication helped only a little.

And through all this, Lorraine had stood staunchly by him, knowing all the while that he had never ceased to love Julie.

Then, when it appeared that Jon was in the depths of despair, tragedy struck. Julie was killed in an automobile accident following a drunken weekend party. Jon's grief was real. But at the same time, realizing that there was no further chance of being with Julie again, his depression lifted. He began to take note of Lorraine, to appreciate her unfailing kindness and understanding, and even to love her. His work slowly improved and he settled into a happy life.

CHILDREN ARE PRONE TO DEPRESSION

Depression can strike children and adolescents just as it afflicts adults. However, depression reveals itself in somewhat different ways in the young, depending upon the stage of their social and emotional development. Depression can strike a child because of failure to achieve a desired goal or because of a loss, actual or imaginary. While the depression is a result of the loss, it also represents, in a sense, a defense against the loss. It depends on the severity of the loss and on the individual's capability of coping with it and with other tensions. Since a child's emotional defenses involve dependence on the parents, the quality of support he receives from his parents sustains him in resisting environmental influences. It also helps him defend himself against his own inner demands and conflicts.

Loss of parents is often responsible for a child's depression. The child exposed to such a loss can't defend himself. His self-esteem is lowered. He expresses his insecurity, his inadequacy, his helplessness, and shows that he has lost hope. He may isolate himself. He may admit he is sad, or he may deny it. The depressed child may manifest aggressive behavior. His intellectual achievement is lowered.

Even small babies can become depressed. They don't thrive; they cry, have sleep disturbances, bang their heads, or have colic. They may undergo severe loss of appetite and weight. Depression in infants can occur when the mother is anxious or when she herself is depressed. A baby who loses his mother quite early in life but who gets a suitable substitute does better at avoiding depression than one who is exposed to a sudden loss at the age of six months. Then the symptoms can consist of progressive weakness, lying motionless in bed, and refusing to respond to adults. The baby has loss of appetite and inadequate weight gain, followed by weight loss. He has severe disturbance of sleep, is susceptible to frequent colds and other infections, and skin eruptions are pronounced. As time goes on, symptoms become more profound and the baby may lie rigidly in bed, becoming increasingly apathetic as marasmus finally ends in death.

Childhood depression shows the same symptoms seen in infants, but in addition there is restraint of physical, emotional, and even intellectual growth. And in children, depression may be replaced by behavioral disturbances, temper tantrums, and disobedience. Inability to get along with others and to socialize may occur. This results in isolation of the child. Sometimes he appears afraid to go to school; his attendance record at school may reveal excessive truancy. He may even run away from home. He appears unable to learn from experience, and he may become accident prone. He may be convinced that he is worthless and unacceptable to others. Some children even have suicidal tendencies. Scholastic progress, including reading ability, is poor. The child is unable to be attentive or to concentrate. He is hyperactive. He usually plays by himself and reveals little initiative. He is not interested in toys. He may steal things, even useless objects. Depressed children crave sweets with a fondness resembling addiction, so they sometimes steal money from parents to purchase candy.

Adolescents

Adolescents, too, are prone to become depressed. It may be difficult for them to admit that they are depressed, so they become jocular, or they clown. The adolescent may be extremely bored or destructive. Some depressed adolescents listen to records or stay with others till the early morning. Some are tired; some are overly-concerned with their health. They don't do well in school, or they may fail. They sometimes become dropouts. In the 15-19 age group, suicide has been reported as the fifth highest ranking cause of death.

Childhood depression cannot be managed unless it is recognized. Teachers, as well as parents, should be on the alert for the depressed child. Such a child is a disturbing element in the classroom, a poor student. The help of the pediatrician, family physician, or psychotherapist should be promptly sought when childhood depression is suspected.

HOW TO TEST YOURSELF

You can get a rough idea as to whether you are truly depressed or not by asking yourself the following questions: (Write the answers on a separate sheet of paper.)

1. Do you get tired for no reason?
   Seldom or never___   Some of the time___
   Quite often___   Almost always___

2. Do you feel downhearted and blue?
   Seldom or never___   Some of the time___
   Quite often___   Almost always___

3. Do you feel particularly discouraged of a morning?
   Seldom or never___   Some of the time___
   Quite often___   Almost always___

4. Do you have crying spells or feel like crying?
   Seldom or never___   Some of the time___
   Quite often___   Almost always___

5. Do you wake very early and have difficulty falling back to sleep?
   Seldom or never___   Some of the time___
   Quite often___   Almost always___

6. Do you have a poor appetite for food?
   Seldom or never___   Some of the time___
   Quite often___   Almost always___

7. Do you feel your life is empty?
   Seldom or never___   Some of the time___
   Quite often___   Almost always___

8. Do you find it difficult to think clearly?
   Seldom or never___   Some of the time___
   Quite often___   Almost always___

9. Do you avoid other people and social activities?
   Seldom or never____   Some of the time____
   Quite often____   Almost always____

10. Do you feel that others would be better off if you were dead?
   Seldom or never____   Some of the time____
   Quite often____   Almost always____

11. Do you find you no longer enjoy the things you used to do?
   Seldom or never____   Some of the time____
   Quite often____   Almost always____

12. Do you feel you are not worth much as a person?
   Seldom or never____   Some of the time____
   Quite often____   Almost always____

Give yourself 0 for every question answered "seldom or never"; 1 point for those answered "some of the time"; 2 points for "quite often"; and 3 points for "almost always." This questionnaire represents an extremely general test, and it can do no more than give you an idea as to whether you *might* be depressed or not. Normal persons average about 3 points on the test, and the person with depression about 18. If you have a score of 12 or more, it is quite possible that you have a depression. On the other hand, a low score doesn't necessarily exclude depression, because many depressed persons hide their true feelings even from themselves. The questionnaire and its results are nothing more than an extremely general guide.

The questionnaire presented above is adapted from an article by Burton W. Rockliff, M.D.: *A Brief Self-Rating Questionnaire for Depression,* which appeared in the July-August, 1969, *Psychosomatics* journal. Concerning the questionnaire the author cautions: ". . . it should be emphasized that no self-administered questionnaire should be relied upon uncritically as the basis for making a diagnosis . . . The implication that any self-rating scale provides 'do-it-yourself' diagnosis . . . must be considered deplorably naive and misleading."

WHAT TO DO IF YOU HAVE A DEPRESSION

Again, the approach for anyone who suspects he has a depression is to consult a doctor and have a thorough medical checkup. Various organic ailments can cause depression. Among these are lesions of the brain, such as brain tumor. Various physical illnesses are often accompanied by depression. These include influenza, liver infection; disturbances of the endocrine glands, especially of the adrenal gland or of the parathyroid glands; and the period following delivery of a baby. Degeneration of the brain substance can cause depression. And, of course, depression is a leading feature of manic-depressive psychosis, or serious mental disease. Depression is also a frequent emotional response in patients with fatal disease. Almost 50 per cent of a large group of fatally ill patients experienced depression to a distressing degree. So, a thorough physical examination would be the first step for a person with depression. Next, a careful psychologic inventory should be taken to determine if events to which the individual has been subjected will account for the depression.

Let us suppose now that organic conditions have been ruled out as the cause of your depression and that it is due to a shower of unhappy events such as can hit anyone over a course of time. You should always keep in mind that anyone with depression can recover, however deep the depression. Severe depression is sometimes treated by shock therapy, but this is not often necessary. Various effective antidepressant drugs have been developed recently, and these can be prescribed by your doctor. You should realize that it will take time for you to recover from the depression. During that time, it is most important for you to have something to occupy your time. You should not attempt to recover by sitting around the house watching the days pass, trying to fill each hour as it comes. You should have an organized program so that you can look ahead and know how each day will be filled. Max Lerner said, "Tragedy comes to all of us and this we cannot prevent; apathy, however, we can prevent." Edmund Burke said to a friend once, "Never despair, but if you do, work on in despair." That advice is extremely worthwhile, although easier to state than to carry out.

Small pleasures

Taking pleasure in small daily experiences can help. Try to enjoy a beautiful sunrise, the sun shining on the flowers outside, a willow tree waving in the breeze, the sparkling of waves on a lake stirred by the wind. These small happy experiences help lift the spirit. Working out of doors is especially helpful to some persons who are depressed. You must depend on a cheerful environment to help you.

Do not live alone

If at all possible, you should not live alone. Stay with relatives, friends, or even at a boarding house. Anywhere that you can live with other people is better than living alone. However, you should make no impulsive, irretrievable arrangements. When your depression has disappeared, and it will, your own home will probably be a source of great joy and comfort to you. Remember that the depression is you; it is not the world that is so terrible. *Depression is an illness, just as influenza is an illness.*

Do not harbor negative memories

The memory of yesterday's suffering makes a bad start for today. One can concede that yesterday was a bad day, that today may not be too good; but you should also keep ever in mind that as the days go by, they *will* get better. Naturally, every possible step should be taken to relieve the circumstances that caused the depression in the first place.

Change your attitude to positive ones

Depression involves emotional depletion, and as emotional reserves rebuild—which they will—spirits rise. One morning you will find life somewhat better, and that may be the beginning of recovery. This is particularly true if you have been able to eliminate or in some other way cope with the sources of psychic tension that gave you the depression in the first place. As you come out of the depression, you should resort to change—interesting occupations, and company. If you face the morning with a leaden heart, get out of bed as soon as you wake up, take a shower, fix a cup of coffee and, if at all possible, go for a walk. If you have work to do or if there are meetings you can attend, the earlier the better. Having something even mildly pleasurable to look forward to helps you to start the day in far better spirits. And, of course, your ace in the hole in escaping from depression is psychotherapy. The psychotherapist will help you analyze the events that brought on the depression, and he can provide reassurance and attention. Indeed, a goal of psychotherapy in depression is to help the patient gain insight into what brought about his depression. But even if insight can't be achieved, supportive psychotherapy can shorten the course of the depression.

Depression is, of course, only one of many psychosomatic reactions to psychic tension. One individual may react with peptic ulcer, another with high blood pressure, another with over-breathing, and another with disorders of the sense organs. In still others, the endocrine glands may be affected. Some develop depression, or melancholy. The same general principles apply to the management of depression as to the management of all psychosomatic ailments. And for this, the reader is again referred to the last chapter.

seventeen

Healing without drugs

> Despair is better treated with hope, not
> dope.
>
> Richard Asher, 1912-

Via our mass media (chiefly television), we are bombarded with commercials proclaiming the merits of numerous drugs. We are thus brainwashed into believing that there is a drug for every need. If you can't sleep, take this. If you need to stay awake, take that. Another will make you irresistible to girls. Another is designed to make you more kissable, and still another professes to increase the sexual urge. And so on, without limit.

We are assuredly a drug-oriented society, and to a far greater extent than when the great Dr. John Shaw Billings said near the turn of the century that: "We are a bitters-and-pill-taking people." In 1970 alone, Americans consumed 17,500 tons of aspirins, either plain or in combination formulations. That is some 46 billion tablets or an average per person of about 225 tablets per year.

Being drug-oriented would not be so bad if drugs in their almost unlimited variety were harmless. In fact, they are frequently helpful, even life-saving. But, unfortunately, these same drugs can be extremely dangerous. We don't have to rely on modern scientific knowledge to learn this. Shakespeare, who apparently had some amazing medical knowledge or instincts, assured us that "antidotes are poisons"—meaning, of course, that a substance that heals can also harm. Then in *Cymbeline*, Shakespeare imparted some further knowledge: "The drug he gave me,

which he said was precious, and cordial to me, have I not found it
murd'rous to th' senses?"

Unfortunately, many persons, perhaps millions, abuse drugs.
They are, in the real sense of the word, drug dependent. How did
this come about?

THE STRANGE DEVELOPMENT OF OUR RELIANCE ON DRUGS

Drugs, using the term in the broad sense of any substance
taken internally to influence body processes, date back to prehis-
toric times. A few of the ancient remedies—quinine, for example—
were undoubtedly effective. But in all probability, most of them
depended upon the patient's faith for any curative effect.

Rather than review the long history of drug development
over the centuries, let's take a quick look at the state of drug
treatment a century ago, for it is within the past century that most
of the startling developments in medicinal therapy have taken
place—and it is because of these startling developments, many of
which unquestionably represent enormous advances, that we have
become a society that takes drugs unwisely and excessively.

A Currier & Ives view of the 19th century and a look at today

Let's first view the 19th century through the eyes of Currier
and Ives. As we leaf through an album of their prints, we are
regaled by wintertime vignettes of snow, sleigh bells, and bounti-
fully festive tables. We view colorful pictures of hunting in the
virgin forests, fishing in rolling streams, riding pell mell after
buffalo on the broad prairies. Scenes with comfortable titles such
as "Home for Thanksgiving," "A Home in the Country," and
"Skating in Central Park" are heartwarming.

Now consider the world of today. Most of us feel that we are
living in hazardous times. The toll of injuries and death from
automobile accidents is appalling. We find our world in a state of
disruption, abounding in wars and in threats of wars. The menace
of bombs of unimaginable power riding intercontinental missiles
hangs over us. We face the problems of overpopulation, over-

crowding, and pollution, to name just a few. The countless
tensions of modern living contribute to a host of ailments, such as
we have read about in earlier chapters.

... But behind the scenes we see a grim picture

Perhaps by now you are gazing nostalgically at the 19th
century. By comparison, life in the 19th century as portrayed by
Currier and Ives appears to have been uncomplicated, serene, and
happy. But, all unnoticed, a grim spectre stands behind every
cheery scene, its forbidding presence representing more of a threat
to life and limb than all of today's hazards added together and
multiplied many times. That spectre was disease—but not disease
as we know it today.

A century ago, disease—and we refer to disease in the most
enlightened countries of the world—revealed its ugly head in many
disorders, most of them focusing on infants, children, and young
adults. An appalling percentage of infants died, largely because of
primitive sanitation and fulminating infections. The grisly hand of
disease might seize anyone at any time with ague (malaria),
abscesses, consumption (tuberculosis), Asiatic cholera, milk sickness, pneumonia, scarlet fever, tuberculosis of the neck glands, all
sorts of vitamin deficiencies, and, in a sense the most terrible of
all, the strangling diphtheria. Surgery, which was performed only
as a last resort, was primitive and carried in its train an awesome
death rate. Inevitably, every family was deeply involved with
disease. Its onset could never be predicted or prevented.

Remedies were scarce

The doctors of the 19th century were usually the most
learned men of the community, possessed of high intelligence and
strong devotion. To most of them, death was as light as a feather
and duty heavier than a mountain. Their harsh days were laced
with searing heartbreak. They began at the crack of dawn or
earlier and continued through the night. But medicine, while a
respected profession, was mostly art mixed with just a little
science. Too few relevant facts had been scientifically established

to provide a basis for effective treatment, and, in a real sense, the doctor's cupboard of effective remedies was about as bare as Old Mother Hubbard's cupboard.

Just how valuable were medications of a century ago? We can get some idea from a fairly precise and authoritative statement written just a decade more than a century ago by the physician-poet Oliver Wendel Holmes: "Excluding opium, which the creator, Himself, seems to prescribe and excluding wine, which is a food, and excluding the vapors which produce the miracle of anesthesia, I firmly believe that if the whole materia medica, as now used, could be sunk to the bottom of the sea, it would be all the better for mankind and all the worse for the fishes." The miracle drugs with which we are blessed could be formulated only after the real scientific basis for medical practice was established and after modern chemistry and its industrial counterparts had appeared on the scene. So, effective treatment had to wait. But patients could not wait. They sickened, and all too frequently they died.

Medical breakthrough

Almost fifty years passed before there were any real advances in the development of medications. Then, during the first decade of the 20th century an impressive breakthrough was achieved in the development of a medication for the treatment of syphilis. Then, about 1915, pioneer work was done in the clinical application of knowledge of body fluids. Other developments followed rapidly.

The theory of vitamins promulgated in 1912 resulted in production of important vitamin products, beginning in the third decade of the century. A host of pharmaceuticals affecting various body processes and contributing greatly to the management of disease followed in the 1930's. Then, toward the end of that decade, new broadly useful agents to combat infection were discovered and introduced. Developing the sulfonamides, then the antibiotics, probably represented the greatest advances in medical treatment since the beginning of time. Modern medical knowledge, and with it enormously improved drugs, continued to burgeon. In the 1970's we find ourselves surrounded by a wealth of valuable treatment agents that were not even dreamed of half a century ago.

But we tend to go overboard . . .

The quite natural result of these developments has been an enormously heightened respect for drugs. It is almost as if mankind had been waiting untold centuries for real help in a battle against disease. When the help finally came, it was a natural tendency to go overboard and to believe that there was indeed a drug to cure every ailment. In many instances, this overenthusiasm was encouraged by unscrupulous commercial interests (not to be confused with the magnificent pharmaceutical companies that were so largely responsible for the true advances in drug therapy).

Today, we find ourselves in a position where it behooves all to take a careful look at the contribution of drugs, the hazards, the side effects, the reactions, and the disadvantages of relying too heavily on artificial aids either to health or tranquility. A whole category of diseases, the so-called iatrogenic ailments, has resulted from overuse of powerful drug agents. Perhaps it is time that we relied more on our natural, psychologic forces and less on the products of modern chemistry, even though they are often beneficial and can be life-saving.

THE GOOD AND THE BAD

Patients with psychosomatic ailments have a more or less natural tendency to rely excessively on drugs. But while medicinal agents used thoughtfully and on proper indication can be helpful in the management of psychosomatic ailments, particularly management of the organic aspects of psychosomatic disease, drugs do not represent the real answer. As we have repeatedly emphasized, and will cover in still more detail in the next chapter, what is really needed is revised life situations—usually brought about by careful psychological analysis and a new approach to living. We must not, however, lightly dismiss the pitfalls of excessive reliance on drugs. Let's examine these from the standpoint of various drugs that are seriously overused in present-day society.

THE UNTENDER TRAP OF ALCOHOL

Love has been referred to as a tender trap. Alcohol certainly deserves the designation of an untender trap. It is probably our number one drug problem. Some would maintain that the damage it causes outweighs the harm from all other drugs added together. On a positive side, alcohol used in moderation offers relaxation, even solace. The opinions of people from the past concerning alcohol's value have varied greatly. Homer, who lived around 850 B.C., said in *The Iliad:* "Inflaming wine, pernicious to mankind, unnerves the limbs, and dulls the noble mind." Louis Pasteur, 1822-1895, said: "Wine is the most healthful and most hygienic of beverages." Stonewall Jackson, 1824-1863, on being ordered by his physician to take brandy, answered: "I like liquor—its taste and its effects—and that is just the reason why I never drink it." Sir Winston Churchill, a heavy user of alcohol, said: "Always remember . . . that I have taken more out of alcohol than alcohol has taken out of me." Obviously, opinions of the true worth of alcohol varied enormously, and they still do.

But even those of us who look forward to an occasional cocktail must admit that alcohol is by no means an unmixed blessing. Consider briefly a few facts: There are at least 6.5 million alcoholics in the United States. Alcoholism costs industry between four and six billion dollars a year through work absences, time and material wasted by workers suffering on-the-job effects of drinks, and the cost of training employees to replace alcoholics discharged. Alcoholism ranks only behind heart disease and cancer as a killer in the United States. Drunkenness is the reason for more arrests than any other infraction. Dr. Stanley Einstein, Associate Director of the New Jersey College of Medicine and Dentistry's Drug Addiction Division, calls alcohol "the most dangerous drug in terms of medical, psychological, and social consequences."

A social drinker or an alcoholic?

Dr. Luther Cloud, President of the National Council on Alcoholism, explains the distinction between drinking alcohol and being an alcoholic: "You can use alcohol socially as a beverage without being in any trouble. The problem comes when you use it as a drug, when you say to yourself, 'I can't face my job in the morning or the old battleaxe at night without a drink.'"

There are no certain answers as to why some individuals become alcoholics and why others do not. It would certainly appear that heredity has a great deal to do with it. So does one's national or social background. For example, there are remarkably few alcoholics among Jewish people and among Mormons, but the rate of alcoholism among the Irish is notoriously high. Many people seek solace in alcohol and drink when beset by psychic tension. One page of a recent newspaper carried an article entitled "Alcohol the Most Potent Drug" and another titled "I Am an Alcoholic." On the same page is an advertisement for whiskey, which states: "When the going gets hard, the whiskey should be soft."

It may well be that some individuals have a biochemical predisposition to become alcoholics. After they have drunk more or less socially for a while, they appear to cross an invisible line. After that, they cannot take just one drink, even if that was their original intention, without having another and another. They drink themselves into a stupor for the next day or two or three—all as a result of having *decided* to take that drink.

There has been an enormous amount of research and many arguments concerning chemical changes that occur in the alcoholic. The present-day consensus is that such changes do occur and that an alcoholic can never become a social drinker again. Most so-called reformed alcoholics do not refer to themselves as former alcoholics or ex-alcoholics, but as *alcoholics*. They do this to emphasize that they cannot drink. The road to alcoholism appears to be an easy one. The road back is by no means easy. Perhaps the most successful route yet is that followed by the great organization Alcoholics Anonymous, that emphasizes one should live a day at a time. It is possible to shake oneself free of the habit by accumulating a series of days, then weeks, then months without alcohol. But even after years of complete sobriety, it might take only one drink to send the alcoholic spiraling back down the road to Skid Row, or to the social equivalent of that sad place.

History of an alcoholic

It is not difficult to find examples of persons who suffer, or have suffered, from alcoholism. Indeed, it is far too easy. George, or so we will call him, represents a fairly typical victim. He had grown up with a persecution complex, feeling quite inferior to his fellow workers and associates. Even to his wife. But a few drinks of alcohol (wine, whiskey, beer, gin, he liked them all) and he felt much bolder, much bigger, and his problems seemed to shrink accordingly. It soon became a habit but he argued that he could stop anytime he wanted. He was certainly not an alcoholic and had no intentions of becoming one, or so he insisted.

But George's problems seemed to grow bigger and consequently he began to drink more frequently. Just a small drink before breakfast and a "nip" at noon helped immensely to carry him through the day's work. Then one night he didn't come home after work. Only a few hours late, but it was the beginning of a habit that would be his undoing. For his stay at the corner tavern became longer each week. His work began to suffer; he missed frequently because of his drinking. But he insisted he "still was not an alcoholic. I just drink to solve my problems. I could stop if I wanted to. I just don't want to now."

And unlike many who found much-needed assistance by calling a phone number of an Alcoholics Anonymous member, George never sought help, and he never accepted advice. He had actually been an alcoholic for over ten years, perhaps longer, when physical ailments began to appear. Then it was too late. Diabetes, ulcers, heart trouble, and finally cirrhosis of the liver combined to end his problems with alcoholism—and his life—at the age of 55.

Fortunately, many persons are able to control their intake of alcoholic beverages, and many alcoholics have been cured. But the prime factor behind either control or cure is a relatively stable mental state. As problems become unmanageable, some persons will develop an ulcer, others will suffer allergies or skin ailments, and some will turn to drinking. And relief can be attained only when mental stability is restored; life situations must be faced and adjusted or perhaps viewed in a new light. Drugs are not the answer!

BARBITURATES

Barbiturates, while non-narcotic drugs, can cause dependence, or addiction. They are especially dangerous since they are often employed to provide tranquility or sedation. Any medication that relieves pain, tension, and anxiety can cause addiction when it is abused, and abuse of barbiturates occurs frequently among all classes of our society. When the individual attempts to discontinue use of the drug, he may experience untoward symptoms, so-called withdrawal symptoms. Moreover, damage to the brain can result from prolonged use of barbiturates. Misuse of them causes accidental death, as well as suicide.

Most persons who abuse barbiturates are individuals who find life's tensions and anxieties unbearable. Like alcoholics, they need the feeling of security and well being that they think the drug will give them. But there are other effects. They become confused, excessively irritable, and depressed, and they lose their coordination. When the effects wear off, the person is faced with the same old tensions and anxieties, plus a hangover. So, while barbiturates can be useful drugs in medical practice, they are potentially dangerous and can result in addiction.

Tranquilizers

Tranquilizers have seen wide use for control of psychic tension. As the name implies, they are designed to produce tranquility, and so they often do—but not always. Far from producing tranquility, they sometimes increase hostility, perhaps even to a dangerous level. Along with this hostility may well go an increase in anxiety.

A group of students who took two commonly-used tranquilizers for a week were found to have increased hostility in three separate areas: (1) Their verbal hostility was increased. (2) They had an increase in what is called indirect hostility, a tendency to slam doors and kick dogs. (3) They tended to get into heated arguments readily. Those showing little or no signs of anxiety before taking the tranquilizers developed striking anxieties. Certainly the type of person who takes tranquilizers has much to do with the reaction he will get from them. But Dr. J. E. P. Butler of the Psychiatry Department of London University, London, England, said: "The tests we have carried out show that a person inclined to be aggressive and impulsive will sometimes lose control of himself when using tranquilizers." Apparently, tranquilizers are particularly useful for the person who is notably unaggressive but at the same time suffering from deep anxiety. Obviously, there are great dangers inherent in trying to drug your fears away.

Energizers

Some thirty years ago, the amphetamines, drugs that cause an enormous increase in energy, were introduced. These drugs subsequently became known as pep pills or bennies. As the years went by, it became all too clear that the amphetamines can be abused and are addictive. They can now be sold only on prescription, and doctors have been advised to prescribe them only for specific brain ailments or for short-term weight reduction, but no longer as a stimulant for mild depressive states. The warning on the label now reads: "Amphetamines have a significant potential for abuse."

But illegal use of bennies is widespread. They have sometimes been taken by truck drivers to postpone fatigue and to keep them awake. Recent reports state that American drug companies produce eight billion pep pills a year, or forty for every man, woman, and child in the country. Apparently half of this production ultimately is used illegally. Large quantities of the pills have been legally exported to Mexico and then smuggled back into the United States for sale to truck drivers, hippies, and addicts. The movie that ran successfully during the late 1960's, "Valley of the Dolls," portrayed well the tragic results of addiction to amphetamines, also known as "dolls."

Words of a bennie addict

A statement from an addict who had been taking four or five *dozen* bennies a day (the normal dose is not more than one to four) reads:

> "I was taking bennies, sometimes as many as four or five dozen a day, and was drinking a lot, too. I was smoking pot a little bit, but mostly I was drinking and taking bennies. . . . Three of us were arrested for peace disturbance and investigation. After they put me in the jail cell, I

started hallucinating. There was a little light above the door, and I thought there were cannon balls coming out of it. I got up into a corner since that was the only place they couldn't get me. After three days, the charges were dropped and they let me go.

"As I walked home from the precinct station, I thought I could see through walls. In addition, I thought everyone was trying to kill me, and I could see guns sticking out of windows. Every time someone would shoot at me, I would hear 'click, click.' All the time I kept thinking how lucky I was there were no bullets in the guns. Before I got back to my neighborhood, I was out in the street directing traffic. The police came, and I ran over and grabbed a lamp post. They had to break my hand to get me loose. I was put into a strait jacket and put into the psychiatric ward of . . . hospital, where I was packed in ice.

"For 18 days, I was under observation. The doctor wasn't really sure what had happened, but he thought I had just lost my mind. But my mother and sister knew what I had been doing, and after about a week, my mother told the doctor. When he found out I had been taking bennies all that time, he told me that the central nervous system is affected by amphetamines and I had probably had a nervous breakdown. So, he started treating me differently, and after 18 days I was released. I couldn't see through walls anymore, but I still heard voices, and I heard people calling my name."

Such experiences as these are not at all unusual in regard to hallucinations and central nervous system effects. Suicides are not unusual among amphetamine addicts.

NARCOTICS & COMPANY

We have previously discussed alcohol, barbiturates, tranquilizers, and energizers. Here we should mention narcotics, the drugs usually associated in our minds with drug abuse and drug dependency. Beginning in 1964, there was a pronounced increase in the use of narcotics in the United States. Recently, morphine and the synthetic derivatives of these products have been used more and more. Starting in the cities, abuse has extended to the countryside. It is a symptom of the troubled times in which we live; heavy drug use is more than casually associated with the riots, bombings, ritualistic slayings, protests, and chaos. There can be no question, we are indeed in the midst of an epidemic.

GET HIGH ON LIFE

The real experts in the drug abuse field are ex-addicts, persons who have been there and have somehow managed to escape. A group of such experts, who dub themselves "The Family" at Mendocino State Hospital in California, have set forth what they believe to be a cure for drug abuse. We mentioned their philosophy in a previous chapter because we feel it is of value not only for drug abusers but for individuals with psychic tension who find themselves in unpleasant, even unbearable, life situations. And it is worthy of repetition. The Family wrote their prescription, based on depth of experience and sincerity, in this way:

"The cure for drug abuse is a meaningful life. The creation of a meaningful life is a goal for all of us, drug abusers or not. We assume it should have some of the following characteristics:

- It should have some warm, human relationships.
- It should have in it the opportunity for self-expression and honesty without penalty.
- It should have a sense of structure and hope for the future.
- It should provide a person with a sense of belonging to something larger than himself that is worthwhile.
- It should be a life that the individual feels he has made through his own efforts."

The formula set forth by The Family advises us, in effect, to seek solace by becoming more deeply involved in life. It really says, "Get high on life rather than on drugs."

DRUGS ARE TO BE USED, NOT ABUSED!

We have not meant for this chapter to represent a wholesale condemnation of drugs. Drugs as a whole have made our lives infinitely more pleasant or bearable than they would have been otherwise. But drugs, like fire, can be misused. The misuse, however, lies primarily in the individual rather than in the product. A letter to the editor of the *New England Journal of Medicine* on December 5, 1968, brings this point home. The letter was written by several doctors practicing in South Vietnam:

"To the Editor: During the past few months we have had the opportunity to observe an unusual set of circumstances in a fellow colleague stationed in South Vietnam. He is a 31-year-old internist with an unusual and seemingly insatiable appetite for small red candy, cinnamon flavored red hots. Since such luxuries are seldom available in the war zone, he has organized a complex set of supply channels from the continental United States. His desire for red hots is best demonstrated by his continued need for them after he has eaten enough to turn his stool red. He expressed concern over the stools, but he found that by mixing red hots with roasted peanuts he could increase his intake without having the problem of red stools. His problem, or pica, has been present for about twenty years with a gradual increase noted over the past two years. Over all, he is best described as a [hyperactive] individual, especially during times of plentiful supply, but he has been observed to be withdrawn, irritable, and short-tempered when the supply has been exhausted for a few days. Cinnamon red hots contain sugar, corn syrup, cornstarch, imitation flavors and certified food coloring. To the best of our knowledge, none of the ingredients are considered harmful but we are unaware of a similar pica [desire for a certain food substance]."

This letter emphasizes the fact that the problems revolving about drugs are not with the drugs themselves but with the people who use them unwisely. Although no two individuals will suffer from the same problems, we hope that in the next chapter, "A Treasury of Wonder-Working Remedies," there will be resources to which all persons can relate meaningfully.

According to a late 1970 Gallup Poll, 42 per cent of college students said they had tried marijuana; 14 per cent said they had used LSD or some other hallucinogen. Hallucinogens, which have been called "the sacred biochemicals," have captured the interest of drug users. Marijuana is a mild hallucinogen. LSD has lost some of its popularity because of adverse publicity, but numerous derivatives of this dangerous drug have taken its place.

Another category of "drugs"

There is a frightening and bewildering category of drugs that Dr. Darold A. Treffert, Superintendent of the Winnebago Hospital, Winnebago, Wisconsin, has called the "God-knows-what" drugs. It includes such products as glue, gasoline, aerosol propellants, cocktail glass chiller, lighter fluid, and various over-the-counter remedies. Some people have even injected ice water, peanut butter, and mayonnaise into their veins. The latter caused death in three young people recently.

As Dr. Treffert points out, we are never going to pass laws against peanut butter or mayonnaise. Instead, he states, "We are going to have to be more creative in our legislative, educative and treatment programs than to simply think we can solve the problem by passing more new laws or creating more new schedules. Rather, with respect to the drugs themselves, our task is simply to point out as realistically and as honestly and as objectively as possible, the real dangers that many of these products have when abused, and hope that our entire society can come to use drugs, including alcohol, responsibly." Dr. Treffert emphasizes that we should examine the individuals who use drugs rather than the drugs themselves. He points out that 80 per cent of the users of the drugs being discussed in this section are casual experimenters and 20 per cent long-term users.

Some of the casual experimenters use drugs because they are bored or because other people, usually youngsters, use them. All too frequently, they use them with fatal or long-term adverse effects. Others in this group can be called protesters. They are characterized by alienation. They use drugs simply because it irritates the rest of us. Marijuana has become an effective symbol of protest.

In the long-term user group, there are seekers and losers. The seekers believe that man should rise above his present predicament by using drugs. Their motto is "Better living through chemistry." These people believe that the risk is worth the possible rewards. Curiosity is their watchword. The losers might be called the fallout from the other groups. They started out by joining a protesting or seeking group, but they became dependent on drugs. Members of this group often end up in psychiatric hospitals or clinics or some other kind of care-giving facility. They take drugs because it hurts too much not to take them. Drug use by these persons represents a sickness. They were sick to begin with, and drugs only complicated their problem.

There is another group, which might be designated the recreation group. Individuals in this group, which includes older adolescents, young adults, and some older adults, have chosen deliberately and with knowledge and forethought to use drugs as a recreation. They usually exclude alcohol.

eighteen

A treasury of
wonder-working remedies

Stay with me, God. The night is dark,
The night is cold: my little spark
Of courage dies. The night is long;
Be with me God, and make me strong.
> A Soldier—His Prayer
> Found on a scrap of paper
> in a trench in Tunisia during
> the battle of El Agheila

When I consider the short duration of my
life, swallowed up in the eternity before and
after, the little space which I fill, and even
can see, engulfed in the infinite immensity
of space of which I am ignorant, and which
knows me not, I am frightened, and am
astonished being here rather than there, why
now rather than then.
> Blaise Pascal (1623-1662)

Sometimes we may well feel like Pascal, wondering why we are here rather than there, why we are living now rather than at another time, why certain events strike us where and when and how they do. Most psychic tension arises in our environment, even though other factors, such as our heredity and personality make-up have much to do with how we handle tension. But for the most part, well-adjusted individuals become troubled when they have *troubles*. Most of the troubles are real, whether acute and overwhelming, or long drawn out and just as overwhelming.

242

There are all sorts of steps that one can take to help relieve the impact of unhappy events. Writing down the problems and thinking long and hard concerning what can be done about them sometimes helps. Even action that is only partially successful may represent an enormously important step forward. But the best path leading from the morass of psychosomatic disease incorporates six essential steps as set out below. Naturally the order in which the steps are taken and the degree of emphasis placed on the various steps will vary with one's personality and with the situation in which he finds himself. The steps are embodied in a program that is positive in every respect.

Perhaps some of us have as our primary problem a hard, driving personality. We hit the ball too hard and too often, pursue our ambitions too hard and too vigorously. As a result we are up-tight a good part of the time. Perhaps merely slowing down is what this type of person needs most. And although "slowing down" may be easier said than done, this prayer by an anonymous author may help:

Slow Me Down, Lord

Slow me down, Lord! Ease the pounding of my heart by the quieting of my mind. Steady my hurried pace with a vision of the eternal reach of time.

Give me, amid the confusion of the day, the calmness of the everlasting hills. Break the tensions of my nerves and muscles with the soothing music of the singing streams that still lives in my memory. Help me to know the magical, restoring power of sleep.

Teach me the art of taking minute vacations—of slowing down to look at a flower, to chat with a friend, to pat a dog, to answer a child's question, to read a few lines from a good book.

Remind me each day of the fable of the hare and the tortoise, that I may know that the race is not always to the swift—that there is more to life than increasing its speed. Let me look upward into the branches of the towering oak and know that it grew slowly and well.

Slow me down, Lord, and inspire me to send my roots deep into the soil of life's enduring values, that I may grow more surely toward the stars.

Author Unknown

STEP I FOR RECOVERY:
UNDERSTANDING THE ROOTS OF THE ILLNESS

Since psychosomatic disease usually results from autonomic nerve impulses of which the victim is quite unconscious, it is of the very first importance for him to understand, insofar as is possible, the hidden roots of his ailment. When he has seen the relationship between the psychic tensions that have assailed him and his psychosomatic illness, then he will have taken an essential step toward recovery.

Because of the limitations of our current knowledge of psychosomatic disease we cannot understand precisely why this should be true. But the records of patient after patient make it clear beyond any reasonable doubt that it is true. Understanding, even though only vaguely, the basis of a psychosomatic illness, removes the disease from the shadowland of the unknown. For now the unconscious nerve impulses that have been generating the illness have been, at least partially, unmasked; for the first time the patient can take positive steps toward eliminating the original cause of the illness. He can begin to discern, however faintly, a tenuous and somewhat obscure path from the forest of despair to the sunlit meadows of health and happiness.

Common experiences help us in understanding how emotionally colored experiences can cause disease. Remember the way in which a fearful nightmare wakens you with a furiously pounding heart and an unshakable and ominous dread. Realizing that it was only a nightmare helps some but doesn't put you completely at ease. The foreboding and the undercurrent of dread remains.

Why might you be affected by such a nightmare while John or Mary only regards it as a source of amusement? Different persons are blessed—or cursed—with quite different nervous systems. Some can pass through fearful events with little effect on the pulse rate and peace of mind; others might be greatly upset by the thought of merely being introduced to a stranger or going on a routine journey. Those of us who are born with a sensitive type of nervous system will simply have to learn to live with it.

What we are saying is that the victim of psychosomatic

disease must become aware of the relationship between his psychic tensions and his ulcer, high blood pressure or skin rash. Often the relationship between cause and effect is far from obvious. And no wonder, for different persons react so differently to identical tensions. A reprimand by the boss (possibly justified, possibly not) may cause the stomach of one person to secrete great amounts of corrosive hydrochloric acid, may stimulate the heart of another to race at breakneck speed, make tense the muscles and tendons of the neck of another. Or, an individual may develop a given psychosomatic symptom or ailment from different causes. Robert—or Susan—can acquire a splitting tension headache from competition in an athletic event or debate, from being rejected by a sweetheart, from flunking a course in school or from receiving a ticket for "reckless driving." To complicate matters further, the same person might well develop a headache from one of these events and diarrhea from others.

STEP II FOR RECOVERY:
COOPERATING FULLY IN TREATMENT OF ORGANIC ILLNESS

We have seen how established psychosomatic disease all too frequently sets up vicious circles. In such a circle the physical effects of the disease create further psychic rension and thus accentuate the physical or organic changes. The patient is caught up in a circle of events; round and round he goes, becoming worse and worse. He is as certainly doomed as the unfortunate seafarer caught in the eddies of a legendary whirlpool or maelstrom.

It must be emphasized that some persons with psychosomatic disease will require several branches of the medical arts to cope with their psychosomatic problems. Depending upon the circumstances and the patient, needed professionals may include an internist or family physician, a surgeon, and a psychologist or psychiatrist. Nothing is more clear than the truth that in psychosomatic illness, psychic and physiologic disruptions are intimately intertwined. Quite naturally both must receive attention. For however effective psychic therapy may be, it can have no important effect on organic changes that have already occurred.

Energetic treatment of organic disease is, therefore, essential. Here is where modern medicine with its gigantic capabilities in diagnosis and treatment of organic disease can brighten the future for the patient with psychosomatic disease. Psychologic treatment, essential though it is, is not of itself sufficient. Even though the original causative psychic tensions are removed, a stomach ulcer, for example, can proceed to perforation. Chronic diarrhea can continue to deplete the patient. Overactivity of the thyroid gland can wear out the victim. But prompt effective treatment of the organic aspects of the ailment interrupts the circle and permits the patient to win a foothold on the ladder to buoyant health.

STEP III FOR RECOVERY:
ENTERING ENTHUSIASTICALLY INTO
INDICATED PSYCHOTHERAPY

Interrupting the vicious circle by treatment of organic disease is, then, an essential aspect of treatment. Just as important is attention to the psychic problem that started the condition in the first place. Sometimes the patient can analyze his own life situation and take the necessary steps for eliminating the sources of psychic trauma. In other instances the individual will need psychologic help from a professional; the decision as to whether professional help is necessary can well be shared with the family physician. Psychosomatically-oriented family physicians can often provide needed psychologic help. Or, clinical psychologists or psychiatrists may provide needed treatment.

For many years there was a completely unjustified stigma attached to consulting a psychiatrist. Now that we have recognized the enormous importance of this specialty of medicine for virtually everyone, consulting a psychiatrist indicates breadth of understanding and good sense.

Naturally the patient must enter into the psychic aspects of his problem with enthusiasm, devoting to this aspect of treatment all the time required. Psychic factors constitute the roots of psychosomatic disease. Unless the roots are destroyed, the ugly tree will continue to flourish.

One of the most helpful aspects of psychotherapy is provision of an opportunity for the patient to "ventilate," that is, to freely express his ideas to an understanding ear. A good relationship between the patient and the psychotherapist is essential for this.

STEP IV FOR RECOVERY: CHANGING LIFE SITUATIONS OR LEARNING TO COPE WITH THEM

It would be fortunate, indeed, if one could in every instance remove the unhappy life situation that started the individual down the dark path to psychosomatic disease. That is, of course, not always possible. Frequently the situation can be improved; if this is not possible then the individual can learn better to cope with the problems. If he is to cope then he must focus on Step VI.

Just realizing that illness can result from being caught in a trap, and understanding the nature of the trap, can help one to live with it. Also of enormous help is the realization that one is not the first person to have been trapped by a miserable situation. It has been happening for uncounted centuries! The very fact that we are born means that we will encounter obstacles of varying degrees of intensity as long as we draw breath. People have long been coping with problems, many of them horrendous, and in spite of the problems have fought on and won their personal battles. Many have achieved heights of greatness.

STEP V FOR RECOVERY: SETTING THE PROPER LIFE GOALS

Perhaps no aspect of emerging triumphant from psychosomatic illness deserves more attention than setting the proper life goals. Without goals we are like ships set sail on vast oceans without a rudder. Remember the goals set by The Family presented in the chapter concerning drugs. Those goals constitute a worthy nucleus for living.

Biblical wisdom is sound: "Where there is no vision, the people perish." We need goals and dreams to live by; lose the dream and we are sentenced to stumble blindly and hopelessly on—from desperation to desperation. Without dreams and visions and meaningful goals, we are paralyzed by futility.

And it is when life is barren, futile, and meaningless that we become easy prey for psychosomatic symptoms.

STEP VI FOR RECOVERY:
STRENGTHENING THE SELF BY ADOPTING A SOUND PHILOSOPHY

In ancient times, in the middle ages, and in our modern scene many persons have set forth formulas for ·more meaningful, happier living. Consideration of some of these formulas can help the victim of psychosomatic disease adopt a sound and strong inner philosophy that will aid him in triumphantly weathering life's storms. Certainly no one person can profitably use all the formulas, but anyone can gain by a judicious selection. Let us now consider some of these.

A potentate of old was deeply concerned by the succession of problems that continually confronted him. A happy life appeared beyond his grasp. So he called the wisest men in his kingdom to him and asked them for a formula for happiness. They meditated over the matter for a long time, then appeared before him and advised him thus: "When you are confronted with a vexing situation repeat to yourself, 'This, too, will pass away.' " There is truth and validity in this ancient advice. No matter how unhappy and unbearable the situation, it *will*, sooner or later (and quite possibly sooner), pass away. If one can just hang on a little longer the situation, like the New England weather, will surely change.

The rewards of persisting to fight "one more round"

As Dr. Charles L. Copenhaver, senior minister of the Reformed Church of Bronxville, New York, points out: ". . . Life

₁s often harsh. There are things that are incomprehensible; suffering that will not disappear at the command of a smooth saying; pain that will not vanish when rebuked by a feeling of sympathy; injustice that will not be eradicated by the resolution of good will. . . ." We are often tempted to quit. This is exactly what one must not do. Instead, we must pick up the pieces and move ahead. When James J. Corbett, then heavyweight champion of the world, was asked what a person must do to become a champion he replied, "Fight one more round." The Duke of Wellington said that the British soldiers at the Battle of Waterloo were not braver than Napoleon's soldiers, they were just brave for five minutes longer.

Dr. Copenhaver goes on to quote Dag Hammarskjold, one of the great men of our time: "When the morning's freshness has been replaced by the weariness of midday, when the leg muscles quiver under the strain, the climb seems endless, and suddenly nothing will go quite as you wish—it is then that you must not hesitate." For we can profit from adversity, become stronger for our struggles. Every one of us can, like the mythological Phoenix bird, be born anew in the ashes of despair.

Live one day at a time

Another help is the concept of living a day at a time. The great Dr. William Osler strongly recommended this formula, perhaps on the theory that "Sufficient unto the day is the evil thereof." Osler suggested that one cease worrying about the yesterdays or the tomorrows and concentrate on today. He called this approach, "Living in daytight compartments." It worked for him: he became one of the great physicians of all time in spite of discouragements that would have overwhelmed most people. That great organization, Alcoholics Anonymous, which has been so helpful to those with serious drinking problems, bases its program on Osler's philosophy. Members of the group are assured that all they have to do to conquer the alcohol problem is to abstain for 24 hours; at the end of that 24 hours a fresh 24 hour abstention period is started. This formula has been more successful in conquering alcoholism than has any other treatment.

Constructive "escapes"

One excellent way to forget, for a time at least, one's problems is to focus on other areas. This form of escapism helps one to see his situation in better perspective. He may find he is not really as bad off as he thought. How does one escape?

Some persons escape into time, by reading history, studying relics from the past such as old stagecoach inns, ancient trails, log cabins, old battlefields, library archives or museums. Every community has historical groups or societies that facilitate such escape into time. Viewing what some of our forebears had to put up with may make our own lots appear easier.

Or, one can flee into space by reading of far away lands—in the National Geographic Magazine, for example—by attending travelogues, or by making journeys to places close by or far away. Meditating on one's place in the immensity of time and space may provide objectivity, even though it worried Pascal. Ask yourself, "Just how important will this problem be a month from now, a year from now, ten years from now, a century from now?"

Many have found relief in giving aid to others. Hospitals, mental institutions, ghetto projects, the Peace Corps, the good ship Hope, war torn areas are crying for persons to give of themselves. Hans Selye finds his satisfaction in doing the sort of research that quite properly earns him great gratitude. Sometimes, of course, gratitude is not awarded even though richly deserved. That should not deter us.

Faith in adversity

A deep and abiding faith is probably the greatest asset in one's struggle against adversity. Faith has helped many over unspeakably difficult paths, has helped them to take the long view of a situation. For faith is at least partly a mental process involving both the emotions and the will and therefore has a tremendous effect on health of both body and mind. It gives a person a "healthy" outlook on life, the opposite of that which triggers a psychosomatic illness. In other words, as human beings, we are a unique blend of body and mind—soul—and we can best keep them functioning in a well synchronized fashion by seeking the assistance of a power greater than ourselves.

Uses of meditation

Seeking quiet moments for meditation or taking spot or minute vacations can help make one's day more pleasant. Such brief periods consist in taking a moment from the day's activities to view a lovely cloud, to watch a stunning redbird, to glory in a colorful sunrise or sunset. Catherine Marshall describes the mountain housewife, Fairlight, in *Christy* thus: "Often she found time to pause in her dishwashing to let her eyes and her spirit drink in the beauty of a sunset. She would interrupt her work to call the children and revel with them in the grandeur of thunderheads piling up over the mountain peaks, heat lightning flashing behind the clouds like fireworks. 'It lifts the heart,' she would say, and that was explanation enough for any interruption."*

The psychosomatic trap

Whatever your problems they will be worsened if you develop psychosomatic disease. Indeed, even a mild depression induced by psychic tension can impair your success at home, at work, in school. Do not allow yourself to be placed in the position of the great English physician John Hunter who said, "My life is in the hands of any rascal who chooses to annoy or tease me."

It has been well said, "Never despair, but if you do, work on in despair." Dr. Walter Alvarez points out that many famous men, Charles Darwin, Thomas Carlyle, William James, Thomas Huxley, Charles Lamb, Richard Wagner suffered from psychosomatic illness. Yet all kept going, overcame their problems, and made enormous contributions to their work.

Don't bite off more than you can chew

The great psychiatrist Carl Gustav Jung advised: "Fulfill something you are able to fulfill, rather than run after what you

---

*From *Christy* by Catherine Marshall. Copyright 1967 by Catherine Marshall Le Sourd. Used with permission of McGraw-Hill Book Company, Inc.

will never achieve. Nobody is perfect . . . and nobody can be. It is an illusion. We can modestly strive to fulfill ourselves and to be as complete human beings as possible, and that will give us trouble enough." As we have previously emphasized, many persons with psychosomatic disease tend to be perfectionistic, highly-motivated but overconscientious. If you fall into this group, the words of Jung above quoted might have been written just for you. Overconscientious persons are prone to become disturbed, even distraught, when they make an error or do a job poorly. They tend to brood over the incident and this spells psychic tension. What we have called the "swamping effect" can be useful in such instances. This means that one can "swamp" a poor performance by a cluster of good performances. Accomplishing the good work involves energetic action and action is one of the best antidotes for psychic tension.

Although our subconscious mind can contribute to the development of psychosomatic disease, we can put this aspect of our being to good use in solving problems that confront us. Consider what Dr. Albert Szent-Gyorgi, a great scientist, said: "As far as I can remember, it was very rarely that I found the answer to any of my problems by conscious thinking. This conscious thinking only acted as a primer for my brain, which seemed to work much better without my muddling while I was asleep or fishing." When Newton was asked how he made his discoveries, he replied: "By always thinking into them." By thinking about a problem before going to bed we may provide the subconscious the opportunity to give us the solution. The process of before-bedtime meditating may have to be repeated several times if the subconscious is to concentrate on the problem and come up with a solution. This method should be used selectively, however, by those persons who can best utilize it. Those with insomnia or severe anxieties might worsen their condition rather than solve it.

If one could always eliminate the situations that give rise to psychic tension this section on improving one's philosophic approach to life would be largely unnecessary; but situations cannot always be changed or even materially improved. When this is the case then the patient must change, must adapt to the problems so that they do not seriously harm or destroy him.

Nutrition and exercise

All too frequently persons with psychic tension find it difficult both to eat and to exercise. Yet a well-balanced diet and adequate amounts of exercise both represent essentials for health. During the early phases of recovery from a psychosomatic ailment the patient may have to force himself in both these areas. As his condition improves he will find it far easier to meet his dietary requirements and to carry out a program of exercise.

THE MAGIC CARPET OF BOOKS

As we have emphasized, the patient with a psychosomatic ailment should, from time to time, "escape from himself." One of the best, universally available forms of escapism is to lose oneself in a good book. Tastes in reading vary greatly; the following list of books, with brief descriptive comments, have proved most useful in our experience:

Thoreau, H. D.: *Walden or Life in the Woods,* New Edition, New York, Peter Pauper Press, No Date Given for Publication. Perhaps the first philosophic hippie, Thoreau wrote with a seemingly easy skill that has never been surpassed. You don't have to agree with him to appreciate his artistry!

Twain, M.: *The Family Mark Twain.* New York, Harper & Brothers, Publishers, 1936. In his own, inimitable manner, Twain mixed humor with bitter indictment of western civilization. His writings contain far more than might appear to the casual reader.

Kephart, H.: *Our Southern Highlanders,* New York, The Macmillan Company, 1942. Kephart, who fled to the Appalachian Highlands because of a tuberculosis infection of which he ultimately died, gives an exciting, firsthand account of Appalachia, our present-day repository of the language and customs of Chaucerian and Elizabethan England. He paves the way for *Christy,* by Catherine Marshall. (See below.)

Aldrich, E. P.: *As William James Said,* New York, the Vanguard Press, 1942. This book contains a selection of the sayings of the great and compassionate psychologist, William James. Recommended reading for anyone interested in affairs of the mind.

Melville, H.: *Moby Dick; Or, the Whale,* New York, The Heritage Press, 1943. The magnificent word pictures, rather than the narrative, make this book inspiring and fascinating. Consider this quote: "I leave a white and turbid wake; pale waters, paler cheeks, where'er I sail ... Yonder, by ever-brimming goblet's rim, the warm waves blush like wine. The gold brow plumbs the blue."

Pyle, E.: *Brave Men,* New York, Grosset & Dunlap, 1944. War correspondent Pyle, who died on Ie Shima, used active verbs naturally but with superb artistry. His writing bristles with action and compassion.

Adams, H.: *The Education of Henry Adams: An Autobiography,* Boston, Houghton Mifflin Company, 1946. This great man had a facility for explaining complex matters in simple and lucid language. The thread of sadness and futility that runs through the fabric of the book adds to its charm.

Benedict, R.: *The Chrysanthemum and the Sword,* Boston, Houghton Mifflin Company, 1946. This book is more timely today than when it was written. It explains the enigmatic yet formidable Japanese personality in both cultural and psychologic terms. Try laying it down once you have begun it!

Costain, T.B.: *The Conquerors,* Garden City, New York, Doubleday & Company, Inc.,1949. Costain writes history for the escapist! He makes it as enthralling as the most exciting fiction. If you like this book, read Costain's other historical semi-non-fiction novels.

Banta, R. E.: *The Ohio,* New York, Rinehart & Company, Inc., 1957. Fascinating early mid-west history combined with sardonic and even grisly humor that adds to the fascination and readability of the book.

Bibby, G.: *The Testimony of the Spade,* New York, Alfred A. Knopf, 1956. Charmingly written, this book presents the archeology of northern Europe from 15,000 B.C. to the time of the Vikings. The lavish illustrations make the book even more readable. For the first time we obtain a clear view of our Indo-European ancestors.

Eiseley, L.: *The Immense Journey,* New York, Vintage Books, Random House, Inc., 1957. Dr. Eiseley is an eminent naturalist with the soul of a mystic and the pen of an artist. Try putting this book down after you have read the first two chapters! The author's word pictures are bogh vivid and poignant.

Gamow, G.: *One Two Three... Infinity,* New York, The Viking Press, 1957. The prominent mathematician who wrote this book used simple illustrations to excellent effect in explaining complex concepts so anyone can understand them.

Bierce, A.: *The Devil's Dictionary,* New York, Sagamore Press, Ind., 1957. Originally dubbed the "cynic's word book" this little volume contains what H. L. Mencken termed "some of the most gorgeous witticisms in the English language."

Thurber, J.: *The Years with Ross,* Boston, Little Brown and Company, 1959. Written with Thurber's characteristic warmth, humor and clarity this book makes Ross live for the reader.

Carrol, L.: *The Annotated Alice,* New York, Clarkson N. Potter, Inc., 1960. This book is a masterpiece that is required if one is to understand another masterpiece, *Alice in Wonderland.* It will shock and enlighten you—and transport you to magical far-off lands.

Osborn, A. F.: *Applied Imagination: Principles and Procedures of Creative Problem Solving,* New York, Charles Scribner's Sons, 1953. This book is an eminently practical manual on creativity and the harnessing of the subconscious.

Todd, A. L.: *Abandoned,* New York, McGraw Hill Book Company, Inc., 1961. In our opinion one of the finest non-fiction novels ever written. It tells of a saga of courage unsurpassed in American history.

Gann, E. K.: *Fate Is the Hunter,* New York, Simon and Schuster, 1961. Pilot Gann tells true stories of the pioneer days of air transportation that will stand your hair on end. The author has a finely honed sense of the dramatic.

Orwell, G.: *Animal Farm,* New York, The American Library of World Literature, Inc. 1962. Here is a fairy tale with a cogent message for modern society. Orwell's satire is directed, with telling force, against communism.

Gardiner, J. W.: *Self-Renewal,* New York, Harper & Row, 1964. If you haven't already read this book you should! Written with a breadth of understanding of modern society, this volume presents a prescription for rebirth. Especially useful for the person with psychosomatic disease.

Marshall, C.: *Christy,* New York, Avon Books, 1967. Here is a beautiful and inspiring book, semi-non-fiction, of a young girl's experiences in the southern Appalachians during the early years of this century.

Cooper, K. H.: *Aerobics,* New York, M. Evans and Company, Inc., 1968. Exercise is an important facet of treatment of psychosomatic disease. This little book, available in paperback, outlines common sense approaches that anyone can use.

Weekes, C.: *Hope and Help for Your Nerves,* New York, Hawthorn Books, Inc., 1969. This book was written for "the many people whose nerves are often on edge . . ." It explains the basis for nervous disturbances and offers many helpful approaches in overcoming them.

Kroeber, T.: *Ishi in Two Worlds,* Berkeley, Cal., U. of California Press, 1970. This is the enthralling story of the last wild Indian in North America, how he stumbled down into "civilization" after years of living alone, a fugitive from the hated white man, how he made a miraculous recovery from his state of profound physical and psychic depression. It is an inspiring saga of the triumph of the human spirit.

We have not mentioned many of the truly great works such as The Bible, Shakespeare, Dickens and their immortal companion pieces. Certainly there is a wealth in the volumes of literature, true treasure chests. And all can help you in your battle against psychosomatic disease.

Index

Index